Dedicated to
The Most Reverend
and
Most Honourable
The Lord Archbishop
of
Canterbury

THE GIFT OF THE SEA—
ROMNEY MARSH

Birlings (Kent) Ltd., Cobbs Wood House, Chart Road, Ashford, Kent, England.

First Published 1984.

© Anne Roper.

ISBN Number 0 9509736 1 0.

This book has been typeset in 10 on 11 point Times Roman and printed by Geerings of Ashford Ltd., Ashford, Kent, England.

The Gift of the Sea~ Romney Marsh

Anne Roper MBE, MA, FSA

Birlings (Kent) Ltd., Ashford, Kent, England

Anne Roper

MBE, MA, FSA

Coming to Kent more than 57 years ago to recuperate after an accident playing hockey for the University College, Cardiff, Miss Roper spent her convalescence in sorting through the New Romney archives and becoming thoroughly immersed in the history of the Town. She became secretary to the late Major M. Teichman Derville, OBE, DL, JP, FSA, Bailiff of Romney Marsh and for twelve years Mayor of New Romney. Local history became her absorbing interest and she launched a pioneer course of lectures on Romney Marsh in 1936, the first was at Ham Street. Up to 1939 Miss Roper was the driving force behind many local history projects, connected primarily with Romney Marsh and South East Kent, with Churches, exhibitions and archaeological studies.

During the second World War Miss Roper was an Army Welfare Officer not only for the troops stationed in the Marsh, but also for the Women's Land Army. A member of the Oxford University panel of extra-mural lecturers she gave many talks on Marsh History, Kentish Inns, the Cinque Ports and Smuggling. For her services to Army Welfare she was awarded the MBE in 1944.

Since the War, in 1948 she was appointed a delegate to the First World Council of Churches held in Amsterdam and also elected to attend the second council held in the United States. She has been a Vice-President of the Kent Archaeological Society for many years and for three years was the first woman President of the Association of Men of Kent and Kentish Men. For nearly twenty years Honorary Archivist to the Corporation of Hythe, A Fellow of the Society of Antiquaries. A JP for nineteen years, a Churchwarden for fifty years. She has written the guide books for many of the Marsh churches and is a Vice-President of the Romney Marsh Historic Churches Trust.

In 1984, His Grace the Lord Archbishop of Canterbury conferred on her a Lambeth Degree of Master of Arts of Oxford University. The ceremony took place in Lambeth Palace Chapel. As the Archbishop's privilege goes back to pre-Reformation times, it was not surprising that the Service was partly in Latin.

Anne Roper is Lord of the Manor of Eastbridge one of the XXIII Manors of Romney Marsh.

DESCRIPTION OF PAINTING

The painting – The Gift of the Sea – has been especially created for the dust jacket of this book, to portray the title.

It depicts the evolution of the Marsh and within its subtle colouring captures the many moods of the Marsh; the land has gentle overtones of the swirling sea, which once covered the whole area, gradually over the centuries receding to leave this valuable, fertile Marsh, as a "gift of the sea". In the background the verdant range of "little hills" remind us of the ancient coastline, the patches of white, the hawthorn blossom, a tree once so important for its wood for many centuries for the sea-wall, and, in contrast, the vivid yellow of a relative new-comer to Marsh, oil seed rape.

The central shadowy figures show the murder of Archbishop Thomas Becket with the three knights, swords upraised, with his chaplain standing by, holding a cross; the Marsh churches are many in number, but Brookland, because of its situation is probably the best known, and has the original wall painting, which was found so unexpectedly during repair work to the exterior of the Church. The knights' armour suggests the period of the thirteenth century, there is also a glimpse of the Brookland weathervane, dated 1797.

In the foreground the fishes, for fishing has always been carried on to a greater or lesser degree along these shores; and then there are the Phragmites, so well known, fringing the Marsh dykes today just as they have done for centuries past. The whole picture captures the sense of timelessness, with ancient and modern standing side by side.

The artist, Gerda Roper, a niece of the author studied Fine Art at Gloucestershire College of Art, Exeter College of Art and at the University of Reading.

She has recently been appointed as Associate Senior Lecturer and Deputy Course Leader of the MA Fine Art Course at Newcastle Polytechnic.

She has exhibited throughout Great Britain and works mainly with oil on canvas and pencil on paper. Her work is in both public and private collections.

CONTENTS

ACKNOWLEDGEMENTS

I would like to thank the following for their informative and kindly help: – Mr. A. Lackner; Mr. K. M. Steel; Mr. Fred Wood; Mr. Ted Carpenter; Mr. A. J. Core; Mr. Peter Richardson; Mr. & Mrs. Tart; Doctor Felix Hull for permission to reproduce his article from the local history journal, formerly called Cantium about the local smugglers, my niece Gerda Roper who has designed the dust jacket and many other people too numerous to mention who during the past forty years have given me information about Romney Marsh, which they themselves will recognise, and lastly but not least my faithful typist without those constant encouragement this book might not have seen the light of day.

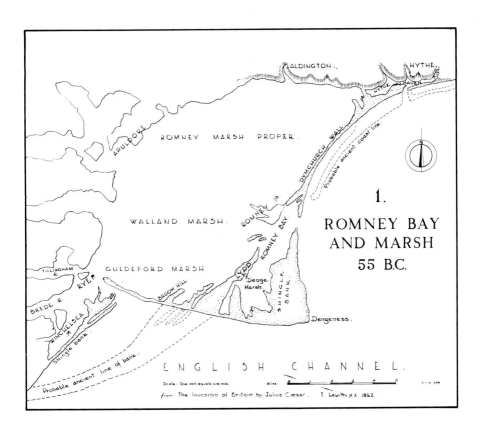

APULDORE

ALDINGTON..

HYTHE.

HYTHE HAVEN

ROMNEY MARSH PROPER.

DYMCHURCH WALL

Probable ancient coast line

WALLAND MARSH.

ROMNEY R

ROMNEY BAY

1.

ROMNEY BAY
AND MARSH
55 B.C.

TILLINGHAM R

GULDEFORD MARSH

RYE

BROOM HILL

LYDD

Denge Marsh

SHINGLE BANK

Dengeness.

BREDE R

WINCHELSEA

Shingle bank

Probable ancient line of bank

E N G L I S H   C H A N N E L.

Scale : One inch equals one mile.

Miles

c.r.a.'44

from The Invasion of Britain by Julius Caesar .   T. Lewin M.A 1862

xi

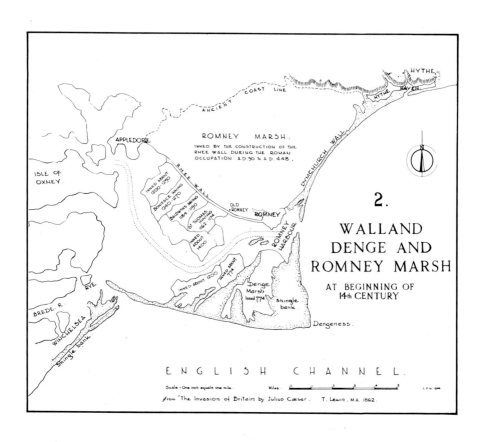

ANCIENT   COAST   LINE

HYTHE

HYTHE HAVEN

DYMCHURCH WALL

ROMNEY   MARSH.

INNED BY THE CONSTRUCTION OF THE
RHEE WALL DURING THE ROMAN
OCCUPATION A.D. 50 to A.D. 448.

APPLEDORE

ISLE OF
OXNEY.

RHEE WALL

INNED ABOUT
1200 1290

BONIFACE INNING
1240 1270

BALDWINS INNING
1184 1190

ST THOMAS
INNING
1662 1714

INNED
ABOUT
1400

OLD
ROMNEY

ROMNEY

ROMNEY HARBOUR

INNED ABOUT 1200

INNED ABOUT
1714

Denge
Marsh
Inned 774

Shingle
bank

Dengeness.

BREDE R.

RYE

WINCHELSEA

Shingle bank

2.

WALLAND
DENGE AND
ROMNEY MARSH

AT BEGINNING OF
14th CENTURY

ENGLISH   CHANNEL.

Scale : One inch equals one mile.   Miles   0   1   2   3   4   5

from "The Invasion of Britain by Julius Cæsar.   T. Lewin. M.A. 1862.

xii

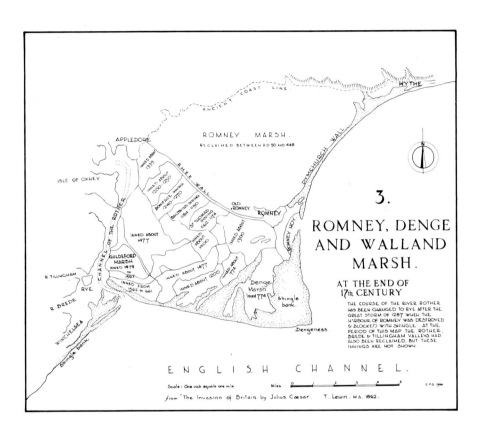

3.

ROMNEY, DENGE AND WALLAND MARSH.

AT THE END OF 17th CENTURY

THE COURSE OF THE RIVER ROTHER HAS BEEN CHANGED TO RYE AFTER THE GREAT STORM OF 1287 WHEN THE HARBOUR OF ROMNEY WAS DESTROYED & BLOCKED WITH SHINGLE. AT THE PERIOD OF THIS MAP THE ROTHER, BREDE & TILLINGHAM VALLEYS HAD ALSO BEEN RECLAIMED, BUT THESE INNINGS ARE NOT SHOWN.

ROMNEY MARSH.
RECLAIMED BETWEEN AD 50 AND 448

ANCIENT COAST LINE

HYTHE

APPLEDORE

ISLE OF OXNEY

INNED ABOUT 1333

RHEE WALL

DYMCHURCH WALL

OLD ROMNEY

ROMNEY

BONIFACE INNING 1240-1270

BALDWINS INNING 1184-1190

St THOMAS INNING 1162-1174

INNED ABOUT 1200-1250

INNED ABOUT 1477

GULDEFORD MARSH INNED 1478 to 552

INNED ABOUT 1400

INNED ABOUT 1300

ROMNEY HOY

CHANNEL OF THE ROTHER

INNED FROM 1562 to 1661

R. TILLINGHAM

RYE

R. BREDE

WINCHELSEA

Shingle bank

INNED ABOUT 1477

INNED ABOUT 1200

INNED ABOUT 774

Denge Marsh Inned 774

Shingle bank

Dengeness

ENGLISH CHANNEL.

Scale : One inch equals one mile   Miles 0 1 2 3 4 5   C.P.O 1966

from "The Invasion of Britain by Julius Caesar". T. Lewin. M.A. 1862.

xiii

CHAPTER 1

The Gift of the Sea

I've loosed my mind
for to out and run
On a Marsh that was old
ere Kings begun.

Kipling

Richard Harris Barham, the author of *Ingoldsby Legends* wrote 'The world according to the best geographers is divided into Europe, Asia, Africa, America and Romney Marsh', and thereby suggested the extraordinary phenomenon of a fifth quarter of the globe.

The name Romney Marsh is misleading, conjuring up as it does great stretches of boggy swamps. Kent's sixteenth century topographer, William Lambarde, described the area in his *Perambulation of Kent* 'The place hath in it sundry villages although not thicke set, nor much inhabited because it is *Hyeme malus, Aestate molestus, Nunquam bonus,* Evill in Winter, grievous in Summer and never good'. For centuries Romney Marsh was believed to be unhealthy, eerie and inhabited by fearsome witches. Today, the reader cannot see such spectacles as described by Barham, of the witches weathering Dungeness Point in their egg-shells or careering across Dymchurch Wall at night on their broomsticks, but there are today many ancient customs and traditions, which make Romney Marsh a place of 'Infinite age and infinite mystery'.

It is situated in the southern corner of the County of Kent and the area extends for some twenty-five miles along the coast from Hythe to Rye, and inland to a depth of ten miles. On the North and North-West it is bounded by the irregular range of hills which marks the ancient coastline and on the South-West by the Rhee Wall, an artificial embankment of early date, constructed from Romney to Snargate.

In early times, the Marsh was entirely under the sea, the waters of which flowed to the foot of Lympne Hills. The River Limen coming down from the Weald debouched into the sea at the foot of the cliffs, making a natural harbour and a safe anchorage for ships. Ceasar when he came in 55 B.C. to reconnoitre for possible landfalls for his planned invasion of Britain chose the harbour of the Limen as one of them. Later, on the hill slopes the Romans built the stout fortress *Portus Lemanis,* which covered eight acres, much of the massive

1

The ruin of the Roman Fortress at Stutfall.

Part of the Roman Fortress at Portus Lemanis, showing the Marsh, which at that time was under the sea.

2

masonry may still be seen, the site is marked on the map today as Stutfall Castle.

Geography is the basis of all history and the history of Romney Marsh can be traced in the long slow story of its changing coastline. The River Limen gradually brought down clay from the Weald, which in course of time spread imperceptibly on the bed of the harbour, and as time went by, the bay became more shallow. This process was hastened by the eastward drift up channel, when the prevailing winds and tides swept shingle round Dungeness Point and into the harbour. As time went on the shingle piled up and formed a natural protective ridge on the seaward side. As the harbour silted up, small sandy islands appeared in the bay and later tracts of land were visible at high water.

The earliest islands of which there are records were Romney and Lydd. A third island formed midway between these two, was called the Middle Isle, recalled in the present parish of Midley. Saxon grants of land as early as the year 697 A.D. and Ethelward's Chronicle of 796 refer to the province of *Mercswari,* or 'men of the marsh'.

Meanwhile the mouth of the Limen had yielded to the pressure of shingle and had found a new channel out to sea carrying the waters of the Weald past Appledore into a broad estuary where Romney now stands. Here on the north bank a Saxon oratory was dedicated to St. Martin and round this, grew up the port of Romney with a busy shipping and fishing trade. From the time of

The irregular range of hills marking the ancient coastline, in winter.

3

Edward the Confessor coins were issued from Romney's own mint and the port became one of the original Cinque Ports.

The sandy islands were now greater in size and became the nuclei of the twenty-three parishes of Romney Marsh, each with its own Lord of the Manor, the manors exist today, although some only in name.

An ingenious system of embanking and draining was carried out, to take the surplus water to the sea. This was done by the cutting of sewers or dykes and the building of defensive 'walls' along the seashore. These walls were made of bundles of thorn faggots, lashed together with enveloping wet clay, which baked hard in the sun. By the thirteenth century with much skillful inning, draining and embanking, a protected area had come into existence. A unique feature of this flat tract of extremely fertile alluvial soil is the fact that it has not been reclaimed from the sea, but the sea has receded from it. The receding waters left behind mineral substances from foreign shores and these combined with the Wealden clay, the sand and the salt gave rise to the growth of that luxuriant green grass which has made Romney Marsh the envy of sheep graziers all over the world. William Camden in *Britannia* wrote 'As Egypt was the gift of the Nile this level tract . . . has by the bounty of the sea been by degrees added to the land, so that I may not without reason call it the Gift of the Sea . . .'.

The peculiar evolution of Romney Marsh and its vulnerable situation, involving constant watch on its drainage and sea defences gave rise to the need for special administration. Scarcely a grant of land was made without some provision for the upkeep of the walls and waterways. This may be seen in the obligations laid down on the tenants. About the year 1120, grants of land at Appledore were made by the Prior of Christchurch, Canterbury, which stipulated 'That the tenants engage to maintain the walls and sewers against the fresh and salt water, and, as often as there shall be need, to repair and to strengthen them according to the law of the Marsh'. So real was the danger of the loss of land by flooding that a lease of 1202 made provision for a decrease in the rent of 6d. for every acre lost by violence of the sea, it is clear that to maintain efficient sea defence, as early as the twelfth century a recognised code had come into existence, referred to as *Lex marisci,* the Law of the Marsh.

By 1250, the special officers who administered the Law of the Marsh consisted of twenty-four sworn men, or Jurats, who were elected by the commonalty. One of their tasks was to see that all holders of land within the Marsh paid their due contributions for the maintenance of the sea walls and watercourses for the common safety. It is interesting to note that after seven centuries, these compulsory levies of 'scots' were still enforced from all landowners in Romney Marsh until 1932.

The threat of inundation was an ever present one and violent storms and tempests in the thirteenth century caused immense havoc. A dreadful tempest in October 1250 was described by Holinshed 'The sea flowed twice without ebbing and appeared in the dark of the night as if it had been on fire and the waves to strive and fight together after a marvelous sort'. This storm, as may be expected necessitated the levying of special contributions for the repair of the walls.

Today Romney Marsh comprises four entirely distinct marshes, Romney Marsh proper, Denge Marsh, which enfolds the town of Lydd and Dungeness, Wallend Marsh, which extends from Lydd to the county boundary, marked on the map as the Kent Ditch, and the fourth lies across the Ditch to Rye and is known as Guilford Level.

CHAPTER 2

The Lords of Romney Marsh

Although there were over thirty manors in Romney Marsh, only twenty-three of them carried the right of representation in the Lathe, and it is curious to find that of these only eleven (of which four were subordinate manors) lay wholly within the boundaries of the Liberty. The manor house, or headquarters of ten others lay outside the Marsh, although the lands extended within it, while in the case of two, Horton and Eastwell, the manors were five and ten miles away, and their interest in the Marsh must have been on account of detached holdings. It is therefore worth while to attempt to identify, if possible, both the marsh holdings and the manors to which they were attached. Sometimes the head manor had the right of representation, in other cases the marshland portion was sufficiently independent to claim for itself the right, while often both head and subordinate manor were represented by Lords of the Marsh. Since the *Lords of the Manors* have played an important part in electing the Bailiff and in attending to the sea defence and land drainage of the district, it is also of interest to trace the early descent of the manors.

New Hall, Dymchurch, the headquarters of The Lords Of Romney Marsh.

7

I. ALDINGTON

Topography. According to Hasted (III, 453) the manor included most of Newchurch parish, the manor of Snargate, most of Ivychurch, including More Court, the manor of Old Langport in Lydd, etc. In 1086 there were in Romney eighty-five burgesses belonging to Aldington, worth £6. (Kent Domesday, ed. Larking, p. 14, line 19). The manor house lay outside the Liberty. Of its subordinate manors in the Marsh only Willop had independent representation.

Descent. A manor of Christ Church Canterbury, to which it was restored in 946. (Birch, *Cart. Sax.* 811.)

1540.   Forced exchange with King.

1547.   Grant to John Dudley, Earl of Warwick.

1549.   To the King, by exchange.

Temp. Charles I, grant to Nicholas Siddenham and Edward Smith.

Eighteenth century.   Held by Thomas Randolph and heirs.

1770, by sale to John Mascall of Ashford. (Hasted, III, 453.)

1804.   To William Deedes.

1919.   J. J. Done.

1929.   M. P. S. White

1965.   P. G. Boulden.

II. BLACKMANSTONE

Topography. A manor lying wholly within the Marsh. In 1346 it included Turnagates, now Marten Farm in Newchurch *(Arch. Cant.* X, 124) which shows that it must have extended beyond the original limits of the Saxon (and still existing) parish of Blackmanstone. It was a fee of the Constable of Dover.

Descent. An important *Saxon manor* granted at the Conquest to Hugh de Montfort.

Temp. Henry I and later held by the de Marinis or Maryns family.

1349.   To Henry Haut and heirs.

1541.   To Sir Thomas Wyatt, by marriage, who exchanged it with the King.

1587.   Queen Elizabeth to Roger Parker, who sold it to William Hall.

1630.   Alienated to Sir Edward Hales, in whose family it descended for over 100 years. (Hasted, III, 431).

1790.   Shoosmith family.

1815.   To Samuel Finn.

1848.   Sir Edward Knatchbull, Bt.

1880.   Sir Edward Knatchbull-Hugesson (first Lord Brabourne).

1913.   Hon. de Grey Beaumont and A. C. Wade.

1919.   Arthur Finn.

1929.   G. F. Finn.

1959.   H. J. Blacklocks.

1962.   Exors of H. J. Blacklocks.

1963. W. C. Blacklocks.
1966. S. H. Blacklocks.
1971. D. J. S. Blacklocks.

III. BILSINGTON INFERIOR
and
IV. BILSINGTON SUPERIOR

Topography. The manor houses of both Upper and Lower Bilsington lie outside the Liberty, but the lands extend into the Marsh. The terrier of the Priory (Bilsington Superior) shows wide possessions in the Marsh in the fifteenth century. (Neilson, *Cartulary of Bilsington Priory,* pp. 148 sq.).

Descent. At the Conquest both Upper and Lower Bilsington were granted to *Odo of Bayeux.*

1090. William de Albeni and heirs, the Earls of Arundel and Sussex. Held by the grand serjeanty of acting as chief butler at the coronations.
1259. The manor was divided.

(a) Bilsington Inferior went to the Fitzalan family.

Temp. Edward III to the Staplegates, who held it by the serjeanty of presenting three maple cups at the coronation.
Temp. Henry VI sold to Sir John Cheney.
1561. To Francis Barnham by conveyance.

(b) Bilsington Superior went to Roger de Somery who sold it to John Mansell.

1253. Foundation of the Priory of Bilsington (cf. Neilson, p. 65). Held by serving the King with his cup on Whit Sunday.
1535. On dissolution leased to Anthony St. Leger.
1568. To Francis Barnham by sale.

The two manors were thus reunited, and remained in the Barnham family, holding by the serjeanty of carrying the last dish of the second course to the King's table, and of presenting three maple cups at coronations.

1700. Passed to Thomas Rider by marriage. (Hasted, III, 468).
1826. To the Cosway family. (Subsequently Halliday).
1905. R. J. Balston.
1930. Hon. Mr. Justice Luxmoore.
1945. Exors of Lord Justice Luxmoore.
1946. Major H. R. Pratt Boorman.
1965. E. R. Pratt Boorman (Bilsington Inferior).

V. BONNINGTON

Topography. The manor house lay outside the Marsh, but the lands extend far into the Liberty. It was a fee of the Constable of Dover.

Descent.

1086. Hugh de Montfort.

Escheat to Henry I, and afterwards granted to the Knights Hospitallers of St. John of Jerusalem.

1540. To John Williams by royal grant, who alienated it to Sir Thomas Moyle, who sold to Sir James Hales.

Temp. Elizabeth to Sir Christopher Mann, by exchange.

1695. Thomas Turner.

1765. Sir Thomas Lombe, by marriage.

1780. David Papillon, by sale (Hasted, III, 461), in whose family it remained. (Holder in 1935 Pelham H. Papillon).

1944. Exors of Colonel P. R. Papillon.

1966. E. M. Boulden.

1974. C. G. Boulden.

VI. BURMARSH

Topography. The manor is also known as Abbats Court. It lies within the Liberty, its subordinate manor of Snave-wick having independent representation.

Descent.

848. To St. Augustine's. (The Abbot held it in Frankalmoigne with view of frankpledge, and claimed sac, sok, thol, theam, infangenethef, girthbreache, hamsoken, etc., in the manor (cf. Thorne's *Chronicle,* ed. Davis, pp. 404, 413).

1538. To King.

1539. Grant to Walter Hendley, and later to Sir William Finch, whose family held it until

Temp. Charles I it passed to Sir Ralph Whitfield. (Hasted, III, 423). In the eighteenth century alienated to the Dering family.

1906. To Thomas Minstrell. (Holder in 1935 Thomas Percy Minstrell).

1961. Exors of T. P. Minstrell.

1969. Brigadier A. S. Ellis, D.S.O.

VII. CRAYTHORNE

Topography. The manor is in the parish of Hope All Saints close to New Romney, and lies wholly within the Marsh. The site of the manor house was represented by a moat, now filled in and ploughed up.

Descent. The early history of the manor is uncertain. It may have been held by a family called Crauthorne.

1467. Held by Sir John Cheney, whose descendant alienated it in
1547. to Sir Walter Hendley.
Temp. Elizabeth sold to Thomas Lord Borough who sold to John Tooke who sold to Edward Choute by devise.
1721. Edward Austin, by devise.
1760. John Amherst, by devise.
1780 (about). William Dunning. (Hasted, III, 506).
1795. Reversion to heirs John Amherst.
1800. By sale to Liberty Taylor.
1885. To Thomas Tunbridge.
1895. Arthur Schreiber.
1920. To T. J. Pearson, in whose family it remained until 1947.
1948. Sir Edward Hardy.
1969. R. M. Older.

VIII. EASTBRIDGE

Topography. A manor lying within the Marsh, including most of Dymchurch and having originally two churches (Eastbridge, now ruined, and Dymchurch). Known as the "Sea-girt manor of Eastbridge" the Homage in the seventeenth century presented "that the royalty and claim of wrecks at sea belong to this Manor and extend along the sea coast from Brockman's Barn wall to Romney Warren Post." (Records of the Court Baron of Eastbridge, 1650-1802).

Descent. A manor of Godwin, Earl of Kent.

1086. Held by Hugh de Montfort.
Temp. Henry I escheat to Crown.
1229. To Hubert de Burgh who gave it to the Maison Dieu, Dover. (Hubert de Burgh held it by the petty serjeanty of a sparrowhawk at Lammas annually. Furley, *Weald of Kent,* 1874, Vol. II, pt. i, p. 71).
At the dissolution passed to the King.
1563. Granted to Cuthbert Vaughan and together with Honeychild passed later to the Twysden family, and then, by marriage, to the Derings. (Hasted, III, 433).
1920. By sale to J. Constantine.
1923. H. W. Henshaw.
1928. To Major Teichman Derville.
1963. Exors of Major Teichman Derville.
1964. Miss Anne Roper, M.B.E., M.A., F.S.A.

IX. EASTWELL

Topography. The parent manor is north of Ashford and west of Wye, nearly ten miles from the Marsh. It owned a detached holding at Schingledehalle *(Arch. Cant.* V, 297) which is probably represented by a field called Shinglehall on the east of the St. Mary-Blackmanstone road, south of Turnagate bridge. The detached portion had no independent representation. It was a fee of the Constable of Dover (cf. Elton, *Tenures of Kent,* p. 210).

Descent.

1086.	Hugh de Montfort.
Temp. Henry I	escheat to the King.
Temp. Henry III	to the Crioil family.
1360.	By marriage to the Poynings.
1447.	By marriage to the Percy family, Earls of Northumberland.
1531.	To Sir Thomas Cheyney, etc., and later to Sir Christopher Hales, whose daughters sold it to Sir Thomas Moyle.
1560.	By marriage to the Finch family, Earls of Winchilsea.
1769.	Finch Hatton family. (Hasted, III, 196).
1827.	Earl of Winchilsea and Nottingham.
1893.	Lord Gerard.
1922.	To Osborne Dan.
1925.	Sir John Pennefather.
1930.	To Viscount and Viscountess Dunsford.
1944.	The Countess of Midleton.
1978.	Messrs. T. Bates & Son.

X. FAWKENHURST

Topography. Falconer's Hurst, or Hurst Manor. The house called Falconhurst near the ruins of St. Leonard's church was probably the manor house. The lands extended into the Marsh and in the eighteenth century the marsh lands amounted to 105 acres. The manor was one of the fees of Dover granted to Fulbert of Dover. (Hasted, IV, 61).

Descent.

Henry II granted the manor to William son of Balderic, to hold by the grand serjeanty of keeping one falcon for the King's pleasure. His descendant Godfrey le Huton took the name of Le Falconer and his family held it under this name till

1394.	when the descendants took the name of Michelgrove. They had free warren, view of frankpledge and assize of Bread and Ale.
1400.	To Sir John Shelley, by marriage.
c.1711.	Alienated to George Carter. (Hasted, III, 459).
1906.	To R. H. Green.

1942. Exors of R. H. Green.
1943. Capt. G. H. Wyndham-Green.
1960. Miss S. F. Wood.
1964. E. R. Wood.
1977. Mrs. Muriel Wood.
1978. J. L. Boulden.

XI. HORTON

Topography. Otherwise known as Monk's Horton, about five miles outside the Marsh to the north-east. In 1140 "the land and men of the marsh" were given with Horton to the newly founded priory of Monk's Horton *(Arch. Cant.* X, 270). There is perhaps a clue to the site of some at least of the marsh lands attached to the manor, in the record of the same date, that the monks held "xxviii solidos terre in marisco de Rumenel, quam Erininilda tenuit" *(Arch. Cant.* X, 271). Erininilda was the wife of Osbert the Mariscall, or Marshall, and among the place names of Dymchurch are Marshalls Bridge, and adjoining it Great Mascall Field (in 1820). Since Dymchurch was part of the land of Hugh de Montfort and Osbert one of his men, this may well retain the memory of that early benefactor of the Priory. Possibly Sutton Farm in Dymchurch represents the original farm house. The priory had a small interest in Eastbridge manor *(cf. Arch. Cant.* X, 271). Tinton manor was also held by the Priory but had separate representation.

Descent.
1086. Hugh de Montfort.
Temp. Henry I, Robert de Ver.
1140. Granted to Horton Priory. The prior owed service for the repair of the Pencester tower in Dover Castle.
1537. To Thomas, Archbishop of Canterbury.
Temp. Elizabeth, to the Queen.
1652. To the Mayor and Commonalty of London.
1654. Sold to George Rooke of Mersham.
Temp. Queen Anne, to Thomas Morris (by alienation) and to his descendants. (Hasted, III, 316).
1795. To the Rt. Hon. Lord Rokeby.
1857. John Kirkpatrick.
1900. G. C. Swindels.
1917. To Lt. Col. E. R. Wayland.
1942. Exors of Lt. Col. E. R. Wayland.
1946. Sir Wm. Wayland.
1951. H. R. Ledham.
1955. J. Davis.
1969. S. Salbstein.

13

XII. HONYCHILD

Topography. A manor in the parishes of St. Mary's in the Marsh and Hope All Saints. The manor house is still on the map and named Old Honychild. There is another house named Honychild Manor, which was also part of the demesnes of Honychild as sold in 1858. But the presence of a field called by the old name of Forstall in relation to Old Honychild, and the way in which its lands, even in 1858, followed closely the parish boundary leaves little doubt that this was the original manor house.

Descent.

1086. Hugh de Montfort, who held by knight service.

Temp. Henry I, Robert de Ver, who held by knight service.

Temp. Henry III, Hubert de Burgh, who gave it in

1247 to the Maison Dieu, Dover, to hold in frankalmoigne.

Temp. Henry VIII, to the King.

1563. Cuthbert Vaughan (with Eastbridge) passed later to Twysden family.

1613. Alienated to Sir William Sedley.

1780. Sold to Jeremiah Curteis and John Waterman, attorneys of Rye, who conveyed it to Sir Edward Dering. (Hasted, III, 505).

1919. To the Rev. E. Owen, in whose family it remained until 1969.

1945. Exors of A. S. Owen.

1961. N. Owen.

1970. Vacant.

1974. K. Armstrong.

XIII. KENARDINGTON

Topography. A boundary manor, with the manor house outside the Marsh and the lands extending into the Liberty. According to Furley (II, 713) originally a den of Aldington. It was a fee of the Constable of Dover.

Descent.

1066. To John de Fiennes, as part of the constabulary of Dover Castle.

Temp. John, William de Normanville by knight and castle guard service.

1283. By marriage to the Basing family.

1446. By marriage to the Machworth family.

Temp. Henry VII, by marriage to the Wise family.

1532. Conveyed to Roger Horne of Horne's Place.

1565. Escheat to Crown because Richard Guldeford, who held it by marriage, refused to take the oath of supremacy.

1597. Queen Elizabeth granted it to Walter Moyle. Held by the Moyle and Moyle-Breton families. (Hasted, III, 115).

1848. To Rev. Edward Moore.

1862. Count Ernest Augustus Bonar.

1893. Charles Orford.

1906. J. H. Lorden.

1960. H. Lorden.

14

XIV. NEWINGTON FEE

Topography. Newington Fee *alias* Dymchurch. According to Hasted a part of the manor of Newington Belhouse near Hythe, which had no representation in the Marsh. Possibly the parts of Dymchurch not in Eastbridge became attached to Newington Belhouse, which, like Eastbridge, was a de Montfort manor. The origin of the manor requires further investigation.

Descent.

1086. Hugh de Montfort.
Temp. John, Baldwin, Earl of Guisnes.
Temp. Henry III, Hubert de Burgh.
1271. Thomas de Belhouse, who held it by knight service.
1374. To the Knevett family by marriage.
1507. To the Clopton family by marriage.
1537. Thomas Lord Cromwell (by alienation).
1540. To the King.
1554. To Edward Lord Clinton and Sale.
1555. Alienated to Henry Herdson.
Temp. James I, alienated to Henry Brockman.
1707. The Rev. Ralph Drake-Brockman (Hasted, III, 392, 427), in whose family it remained until 1970.
1971. Vacant.
1976. D. H. Duff.

XV. ORLESTONE

Topography. A boundary manor, with the manor house outside the Marsh and lands extending into the Liberty. It was a fee of the Constable of Dover.

Descent.

1086. Hugh de Montfort.
Temp. Henry I, William de Orlestone and heirs (held in chief by knight service and castle guard).
1429. To Sir William Scott of Scotts Hall, by marriage.
c.1726. To Sir Philip Boteler (by sale).
1776. To William Bouverie, Earl of Radnor. (Hasted, III, 477).
1824. Thomas Thornhill.
1865. To Thomas Oliver, in whose family it remained until 1965.
1966. Vacant.
1970. J. M. Lancaster.

XVI. PACKMANSTONE

Topography. Hasted says the manor was in Newchurch, but its precise position seems to be unrecorded. It was possibly near Gammon Farm. From the fact that in 1271 it changed hands with Ashford (Brit. Mus. Anc. Deeds, V, A.11766) it is probable that it was subordinate to that manor and represented the marsh holding of Ashford. In 1268 Matilda de Eastwell, widow of Simon de Crioil, held two knights fees in Ashford, Sevington, Packmanstone and Esture. *(Arch. Cant.* V, 297). In this case the head manor had no separate representation.

Descent.

1268.	Part of the Crioil lands.
1271.	Leybourne family.
1367.	Escheat to King, owing to lack of heirs.
1388.	Granted to the Canons of Chiltern Langley, Herts.
1538.	To Richard, Bishop of Dover.
1544.	Sir Thomas Moyle.
1559.	Sir Thomas Kempe (by marriage).
Temp. Elizabeth,	Thomas Smith, by alienation.
1632.	Maurice Barrow by marriage.
c.1660.	To the Godfrey family.
1769.	To William Mackenzie (Hasted, III, 465), (who assumed the name of Godfrey).
1840.	To Archibald Stoakes.
1914.	E. Bath.
1924.	T. N. Cannon (whose executors were the holders in 1935).
1945.	R. N. Cannon.
1947.	H. F. Link.
1952.	A. A. Link.
1967.	Miss H. V. Link (now Mrs. H. V. Langrish).

XVII. RUCKINGE

Topography. A boundary manor, with the manor house outside the Marsh and lands extending into it. It was a fee of the Constable of Dover. It was a subordinate manor of Ickham, near Canterbury, and as such the subject of many Saxon charters. The head manor was unrepresented in the Lathe.

Descent.

791.	To Christ Church, Canterbury, by grant of King Offa.
1066.	To Hugh de Montfort.
1076.	Restored to Christ Church.
1539.	To the King.
1541.	To the Dean and Chapter, Christ Church. (Hasted, III, 472).
1921.	H. J. Body.
1958.	Exors H. J. Body.
1964.	R. S. Body.

XVIII. SNAVE

Topography. The manor lies about St. Augustine's church at Snave, to the east of the Snave-Stockbridge road. Its subordinate manor of Snavewick (Week) had separate representation.

Descent. A fee of the Abbot of St. Augustine's.

Temp. Richard I, John de Snave held of the Abbot.
Temp. Edward III, William de Sokenesse held of the Abbot.
1346. William de Orlaustone.
1475. The Haut family.
Temp. Henry VIII, Sir Thomas Wyatt (by marriage).
1541. Exchanged with the King.
1580. Grant to John Baptist Castillon.
1586. Sir Henry Sidney.
Temp. Charles I, alienated to Sir George Stonehouse, who alienated it to the Marsh family.
1753. John Winchester, by devise.
1781. John Marsh, by devise. (Hasted, III, 494).
1901. By sale to Arthur T. Schreiber.
1920. H. P. Collick.
1931. Major Teichman Derville.
1963. Exors of Major Teichman Derville.
1964. E. S. Buck.
1982. Mrs. M. Buck.

XIX. STREET

Topography. The manor is in Lympne parish. The old house may be represented by Manor Farm. The demesnes sold in 1864 extended over Lower Wall southward into the Marsh. It was a fee of the Constable of Dover.

Descent.

1086. Hugh de Montfort.
Henry I, the Hadloe family. (In 1274 Nicholas de Hadlow was accused of diverting a road used by the marshmen, in order to establish a market place. (Furley, *History of the Weald,* II, 138)).
1346. Divided:
    a. John Colvile and heirs.
    b. Lisle, Laurence, and Spicer.
1492. Reunited in hands of Francis Colvile.
1533. Alienated to Edward Thwayts.
1569. Alienated to Edward Jackman.
Temp. Elizabeth, alienated to William Hewett.
1662. George Lovejoy (by sale).
1694. Sir William Honeywood (alienation). (Hasted, III, 438).
1909. Rt. Hon. Lord Ashburton.

1911. A. B. Wood.
1943. Trustee of A. B. Wood.
1952. Mrs. E. M. A. R. Duthoit.
1953. J. A. Duthoit.
1978. G. W. Duthoit.
1982. J. Duthoit.

XX. TINTON

Topography. The south part of the parish of Warehorne. The manor remains with its old name, its lands extend well into the Marsh and there are also some detached portions, mentioned in Domesday.

Descent.

1086. Hugh de Montfort.
Henry I, Robert de Ver.
Temp. Henry II, granted to Horton Priory.
1535. To the King.
· 1537. To Thomas, Archbishop of Canterbury.
Temp. Elizabeth, to the Queen.
Temp. James I, grant to Sir William Sedley.
c.1780. To Mr. Jeremiah Curteis and John Waterman of Rye, attorneys, who conveyed it to Sir Edward Dering. (Hasted, III, 480).
1930. To Capt. Hon. Michael Knatchbull (Lord Brabourne), in whose family it still remains.

XXI. WAREHORNE

Topography. A border manor.

Descent.

820. Godwine by charter of Egbert.
1010. To Christ Church, Canterbury.
1086. Christ Church (in frankalmoigne).
Temp. John, held of the Archbishop by knight service.
Temp. Henry III, Richard de Bedeford.
Temp. Edward II, Hugh de Windsor.
Temp. Edward III, William de Moraunt.
    James Peckham (by marriage).
    Haut family (by marriage).
1541. Sir Thomas Wyatt (by marriage).
Temp. Elizabeth, Ellis, sold to Thomas Paget and Thomas Twisden.
1600. By alienation to Sir John Tufton (Hasted, III, 479) and his descendants the Earls of Thanet, Lord Hothfield and the Tufton family.
1930. Dr. F. W. Cock.
1944. G. T. Paine.
1983. J. H. Paine.

XXII. WEEK (COURT-AT-WEEK or SNAVE WICK)

Topography. A subordinate manor of Snave, which was also linked to Burmarsh. It lay to the west of the Snave-Stockbridge road.

Descent.

848. To St. Augustine's Abbey. The Abbot had view of frankpledge, wreck of the sea, pleas of felons, gallows, pillory tumbril, etc. (cf. Thorne, pp. 413, 404).
1538. To the King.
1539. To Walter Hendley.
1547. The King — who conveyed it at once to Thomas, Archbishop of Canterbury.
Temp. Elizabeth, the Queen, who granted it for a term of years to Yates.
Temp. Charles I, King granted reversion to Patrick Black. Conveyed by Blake to Sir Robert Austin.
1772. Passed to Sir Francis Dashwood, Lord le Despenser (later to the Stapletons who became lords Despenser). (Hasted, III, 495).
1866. Thomas R. Startup.
1942. Exors of T. R. Startup.
1952. H. S. Buck.
1966. S. P. Buck.

XXIII. WILLOP

Topography. Willop was a manor subordinate to Aldington, probably comprising the detached portions of Aldington in the Watering which perpetuates the name of Willop. The boundaries of this Watering coincide for long distances with those of the detached portion of Aldington by Lympne and Burmarsh. It probably included also land to the east of the two detached parts of Aldington.

Descent. Held by the Archbishop till 1540, when an exchange was made with the King.

1540. Granted for eighty years' lease to John Knatchbull. The Knatchbull family had leased the manor from the Archbishop since at least 1512 (cf. Rental quoted by Furley, *History of the Weald,* II, 425).
1610. To Eldred and Whitmore for sixty years.
Charles I granted to Sir Edward Hales, who sold to George Green who alienated to William Glenvill (and Glanvyl-Evelyn).
1790. Lord Romney and executors of W. Green and William Evelyn. (Hasted, III, 441).
The Earl of Romney in whose family it remains.

19

Above: The nineteenth century Corporation Punch Bowl, still filled at the Lord's annual lunch.

Right: The Great Chair of the Bailiff of Romney Marsh.

The Common Seal of the Bailiff of Romney Marsh. (Actual size) from an impression in the British Museum. (Seal No. 5347).

20

The names given as present holders are those of the Lords summoned to attend the Grand Lath, Whitsuntide, 1984.

All manorial rights, dues and incidents were extinguished by the 31st December 1935 and the manors to all intents and purposes exist in name only. From a Romney Marsh point of view, the fact that the Manors themselves are not extinguished all together is of material importance as the survival of the Lordships in some form would appear essential to the continued existence of the Corporation of the Lords, Bailiff and Jurats. The ceasing of this appointment would affect the sister Corporation of Bailiff, Jurats and Commonalty of Romney Marsh and they would be deprived of their annual meeting on Michaelmas Day.

CHAPTER 3

The Cinque Ports of
New Romney and its Limb of Lydd

The story of the Cinque Ports forms a unique and colourful part of the history of England, and it was the geographical position of the Ports, ringing the south-eastern seaboard, which gave them their history. Their rise and subsequent decline may be traced in the long slow process of a changing coastline.

The Norman French designation, "Cinque Ports", was given to this group of towns, which are in geographical order, from west to east, Hastings, Romney, Hythe, Dover and Sandwich. That is the order in which they appear in early documents and charters.

The origin of the confederation is lost in antiquity, but there is documentary evidence of its sea services from the time of Edward the Confessor.

In the twelfth century the ports of Rye and Winchelsea were added with equal privileges, but the old title of "Cinque Ports" was too firmly rooted to be displaced, so that the two new members, became, officially, the "Two Antient Towns". Later, other towns called "limbs" were added to the head ports and enjoyed the same duties and franchises, so that as time went by the name Cinque Ports came to be used collectively for the whole Confederation.

Their primary duty was that of supplying the King with fifty-seven ships, manned with a crew of twenty men and a "garcon" or "gromet", in time of war to fight his battles, and in times of peace, to provide passage across the Narrow Seas to France. The Five Ports and the Two Antient Towns were equal in status and privilege. They differed in the number of ships they were bound to provide, the larger towns, like Hastings and Dover supplied twenty-one vessels each, while Romney and the smaller ports were called upon to provide five ships.

In return for their responsibilities they enjoyed unrivalled privileges from the Crown, freedom from Royal Taxes, within their liberties, the right to hold their own Courts, independent of Shire and Hundred Courts, the right to land and dry their nets on The Strand at Yarmouth, to regulate the annual Herring Fair there and perhaps the most zealously guarded of all privileges, Honours at Court, this was to bear the canopy over the Sovereign at his or her Coronation.

Most of the Portsmen were fishermen possessing their own boats ready and seaworthy at short notice. To convert these vessels into warships when

23

summoned for duty, fore and stern castles were erected and the crews armed. The Cinque Ports fleet often has been called the cradle of the navy and there is no doubt they formed an important nucleus of the Fleet until they were superseded in later centuries by larger vessels built in the Royal Yards.

The Cinque Port fleet was sometimes summoned to sail to such far away places as Holyhead, to convey troops to Ireland, or to Skynburnesse or to Chester and even to Dublin. Writs were constantly issued to the Ports for their service on the King's various expeditions against the Welsh and the Scots, in fact it was the Cinque Ports fleet that captured the Isle of Anglesey when the Welsh Prince Llewellyn was forced to sue for peace. The Cinque Ports fleet also had a large share in gaining the naval victory at Sluys in 1340, when the Lord Warden himself commanded the sixty Cinque Port ships.

One cannot ignore the naval side of mediaeval wars, the landing of armies and vast stores on the coast of France in The Hundred Years War, or going to the support of land forces in Wales and Scotland with their supplies. They were the only ports legally bound to furnish the King with a number of ships properly manned whenever he had need. Until the fourteenth century these craft were the small fishing boats, familiar on seals and coins. The portsmen so often found themselves matched against greatly superior forces, and larger vessels, but the traditions of centuries and their innate aptitude for seamanship often turned the balance in their favour. They stood a poor chance in violent storms, heavy seas, and the cross tides of the channel, with their single square sail and masses of woodwork at the rising bow and stern. Oars were a poor substitute for a rudder and chroniclers tell of wholesale disasters that sometimes overtook the mediaeval flotillas. Gradually the more roomy "cogs" used by merchants, came into service. With the larger vessels this created the need for more masts, the rudder had now become common, and the compass soon followed. The boats had become ships manned by skilful sailors, even so, they proved no match for the great Spanish Armada Galleons that sailed up Channel in 1588. Each port was ordered to send a ship but few came from the ports themselves, many of them had silted up and to comply with their duty they were forced to hire.

A cess or tax was levied on the inhabitants, over sixteen years of age, of each Port to furnish a ship of fifty tons "warlikely furnished". Romney hired a vessel called "The John of Chichester" for which Lydd, as its Limb, was to contribute half the cost. Lydd has never paid to this day its full share and there are constant references to the debt in their records!

From the responsibilities of the Cinque Ports it is well to consider some of their privileges. Chief of these was the right to hold their own Courts of Justice, which each of the head ports did in its own town. The central law court of the whole Confederation was the ancient Court of Shepway, derived from Ship Way, the way of the ships. For when Lympne was a port, *Portus Lemanis,* the sea lapped against the foot of the hills on which the Shepway Court was held. This was the common Court of Justice and goes back to the year 1150, long before there were judicial courts and over a hundred years

24

before Parliament came into existence. It was a Royal Court, the "King's High Court of Shepway", and this gave the ports a distinct and privileged position. It was held originally in the open air and no place is more closely identified with the Cinque Ports than the site at the top of Lympne Hill, where the beautiful sculptured stone cross, presented by Lord Beauchamp during his Lord Wardenship, and quite mediaeval in character, crowned with the figure of the Blessed Virgin and the Holy Child in her arms, one hand upraised as if in blessing and on the reverse a representation of the Crucifixion. It was erected as a memorial to the men and women of the Cinque Ports who lost their lives during the First World War. The cross was dedicated by the then Archbishop of Canterbury in 1926.

The very existence of Shepway Court was a source of unity to the Ports, an opportunity for closer association. The only person who could summon or preside at Shepway was the Lord Warden, appointed directly by the Sovereign. As the Sovereign's representative the Warden alone could convey royal commands to the Court, was responsible for calling out the Cinque Port fleet and he alone could summon the Barons to the Coronations. The Court was intended primarily as an instrument for administration and control, linking the Ports through him to central government.

A formal summons was necessary for the holding of the Court. The Lord Warden sent writs to the head officers and each corporate Limb, forty days before the appointed date. This was an exceptionally long warning, shire courts required only six days, but attendance was compulsory, defaulters were fined ten marks, and this long interval allowed time to bring back Portsmen who had gone abroad, fishing, trading, or on the King's service.

The Court assembled at nine a.m. and was declared open by solemn proclamation, an inquest of twelve was impannelled, who took the oath upon the Book and sat in the Court behind the bench of Clerks.

Cases of treason, falsifying money, disputes over fishing, the finding of wreckage, disputes always with the men of Yarmouth, another about goods plundered from Flemish merchants, treasure trove, unlicensed change of market days, the return of outlaws, the chattels of fugitives, the sale of ships to enemies, the escape of prisoners and evil doers across the sea, keeping the assize of bread, of ale, and of measures. Wherever Portsmen were, or in what ever part of England they committed an offence, they could always claim to be tried in the *"Curia Regis"* The Cinque Port Court of Shepway, it cannot be emphasised too much the importance and historic interest of this Royal Court.

Apart from judicial matters, special sessions of the Court were held to instal the Lord Warden in office. When he had received his Commission from the King, he directed a letter of Summons to each Port to be present at Shepway forty days later. His commission was read out, he then took the oath to uphold the "Franchises and usages and customs of the Five Ports. Of his power he shall keep and maintain". The Warden then lifted his right hand, breast high,

25

The Shepway Cross at the top of Lympne Hill.

26

and replied "Yes, if God will, I shall to my power". The Ports' representative bowed to him once and presented him with a gift, formerly a hundred marks in a silken purse, but in later years a piece of silver.

Not until the seventeenth century was the Shepway Court moved to Dover, for the greater convenience of the Lord Warden, it was held in St. James' Church, which became known as the Chancery of the Ports.

In the eighteenth century the post of Warden, was almost a close preserve of Prime Ministers. Lord North, Pitt, Lord Liverpool, The Duke of Wellington, Lord Palmerston and Lord Salisbury. The Duke of Wellington was the first Lord Warden to receive no pay, his predecessors had enjoyed a salary of £3,000 a year.

In 1980 Portsmen everywhere rejoiced at the news from Buckingham Palace that Her Majesty the Queen had appointed Her Majesty the Queen Mother as the new Lord Warden of the Cinque Ports. She was installed, at Dover, in August, in her eightieth year, succeeding the late Sir Robert Menzies.

There were two other courts peculiar to the Confederation, the Brodhull and the Guestling. These were pre-eminently the Courts of the Portsmen themselves, for the transaction of their private business and held independently of any officer of the King or of the Lord Warden. They form the most original feature of the constitution of the Cinque Ports and in them was developed the machinery for the exercise of their common rights and the defence of their privileges, it was a more intimate and less formal Court, until the two Courts were combined under the common name, Brotherhood and Guestling.

From the fourteenth century the Courts were held in the parish church of St. Nicholas at New Romney. It was the central port and here the priceless records of the Ports were housed. These included the famous White and Black Books of the Cinque Ports, so called because the earlier volume is bound in white vellum and the continuing volume in black leather; together with the Charters these books are the most important archives of the Ports. They contain the formal minutes of the Brotherhood and Guestlings from 1432 until 1571, the Black Book begins in that year. They are entirely contemporary and present a vivid picture of the assemblies, reflecting the growth in stature of the Ports, their zeal in maintaining precedent, how they appointed their Bailiffs to attend the Herring Fair at Yarmouth, but above all, very detailed accounts of the Coronation service of the Ports, the bearing of the canopies, descriptions of their costumes, the rehearsals, the journeys by barge to Westminster stairs, the procession to the Abbey and the subsequent banquet in Westminster Hall and the sharing of the canopies and bells before they "took their several ways homeward". Early pages of the White Book describe Queen Eleanor's coronation in 1236 and Richard II in 1377. Procedure is much the same as is followed today.

The Courts of Brotherhood and Guestling fill a significant place in English

Constitutional History, for they witness to the strength of democratic institutions in this country in mediaeval times. It is the Portsmen, summoned by their Speaker to manage their own affairs, who largely laid the foundations of popular government, and none need denigrate this old-world ceremonial as a pointless anachronism.

New Romney

Of the two Cinque Ports towns in Romney Marsh, New Romney and Lydd have long vied with each other. There was an old saying "Romney for pride and Lydd for money".

The early history of Romney is bound up with the River Limen, afterwards called the Rother, and the vicissitudes through which it passed. The Limen coming from the Weald of Kent debouched into the sea at the foot of the range of the Lympne hills which formed the ancient coastline. Later on, owing to the pressure of shingle which was swirled into the harbour, the Limen was forced to find another outlet and made its way under the hills to Appledore and thence to Romney, where on the northern bank of the river mouth the Saxons built an Oratory, dedicated to St. Martin. In a grant of King Ethelbert dated 740 A.D. he made reference to the chapel of St. Martin here.

In the time of Edward the Confessor Romney had a flourishing shipping trade. Silver pennies were minted in the town and some have been found as far afield as Norway, showing the extent to which trade went in those days. Romney continued to issue coins from her own mint until the reign of Henry 1st.

In 1066, the Normans who had been planning an invasion of Britain, set out from Wissant and attempted to land at Romney, the gallant Romney sailors, whose sea-worthy boats were ready to go to sea at short notice, repelled the invaders, who were forced to go further along the coast and attempted to land at Rye. Here they were repulsed by the Rye fishermen and eventually made landfall on the deserted shore at Pevensey. It is said that in their anxiety to be the first to set foot on English soil they so jostled each other that William himself fell headlong on the shingle "Making his nose somewhat bloody upon the beach". Apparently he was distressed and took it as a bad omen, but his cheerful steward, FitzOsborn, comforted him and said "Even so my liege, have you sealed England to your posterity with your own blood". After the disastrous battle of Hastings, William marched straight to Romney "To take what vengeance he could for the slaughter of his men". He then went on to Dover, took the keys of the castle and set out for London. One of his trusted followers, Robert, was left in charge of Romney and became known as Robert de Romenal.

It must never be forgotten how much is owed to the Norman masons who built the magnificent Norman church, dedicated to St. Nicholas, the patron

The magnificent Norman Tower of New Romney Church.

29

saint of sailors and of children. The great west entrance is reached by descending a flight of stone steps and one is then at the original floor level of the Norman church. The visitor cannot fail to appreciate this fine example of a Norman doorcase, although sadly, the outer moulding of beaks heads, has weathered badly. Entering the nave immediately one is impressed by the strength and solidarity of the Norman arcading, with its decorated arches and the well preserved clerestory. At the east end are the unusual three conterminous chancels. Above the high altar, the east window has delightful reticulated tracery with Victorian stained glass, commemorating members of the Stringer family, well known in the town for many generations.

On the south wall will be found the Royal Arms of Queen Anne and on the east wall of the south chapel a tablet commemorates Thomas Lancaster, Captain of the Militia and Mayor of the town for many years. As a Baron of the Cinque Ports, he supported the canopy over Queen Caroline at her coronation in 1727. On the floor in the north aisle of the nave there was a mediaeval brass to William Hollingbroke, members of this family played an important part in the town's affairs, unfortunately the brass itself has been lost, but there is an interesting inscription, in Lombardic lettering, written in Old French, dated 1375, which reads:—

"Pries p l'ame willea holingbroke que devia le XVIII jo d'october Pan de grace mcclxxv".

The word "devia" is unique and is not known to occur on any other brass.

Norman arcading and the Queen Anne pews, New Romney church.

30

A brass worthy of note dated 1510, is in the north chancel on the floor, near the fourteenth century recessed Easter sepulchre. Below the figure of Thomas Lamberd is the following, roughly rhymed verse:—

> "Of yl charitie pray for me,
> Thomas Lamberd of Romeney,
> Which died the XXIII day of August,
> In lykewyse so all ye must,
> For dethe is sure to alle mankynde,
> Therefore have my soule in minde,
> Which ended mdx
> i yeres of hym y dyed for alle men."

It is thought he was a relation of Kent's Elizabethan topographer, Thomas Lambarde.

On the wall of the south aisle is an interesting memorial tablet to "Isaac Warquin, who was born at St. Quentin in Picardy and fled from persecution in France after the Revocation of the Edict of Nantes. He found refuge in New Romney in 1689, where he continued in the practise of physic with success and general applause. And adorned this town and Port with useful learning and lively Christian charity. He died in 1725 aged 61.

This tablet is erected by his friend John Deffray."

On the chancel floor of Old Romney church will be seen a large floor slab commemorating John Deffray "the faithful and diligent Rector of this parish for forty-eight years."

These two tablets reveal the story of two friends who fled to England to escape persecution and who were able to spend their lives so usefully and in peace in Romney Marsh.

The Churchwardens' accounts begin in 1663 and are continuous until the present day. In 1739 money was paid to provide a new ladder for the Church. In 1741 money was given "to buy a pair of leather bodices and a linsay woolsay gown and coat for a poor girl of this parish." In 1756 it is ordered "that a box be made with deal for the Minister to stand in, on performing the burial service." This was known as a Hudd, but twenty years later it is named as a "Century (sic) Box." For some time it served as a back porch to a house in the parish, it has now fallen into decay. The Sentry box was superseded by an umbrella bought for the use of the Church at a cost of 15s. in 1788. The oldest Parochial Register dates from 1589, births, deaths and marriages are all recorded in one vellum bound book.

Until the passing of the nineteenth century Municipal Corporations Act the election of the Mayor took place annually in the Church on the 25th of March, the Jurats assembled around the tomb of Richard Stuppenny in the south aisle. He had died in 1526, but his tomb was renewed in 1622, by his great-grandson, Clement Stuppeny. On a brass on this altar tomb is engraved the following:—

"Here lyeth buryed the bodye of Richard Stuppenye, Jurate of the towne in the first yeare of Kg. Hy. Viij in the eighteenth yeare of the sayde Kynges reigne of whose memorye Clement Stuppenye of the same port his great grandsonne hath caused this tombe to be new erected for the use of the ancient meeting and election of Maior and Jurats of the port towne June 10th anno dm 1622."

An interesting feature of the Church was its constant use for the town's business from quite early times. The Jurats in 1393 paid 20d for a "desque", to stand in the church "for their use". In 1405 while the Jurats were holding a session there, a presentment was made respecting the discovery of 250 pounds of wax on the seashore. In the name of the Archbishop, the Bailiff took possession of 88 pounds and the residue was divided among those who found it. One of the Vicars of Romney, John Hacche, was so horrified by the Jurats holding their session in the church during divine service, that in 1407 he gave 3s. 4d. to the Town Funds, on condition that this practice was not repeated.

St. Nicholas is the last remaining church of the five churches that stood in Romney originally. The oldest was St. Martin, possibly built on the site of the Saxon oratory, dedicated to that Saint, which was demolished in the sixteenth century. The churches St. Martin and St. Laurence were appendant chapels to the parish church of St. Nicholas.

St. Laurence stood next to the present Forge at the west end of the High Street. In 1477 the Jurats of the Town went there on Lady Day and for many years following, to elect the Bailiff. This important meeting was later transferred to the south aisle of St. Nicholas church, at the Stuppenye tomb. In St. Laurence's tall tower the town clock was kept.

Coming from the Ivychurch direction, the ruins of the church of Hope All Saints greet the visitor. From 1318 to 1589 this parish had its own Rector, but because of its "slender value" Archbishop Parker joined the benefice to that of New Romney. The church fell into decay in the eighteenth century and the bells were removed to the tower of St. Nicholas.

The Chapel of the Lepers' Hospital provided Romney with its fourth church. According to a decree of Pope Alexander III *"De Leprosis"* all lepers were to have their own chapels and were forbidden to frequent any other church. This chapel founded by Adam de Cherring about 1180, was refounded in 1363 by John Fraunceys, an early Bailiff of Romney, with a chaplain and a master. The name Lepers' Spital survives today in Spitalfield Lane and Spitalfield Villas, which mark the site of the Hospital.

During an excavation of the site in the 1930's, stained glass from the chapel windows was found together with mediaeval keys, a leper token and a tomb of an early founder, possibly a Master, or Chaplain.

At the cross roads in the High Street stood the Priory of St. John the Baptist, with its chapel. It is curious that there never seemed to be a burial

High Street, New Romney, showing on the right the entrance to the Town Hall and on the left the old prison, note the iron barred windows of the cells at ground level, and above, the larger window.

ground attached to this Priory, but a site in St. John's Lane has yielded many skulls and bones, and it is concluded that this was the land used for a burial ground by the Prior of St. John's.

Romney is extremely fortunate in possessing a remarkable collection of records illustrating the Town's history from 1352 to the present day. These records have now been removed from the Town Hall to the County Archives office at Maidstone, where they are properly safeguarded and kept under correct conditions of temperature and humidity. They have now been carefully catalogued.

One of the earliest Assessment Books the Town possessed dates from 1381. This contains a list of inhabitants of Romney, over the age of fifteen and the amount each was assessed for the Poll Tax, which led to Wat Tyler's insurrection. The christian names themselves are of interest, among the more popular men's names were:—

| Hamo | Brice | Odigar |

Among the girls' names are:—

Aghata	Demisia	Matildis
Avice	Elena	Parnel
Bretonissa	Elicia	Sarra
Celestria	Isabel	Tethina
Christina	Magota	

In these early days there were no surnames, but people were identified by their occupations or their place of residence. Lapin ate well, Adam ate bushe (The Inn Keeper) John le sole (John at the pond) John Pastiler (The Pastrycook) Peter Newene (The New Inn).

Other interesting extracts from this assessment book include the following details for the making of a new sluice . . . .

"First, paid for two great trees, called beeches, bought at the wood of Lythelhaie, 18s. 2d. and for cutting them down 8d. and for bringing them on sleds 6s. also for the wages of Thomas Pot and John in making a pit for sawing the said trees, 1 day 8d. also for the wages of the sawyers, sawing the said trees into planks, to be made therefrom for the bottom of the said sluice 14s. 2d., with drink, paying one couple per day 14d. . . . . Also for timber bought at Romene 8s. 2d. and for the carriage of the said timber, together with one piece of timber formerly lying near St. Johns House 2s. 3d. by boat to the sluice . . . . . . Also, for the wages of Henry Smythe for the making of the clenches, agned, and nails with other ironworks there 5Li. 12s. 6d. . . . . Also, for two and a half barrels of pitch and four gallons of tar for the said gates 10s. 4d. And, for eight pitch-crocks bought for boiling the said pitch and tar there 16d. . . . . Also, of the said William Child and Simon Clerk, staying daily at the said work overlooking the workmen with hire of their horses 26s. 11½d." Unfortunately the account for making the sluice is incomplete and ends at this point.

Another interesting account was that for the fitting out of the Town's barge that was to go to France to fetch "The Lady – Queen Eleanor".

"Also, paid to Richard Lullynge, carpenter, for the making of the cabin for the use of The Lady The Queen, and for the stocking of the gun and for mending the lower side of the fane, with his own timber 3s. 8d. and for nails bought for making the cabin 6d. Also, paid for six sprit had of J. Gaioler of Doverre going before at the cabin 12d. Also, paid for one ell and a half of linen cloth for the fane and for making the said fane anew with the said cloth 8d. Also, paid J. Lowys, cooper, for making a new bail and mending the old bail and lantern of the barge 16d. and 2d. . . . . When the said barge was taken from the Pale to Fogelnesse there in a short time it was driven up on the seashore and so, for six shovels, bought for digging beneath it there 10d. Also, for the wages of Laurence and Morice and his fellows in taking out the ballast and digging beneath the barge and getting it back again into the channel 3s. 6d. and in ale 15d. . . . . Also, for victuals bought. First, paid for eight and a half quarters of baked wheaten bread bought for the voyage, 59s. 6d. Also, paid for forty-three barrels of ale of one sort 4Li 19s. and for four barrels of another high sort, 15s. Also, for beef bought wholesale, 37s. 10d. and for two whole steers bought of Thomas Lovecock, alive, 30s. The entrails and the hides of which were sold, as set forth in the account. Also, for one barrel of white herrings bought 13s. 4d. and for a thousand of red herrings 13s. Also, for two bushels of white pease bought 20d. Also, for thirteen and a half pounds of candles bought 2s. 9d. Also, for one quarter of coarse salt bought 5s. 8d. And paid for the washing of certain barrels to hold water for the said barge, 5d. Which victuals were provided and bought by J. Rose and Roger Piers, then Constables of the barge. Given to J. Yve, writing down their expenses, in ale, 3d. . . . ."

For many years the Archbishop of Canterbury was the Overlord of Romney and appointed the Bailiff, the people of Romney resented this as he was primarily the Archbishop's representative and possibly did not have the interest of the people of Romney really at heart. During the troubled and unsettled period of the Wars of the Roses, Romney had become very restive in this matter and decided to set up their own Mayor. In 1484, they even sent to Canterbury and had a silver mace made. After the Battle of Bosworth and the end of the Wars, the King, Richard III, heard of the "bogus" Mayor who had been elected, he sent down "one Adam Tuter, to depose the said Mayor." This was a great blow to the Town and it was not until the reign of Queen Elizabeth, who with womanly diplomacy, in 1575, granted the Town a Royal Charter of Incorporation. This original Charter is in a beautiful gold tooled leather case to which is attached Queen Elizabeth's seal.

The morals of the young men of the Town were also well looked after. In the Town's records we find several references to fines imposed for playing at "Le cards". The New Romney Apprentice Indentures of the fifteenth century, stipulate that the apprentices "Are not to play at dice, chance, nor chess, nor habitually frequent the Tavern." During their apprenticeship they were not only forbidden to contract marriage with any woman, but they might not even "betroth themselves to any". Fines for being out late at night were imposed as late as 1599, with unusual severity, as is shown by an entry "received of John Goddard for a fyne for his night walking contrari to the decrees of this town" xxs.

There are references to Jack Cade's insurrection and it appears apart from the treason of his politics and his use of magical books he was accused of having "Rered upp the divell in the semblance of a blak dogge in his chamber".

But not all the Town Clerks of the day took life too seriously, for at the bottom of a dull series of accounts, written in a fifteenth century hand, we find, *"Dum sumus in Mundo Vivamus Corde Jocundo"* – "So long as we are alive let us live with a joyful heart".

One of our notable Town Clerks was Thomas Caxton, alleged to be a relation of William Caxton, the printer, who had written "I was born in the Weald and lernt mine English there". There are several books written in Thomas Caxton's vigorous and legible hand. The brown ink of the period was made from oak galls, gum arabic and rainwater.

Dogs would appear to have been a source of considerable worry to the Corporation since the earliest days. In 1414, in Henry V's reign, an order was

35

made that "all dogs should be expelled from the Town or safely kept so that they do no harm under a penalty of 20p." Some hundred years later, one Manning was appointed Dog Whipper and paid 12d. for his wages. The following entry will cause no surprise. "payd to Robert Pell for looking to Manning's legges XXs." Mannings evidently recovered from the bite as the Town continued to pay his salary for many subsequent years. In another of the Town's records called the *Book of Notte* is an interesting entry that "On the thirde day of January 1579 was the decree for dogges red and proclaymed in the Churche of St. Nycholas after Evensonge that all inhabitants of New Romney disposed to keep any dogge or curr, shoulde before the twelfth of the said month enter their dogges and observe the decrees upon payne in those decrees expressed." These were admitted to keep dogges:—

"John Cheeseman, Mayor − A great balde branded Mastiff
William Epps, Jurat − Three red spannelles, one bitch all spoted red.
William Southland, Jurat − A white Mastiff dog, with a black eare and a black spot in the rumpe.

Another owner was permitted to keep "A black spannelle with a whyte garland about ye neck, a grey hounde whelp black with iii whyte feete and a whyte typpe of the tail;" another a red curr without a tail, a mongrell bitch, grey faced somewhat whyte upon the brest."

The Town's income was derived mainly from the letting of the Corporation lands, and from the Leases of the various Kiddell or fishing grounds, provided that "The Mayor and Jurats and all other gentlemen of the Town and Port should have all the turbot and mullets as they shall think fit at 3d. per lb for mullet and 1½d. for turbot"! The Town Mill must have been profitable too, for there are continuous references to it from earliest days. A special committee was appointed for its letting and repair. In those days when corn was grown in great quantities on the Marsh it was one of the Town's most valuable possessions. It is amusing to read the almost affectionate terms used in reference to the old mill, when in 1794, it was decided to rebuild it. "She being in a very bad repair, her mainpost being decayed, and she being so old and worn out". In the fourteenth century however, there were no less than five windmills mentioned and the Town mill, which was painted white, must have been the last survival of a flourishing milling trade. Unfortunately this mill had to be burned down during the First World War, as its position on a hillock made it a landmark for any enemy coming across the Channel. Its site is recalled in a bungalow "Mill House" − of which the architect was Ernest Newton, the architect of Regent Street in London.

From time to time quite large sums of money were spent on the Corporation's personal entertainment. In 1646, when Colonel Brown sent a buck to the Corporation, it was "Thereupon ordered that an ordinary of 12d. be provided against tomorrow noon, and that as well the Freemen and their wives be invited to eat thereof and that every couple shall be allowed a pint of wine at the cost and charges of the Corporation". This was probably the origin of the Corporation's famous Venison Feast, held annually on September 22nd and abolished only in 1797. This was only one of the Corporation's feasts and in 1764 a decree was passed that a steady sum should be allowed out of the Town's Funds "To be spent on the entertainment of Kings but only the body corporate invited thereto", although hogsheads of beer were provided for the people.

1530 is the date usually assigned for the introduction of beer into England, owed to the arrival of hops.

Hops and turkeys, Bays and Beer,
Came into England, all in a year.

Romney was well in advance of the times for a hundred years before, in 1427 it was ordered that "two men called Ale Conners shall be chosen to strain and taste the beer made in the Town, the makers of the beer to send for the tasters to approve same, and if good upon proof, they shall sell it for a penny half penny and no more, if not good then at a penny". In another hundred years, in 1528, an enactment provided that all beer is to be sold in Romney at three quarts for a penny, and that any housewife that infringes this order is to be fined 12d. and give up her Tavern.

In early days the sea must have come up eastwards almost to the line of the present Dymchurch road, for permission was granted to place capstans on it for winding up the fishing boats. Here on this reclaimed Warren land was situated the Romney Racecourse, where the race meeting was held annually in the eighteenth century for a cup of Gilt Plate, given by a generous Corporation, who at that time were evidently more sportingly minded. Today, the Warren Inn, has a sign depicting a jockey coming up to the winning post and the bridge that crosses the dyke is still marked on O.S. maps as "Horserace Bridge".

On the Warren also stood a lonely building, known as the "Pest House", built in 1742 as an early isolation hospital for sufferers from any pestilential disorder. There were no medical officers of health in those days, but earlier Mayors did not neglect the health of the Town and in 1609 when the plague was raging, there is an entry of items paid to two men "To mind and keep the people of St. Mary's from coming to this Town for that divers people of St. Mary's have died of the plague".

The conies on the Warren were a source of income to the Town too.

When the Armada invasion appeared to be a serious threat to this country it is interesting to see the plans made for the defence of Romney. As the central Cinque Port it held an important position in the defence of the coastline and in the corresponding measures taken by the men of Romney to prevent an enemy landing on the shallow beaches. A map of 1588 shows the defences of the town in Queen Elizabeth's reign, and a document of the reign of Queen Anne has an estimate of the charges of the ordnance, carriages and ammunition proposed as necessary for the defence of the town "if Her Majesty shall think fit".

"Iron Ordnance:—   Saker 2
                    3 pounders − 3 £55. 4s.
                    Saker − 3 tonns 9 cwt at 16 Li a tonn £3. 3s.
                    Round shot for saker 3 pounder
                    Bedds Coins and breechings
                    Ladle and sponges − Saker 2
                    3 pounds bullets
                    Ladle staves 3 at 12d. each   3s.
                    Saker 2
                    Pounders 3
                    Cases of wood for cartridges
                    Funnells of Plate
                    Corn Powder
                    Match
                    Aprons of lead
                    Crows of Iron
                    Linch pins
                    4 Lockeys
                    Small melt ladles
                    6d. nails"

This document is undated, but it would seem to be about 1708 when the French collected an invasion fleet at Dunkirk, which was bound for Scotland. The English had no idea where the threat of invasion would fall, hence the careful preparation.

When Pitt was Lord Warden of the Cinque Ports, during the wars of the French Revolution and of the Irish Rebellion in 1798 a general deputation of the Cinque Ports and their members met the Lord Warden at Dover Castle, as a result of which £6,500 was secured to form units within the Ports. The Cinque Ports contributed *"two units − The Cinque Ports Fencible Cavalry and the New Romney Fencible Cavalry"*. Troops of Yeomanry and companies of Volunteers were also raised within the Ports, Pitt himself subscribing £1,000, and the Port of Romney raised £104. 17s. 6d.

Ten years earlier when Lord North was Lord Warden there was in existence during the War of American Independence *"A Cinque Ports Battalion of Fencible Infantry"*, which was commanded by the Lord Warden himself, and was often referred to as *"North's Cinque Ports"*. The Battalion was reviewed at Dover Castle on the 6th May 1780 and received a very favourable report, being complete to its establishment of 414 Officers, N.C.O. and Men. The unit served at Maidstone and in the Sittingbourne area and was disbanded in May 1783.

In 1927 the Romney, Hythe and Dymchurch Light Railway with an 18 inch gauge was opened by the then Lord Warden, the Earl Beauchamp. How little could anyone have thought of the important part this railway with its diminutive coaches was to play in the defence of the Marsh, in the Second

World War. The tiny engines such as, "Doctor Syn" and "Hurricane", were now employed in pulling gun-mounted platforms along the track from New Romney to Dungeness, and westward to Hythe, in contrast to the trainloads of laughing holiday makers. Apart from patrolling this track they were also used for transporting ammunition etc., and other military stores.

The Southern Railway trucks, in contrast, were engaged in evacuating hundreds of sheep from this vulnerable coastline long before the evacuation of women and children.

John Southland, son of William Southland was born in the 1540's at Honeychild Manor in the parish of Hope All Saints, he came of one of the wealthiest and most active families of New Romney. His father was Mayor. John was a Magistrate and a member of the "Select Band", in a Muster Roll of 1583 he is mentioned as answering correctly for "a bill, a bow, a sheaff of arrows, a spade and a shovell". In 1588 William Southland, his brother, was Captain of the "Select Band" and had the oversight of the Beacon and of The Helmes Beacon. Great importance was attached to the system of beacons along the coast "paid to a man bringing a letter from Lord Howard, the Admiral, for watching the bekons for the Scots and Frenchmen".

John Southland died in 1610 and in his will, left a messuage or house in New Romney in which Jonas Adams did dwell at the time of John Southland's death and also the house wherein the said two couple of poor people of the said John Southland, viz Edward Mitchell and his wife, wydow Springate and Wydow Edes at the time of the death of John Southland did and yet do now inhabit and dwell to be from henceforth an Hospitall or a biding place for the poor to have forever. After three hundred and seventy years "Southland Hospital" or the "abiding house" for the poor is situated in West Street, New Romney and from the plaque on the wall a seventeenth century Mayor, Robert Austen, paid for the houses to be repaired and put in good order. In this present year, 1983, The Trustees of the Hospital are very active in looking after the inmates of the houses which have recently had Central Heating installed, a more shallow staircase and other necessary modern facilities.

In addition to the "abiding house" for the poor, John Southland had directed "that the Governor was to take an interest in the welfare of the old people, accompanying them to Church on the greater festivals, entertaining them to dinner at the "Governor's" house afterwards and dividing the sum of Five Pounds a year among them, by half yearly payments of twelve shillings and sixpence each", he was to take great care of all the Charity's property, leasing the farms out profitably and seeing that the New Romney houses were kept in first rate repair. "He was freely to teach two poor children until they were fourteen years of age." From these small beginnings it is wonderful to see how the new Southland's Comprehensive School and the Lower School with over a thousand pupils has evolved today, with the many and varied activities of twentieth century education.

It is good to feel that the name of John Southland is alive today, both in the Almshouses and in this extremely well-equipped modern Comprehensive School.

In spite of the great changes which have taken place in almost two thousand years, New Romney still is one of the head Cinque Ports. No longer do two representatives sit in Parliament in accordance with the nineteenth century Reform Bill; no longer is there a Market Cross; no longer does the Town Hall stand on pillars with an open market beneath; and no longer is the Mayor elected in the parish Church annually; no longer are the children taken to school on buses, except from the outlying districts, but they now travel on the Hythe and Dymchurch Light Railway, between Hythe and Dungeness. No longer can the fisherman depend on the thriving and lucrative herring fishery, yet, the Town is busy and flourishing, although its trades and crafts have changed greatly.

Today there is no harbour, but Rudyard Kipling succinctly wrote:

And East till Doubling Rother crawls
To meet the fickle tide,
By dry and sea-forgotten walls
Our Ports of stranded pride.

Romney in America

It is interesting to recall that in West Virginia, in Hampshire county, there is a town called Romney. No records of the town give any indication of the connexion with Romney in Kent, except the brief words . . . . "A ten acres plat was surveyed and laid off into lots of half an acre each and the Town named Romney for one of the Cinque Ports of the English Channel".

From the beginning, the settlers wished Romney to be a *town* which carried certain privileges. Lord Fairfax was responsible for the initial move and on this ten acre plat, he sold half acre plots. The streets were made sixty feet broad, intersecting each other at right angles. At each corner is a "stake" named after the trees planted there:— Five Sycamores Corner; Spanish Oak Bushes; the North Corner has a "stake" between Two Black Oaks and another corner is called White Oaks. The half acre plots were divided into blocks, as they are still, by lanes, Birch Lane, Rosemary Lane, Grubb Lane and now Court House Lane.

The Hampshire County Court House was built in 1922 to replace the older Court House built a hundred years earlier.

There is no doubt, as a Town, Romney has played a significant part in the business, political, social and religious development of the beautiful South Branch Valley.

Romney too was an early seat of learning and culture, with its Classical Institute, its Potomac Seminary and its Literary Hall. Around the Institute and the Seminary the State developed the schools for the deaf and blind. The Literary Hall is now the Library.

Lydd

Lydd has a long history from Saxon times and is a "limb" of the Cinque Port of New Romney. This great tract of land originally was one vast bay of the sea, over the waters of which vessels sailed to the old port at the foot of the Lympne hills.

By Saxon times some sandy islands had increased and some existed above high water level. The islands where Romney and Lydd now stand were the earliest to be inned and protected, with Midley, "the middle island" situated between them.

As early as the eighth century, Saxon charters refer to "Hlyda", a word derived from the Latin *"littus"* meaning shore. When Aethilbert, King of Kent, granted certain lands and rights here to the Monastery at Lyminge, including "the right to pasturing a hundred and fifty cattle, next to the marsh which is called Bishopswick, as far as the wood called Ripp." This mention of the Ripp Wood is significant as the Ripp or Rype, today includes the Holmstone, or Holly stone, "Holen" is the Saxon word for holly, and there are still traces of this remarkable Holly wood on the unfertile, inhospitable shingle, which establishes the site of the wood called Ripp, in this charter of 740 A.D.

The charter of 744 A.D., is even more interesting, for it is endorsed *"Ad hlidum in marisco de romenal"*. This is a grant from King Offa to the Archbishop of Canterbury, of the right to "wreck of the sea and stranded monsters". There is too evidence of a stone Saxon church at Lydd, remains of which may be traced in the north west walling of the nave, which sets beyond all doubt Lydd's existence before 740 A.D.

Hardy seafarers and traders settled here attracted by the rich fishing grounds and convenient haven. Early records tell of battles between Saxons and Danes, fought at the Wick and Holmstone in 904 A.D., when the Barons of Lydd so distinguished themselves that the Archbishop of Canterbury granted them the Rypes as a reward for their valour. The boundary of this gift is described as Stone End, now modern Greatstone.

In the great Domesday survey Lydd is recorded in the Hundred of Langport and reference is made to its twenty-one Burgesses and its seven salt pits, a precious commodity of those days.

But it was during the thirteenth century that Lydd reached the height of her prosperity and was so flourishing in trade and importance that she became a

"Limb" of the neighbouring Cinque Port of New Romney and was called upon to help with the provision of men and ships before the days of a regular navy.

In Queen Elizabeth's reign, Lydd and Romney were ordered to provide a ship to join the fleet in the Channel when the Spanish Armada had been sighted off The Lizard. By this time the small fishing boats were totally inadequate and too small to be "warlikely furnished" that it was necessary to hire a ship, "The John of Chichester", at a cost of three hundred pounds. Lydd contributed only a fifth of this amount and it is doubtful whether the owner ever received full payment. Romney commented ruefully "It is well known that Lydd is treble as wealthy as Romney".

Thomas Caxton, alleged to be a brother of the famous printer was appointed Town Clerk at Lydd in 1458 at a princely salary of £3. 13s. 4d. and "a new stuffe gowne" a year. The Town's affairs were administered by a Bailiff and twelve Jurats, not very successfully perhaps, for during the Wars of the Roses, Lydd sent men to fight under the Earl of Warwick and then paid troops to help the King. Caxton's appointment as Treasurer soon put matters right. He died in 1495 and is buried in the churchyard.

On one occasion a hasty tempered sailor, John Dyne, quarrelled with the Vicar, who rejoiced in the name of William Love, Dyne smote him and was promptly put in the stocks. At night his fellow mariners came secretly and released him. The Jurats of Lydd had to appear before the Archbishop and the Town Clerk was summoned to Rome to answer for the offence. When he returned he tried to be equal with the next Vicar of Lydd by opening his love letters, for which he was arrested and put in fetters.

During the Napoleonic Wars barracks were built at Lydd and Dungeness and among the contemporary lists of those volunteering for service are familiar names:— Finns, Cobbs, Tourneys and Terrys. Before the First World War, when Lydd was an important artillery practice camp, the shingle wastes were used for carrying out experiments with high explosives. It is difficult to believe this now peaceful town gave its name to that destructive explosive "Lydite".

Lydd is the most southerly Town in Kent and although its area is large from the point of view of population, it is one of the smallest boroughs in England, with 5,000 inhabitants.

The glory of Lydd is its magnificent mediaeval church, lofty and spacious, dedicated to All Saints. It is the longest, nearly two hundred feet, and one of the highest in Kent, and locally known as "The Cathedral of the Marsh". The church stands at a corner of the High Street with its imposing fifteenth century tower, one hundred and thirty-two feet high. Cardinal Wolsey was the Rector here, and during his incumbency, it is alleged that he was responsible for adding the final stage to the tower, with the delicate pinnacles. The commanding view from this topmost stage made the Tower an admirable

All Saints Church Lydd, from the east, showing the rebuilt chancel.

The unusual double entrance doors of the Tower into the church, Lydd.

43

lookout for observers searching for the enemy, all down the centuries. The Church is entered by an unusual pair of double doors leading into this massive tower.

At the north-west corner of the nave will be seen some Saxon arcading *"in situ"*, all that remains of the Saxon church which stood on this spot a thousand years ago. In the nave the Early English arcades consist of seven arches supported by circular pillars with large octagonal bases, which were used to provide seating for the elderly and infirm in the Middle Ages. This custom gave rise to the expression "Let the weakest go to the wall", an expression of courtesy, today alas, one of contempt.

The splendid roof, an exceptionally fine example of octagonal king-posts and tie-beam roof. The moulded and battlemented tie-beams rest on ornamental wall pieces.

On the 15th of October, 1940, the church clock stopped at 4.07 p.m., the elegant Early English chancel had been completely destroyed by a direct hit from a High Explosive bomb. Sadly, in addition, the church received much subsequent damage from Flying Bomb attacks in 1944. Protective repairs were carried out, and damaged ceilings removed and timber for the choir roof was made available for work to begin; the parishioners of Lydd were determined the Church should be restored to its original glory. Intensive fund raising efforts were made over the years, the estimate for repairs was Forty thousand pounds. Contrary to the advice of the Diocesan Advisory Committee, that a new chancel should be formed from the east end section of the nave, the parishioners themselves set to work to raise the necessary money to rebuild the chancel and to furnish it; this large sum increased, but they were greatly helped by a devoted and generous churchwarden. The modern craftsmanship is in complete harmony with the architecture of the Church.

The north and south chapels are interesting and in the south chapel is a remarkable thirteenth century double *piscina,* with two deeply chiselled drain basins, and one basin was for the ceremonial washing of the celebrant's hands before he consecrated the Holy Elements, the other for the washing of the Chalice after the Communion, so that no drop of water that touched such a sacred vessel should go anywhere but into consecrated ground. In 1300 the Pope decreed that the Celebrant at Mass might drink the ablutions, as is done today. The only other example of double drains in Romney Marsh is at St. Mary-in-the-Marsh.

On the north wall of the Chancel is a memorial tablet to Thomas Godfrey born in 1553 and who died in 1632, it was little short of a miracle that this carved memorial escaped destruction. He was a member of one of the oldest families in Lydd and there are Godfreys still living in the Town. There are several brasses to members of this family, the earliest dates from 1430, but the oldest brass commemorates John Mottesfont, a vicar, who died on November 6th 1420, several church brasses were badly mutilated after the bombing, but these have been carefully restored and set in a wooden framework on the north wall. It is interesting to note that it was round the Stuppenny tomb of 1608 the Jurats and Commonalty of Lydd assembled yearly, on St. Mary Magdalene's day to elect the Bailiff and Jurats. This custom was carried out until 1885, when the then Bailiff became the first chartered Mayor of Lydd.

In the churchyard lies Lieutenant Thomas Edgar, one of Captain Cook's companions on his voyage round the world, he was with him when he was killed by cannibals in Karakakoa Bay in February 1778, the inscription on his tombstone reads:—

"Lieut. Thomas Edgar of Royal Navy who died October 17th, 1801 Aged 56. He came into the Navy at ten years of age, was in that memorable engagement with Admiral Hawk, and sailed round the world with the unfortunate Captain Cook of the "Resolution" in his last voyage when he was killed by the Indians at the Island of Owhie in the South Seas 1778.

Tom Edgar at last has sailed out of this world,
His shroud is put on and his topsails are furled,
He lies snug in death's boat without any concern,
And is moored for a full due a'head and a'stern,
O'er the Compass of life he has merrily run,
His voyage is completed his reckoning is done."

There are many other interesting old tombstones in the churchyard, one to Samuel Finn, who commanded the battery at Dungeness in the early nineteenth century, and was Captain of the Lydd Volunteers. Several memorial stones commemorate members of the Lydd smuggling gangs.

The Town Hall is in the High Street and now incorporates in its building the old "Lock-up". Here are preserved a splendid collection of archives, properly housed, including a fourteenth century Charter, Elizabethan books of Chamberlain's accounts, a silver Mace with an Elizabethan Loving-Cup cunningly concealed in the top. There are too the old branding irons for the Town's flock of sheep, and many maps, prints and books of great interest.

At the end of Cannon Street is the original mediaeval Court House, now in use as a shop. One of the bedrooms, formerly the Court Room, boasts of a fine King post and tie-beam, and in plaster-work, the Royal Arms of Queen Elizabeth I. The ground rent, under a nine hundred and ninety-nine years Lease, a peppercorn, is paid annually to the Corporation.

There are many interesting old houses and shops in the High Street and adjoining streets, some with the typical Kentish weatherboarding, others tile-hung, some with attractively carved doorways with hoods, some are timber-framed, but were re-fronted with stucco in the eighteenth century, many have hip-tiled roofs and hipped dormers.

45

On the outskirts of the Town are several charming old Farmhouses, Dengemarsh Farm, the manor is mentioned in Domesday Book, the house is built of mellow seventeenth century brick, with hipped tile roof and dormers; Boulderwall Farm, an earlier house re-faced, has casement windows with small leaded panes and some old green glass. Tourney Hall is an early eighteenth century house with a delightful doorway with brick pilasters and entablature. Much of Vine House dates from the seventeenth century and was enlarged in the late eighteenth century, the original is of warm red brick with grey stone headers and the doorway has a flat hood supported on brackets. Jacques Court is one of the older houses of the Town and parts of it remain from the fifteenth century. Traces of the moat can still be seen. In the church, in the north wall, lies the tomb of Sir Walter Menil, who lived here, he died in 1333. It is an interesting stone figure, in fourteenth century armour.

One of the most notable characters in Lydd in the eighteenth century was William Waylett, the Man-midwife, he was the son of an apothecary of Rye, where he was born on December 3rd 1728 and he was buried in Lydd church, October 25th 1815, aged 86 years, as by Law, he was buried in woollen, "6 yards superfine flannel at 3s. 6d. – £1.1s.", this was for the shroud, and "5 yards fine ditto at 2s. 6d." this was to line the coffin. The total funeral expenses amounted to £32. 10s.

Men midwives were customary at this time, and it is interesting to find that Waylett kept a day book, "A list of Women delivered by William Waylett since settled at Lydd". He divided his headlines into columns – Date; Name; Place; Month of Pregnancy; Character of labour and presentation; Sex of child; Number of Pregnancy; and the last column of all "The Fees, paid or unpaid". During the last twenty years he was assisted by Thomas Sargent, his nephew, who suceeded him finally in the practice. The ordinary fee was half-a-guinea, which was the Poor Law fee at that time. The highest fee received was four guineas and that apparently for a special case, a six-mile journey across the Marsh brought in an extra five shillings, a ten-mile trip along the coast produced a whole guinea or now and then a guinea and a half. There were absolutely no hard roads then, and all journeys had to be made on horseback. He considered the practice one of the hardest and poorest in the south of England. Dr. Waylett was the last man in the neighbourhood to wear a "Double-decker" wig, one with two rows of curls at the bottom, like that still worn by State Coachmen and he always walked about with a daisy in his mouth. This practice was kept up by several old gentlemen in Lydd, one in particular carried a piece of Lavender in his mouth to Church, this was done by way of prophylaxis, reminiscent of the herbs strewn on the ledge of the dock, in front of prisoners, and by nosegays of the same, presented to the Judge at the trial, to ward off jail fever.

In the fifteenth century men were paid by the Town for watching in the steeple of the church against "the approach of foreign foes". From the church accounts it is noted that new organs were purchased in 1428 which seem to

Jacques Court one of the oldest houses in Lydd, believed to be the home of the Menil family.

An upstair room at Jacques Court, showing the timber framing and the lathe and plaster walling.

47

have been renewed or repaired twenty-six years later. In 1465 mention is made for rent paid for the house in which were "the great organs". At the church stile Royal proclamations and important municipal notices were announced or "cried". As was customary in the Middle Ages there were several altars in the Church. There were at least ten different shrines in which lighted tapers were kept burning to honour the Saints most revered in Lydd. The Saints thus honoured were:—

The Virgin Mary; All Saints; John the Baptist; St. Peter; St. Katherine and St. George.

There was also a light called the "light of Dengemershe" and another called the "light of Westbrook". There were several fraternities or Guilds of lay-parishioners which were connected with the Church. Various bequests and gifts were made to the Church and by this means many alterations and additions of a minor kind were able to be provided. The donors often stipulated that in acknowledgement of their gifts their names should be recited every Sunday from the pulpit by the parish priest, who commended them especially to the prayers of the congregation. In 1746, John Seawlys left ten marks for the pewing of a large part of the Church. In the south aisle there were traces of frescoes, it was possible to discern a circular roundel upon which was a crowned king in a sitting position. On the north wall are the remains of some remarkable carved screenwork, which survived the bombing. On the south wall in the vestry is the very fine Russell memorial, to a beloved daughter, Ann, who died in 1780, and to her only child Henry who died in January 1781. She is holding up the child to the angels who are waiting to receive him. This is a remarkably fine example of Flaxman's art.

In the Middle Ages, annually on the Feast of St. Nicholas, the 6th of December, the Boy Bishop was elected. He was robed in episcopal vestments and his two attendants were chosen. They usually processed round the Town and during the period of his office he was lavishly entertained with his attendants wherever he went. Lydd records contain fascinating details of his visits to various parishes, involving in some cases quite long journeys. He gave his blessing wherever he went. His office came to an end on Holy Innocents day, December 28th. New Romney parish also elected a Boy Bishop at the feast of St. Nicholas, who with his attendants enjoyed much entertainment on his various visits, including several to Lydd. Before the destruction of the chancel in 1940, on the east wall there was a stained glass roundel with the head of a Boy Bishop.

A Typical entry reads . . . . "item paid on St. Nicholas' Day for expenses incurred over the Bishop of St. Nicholas of the town of Romney, in bread, wine, ale and other victuals".

For the last hundred years Lydd has been an important Army Camp. At first only during the summer months when the firing took place from a position near Boulderwall Farm directed towards Dungeness, later it was carried out over the Holm Stone. The troops were entirely under canvas. In 1893, soon

48

after the railway was opened, a line was extended to the Camp and round the ranges to the sea, this line was constructed of the lines laid down by the British Army from Suakim to Berber to relieve General Gordon at Khartoum. In 1906, huts were built and Lydd became a Siege Artillery School and was permanently occupied, later owing to the great increase in the range of guns, its available ranges of 4-5,000 yards became useless. The artillery moved to Salisbury Plain, while Lydd became a permanent station for the Tank Corps. At Lydd too in 1910, the first experiments were carried out in observation from the air, before the days of flying. A flight of kites was sent up which strained a wire and along this was sent another kite with a man carried in a basket, who clamped himself at whatever height he wished and was later hauled down by a ground line, when he had completed his task.

After the Second World War a great many returned officers who had been prisoners since the beginning of the war had a course of rehabilitation at this Camp, to help them to take their places in civilian life again.

How the people of Lydd must regret the passing of the old Lydd Brewery, which once supplied such good beer to the neighbourhood, the water was found to be especially suitable for brewing and for many centuries one of the town's important decrees forbade anyone who kept a tavern or tippling house to put out for sale beer brewed out of the Town. It was at this brewery the first experiments were initiated in using carbonic acid gas given off from the vats to make soda water. There are a number of attractive Inns in Lydd today. It was to the George Inn in the High Street two German spies, in the early days of the war tried to gain admittance, early one Sunday morning, the fact that they knew nothing of closing hours gave them away and the military were called in and took them back to Intelligence Headquarters for questioning. They were equipped with a hundred pounds each in English money and a radio set, and had come ashore near Jury's Gap and walked to Lydd.

Another feature of this ancient Cinque Port is the Lydditte hatchery, the largest in South East England, handling some thousands of Day-old chicks each week.

Ferryfield Airport midway between Romney and Lydd will be seen, the wide and spacious entrance to one of the world's busiest airports, Lydd Airport. The air ferry was inaugurated in 1948, its two terminal airports, Lympne and Le Touquet in France, were chosen because they formed the closest possible cross channel link, by 1953 it was clear that Lympne could no longer cope with the volume of traffic and the only alternative was for Silver Cities to have its own Airport, work began in January, 1954, and in less than six months Ferryfield was ready for its first commercial flight, which took place on July 13th, 1954. There were two runways, three thousand six hundred feet and three thousand two hundred feet, both one hundred and twenty feet wide. On the 345 acre site was built a two-storey terminal building, the new airport had cost £320,000. By the end of July 1954 the airport was in full operation, over 112,000 passengers and 42,500 vehicles were flown across the channel. One day in July there was a record of 222 crossings. In 1956, H.R.H. The Duke of Edinburgh flew his personal D.H. Heron aircraft to Ferryfield and toured the airport. Today, the airport still functions both commercially and for private users.

One of the most interesting installations associated with the linking of the electrical power systems of Great Britain and France was the installation of the Cross-Channel cable, laid in 1961. Most of the electricity supplies of Europe are interlinked and many advantages are obtained, until the early 1960's Great Britain was not able to share in these undertakings because the connection of two large alternating systems by a submarine cable would introduce serious problems in the control of power, if the transfer of power was in another form, i.e. direct current, most of these problems would not exist. Technical developments have made possible the rectification and inversion of power at very high voltage by means of giant mercury vapour valves, thus enabling electricity to pass between England and France in the form of direct current. From Lydd the current, now direct flowed along two cables, entering the sea at Dungeness, emerging in France at Le Portel, and finally was converted back to alternating current near Boulogne, for connexion with the French grid system. This unusual installation at Lydd was known as "The Converter Station". It seems very sad that these buildings, beautifully constructed and so well equipped should now be closed, but the need for exchange of electric current has diminished.

The great day in the lives of the men and women of Lydd of bygone days, was July 13th. The date of the Annual Fair, which was changed later to the first Monday in September for the convenience of graziers, butchers and buyers of cattle. In addition there was a weekly market, for which Royal consent was essential, Lydd, always fiercely independent, and tired of waiting for the Royal privilege to be granted, took matters into its own hands and held a market for many years. Within living memory Lydd held its Fair too in the High Street, with coconut shies against the Churchyard walls, skittles and even a horse-powered roundabout machine in the middle of the road. The drinking and dancing took place until the early hours of the morning in the yard of the George Hotel, the stalls were arranged along the High Street and under the pillared Guildhall. Pedlars came with their loaded packs and left their caravans near Jacques Court, and retailed all the latest news while they did business. Prices of goods scarcely bear comparison with present day costs . . . . "Bought half a dozen knives and forks for four shillings and sixpence". "I bought me a new wig cost three shillings and sixpence". "Thomas and Isaac, my sons, had each new leather breeches at Lid four shillings and sixpence each". There were also delicious brandy snaps and boiled sweets, home-made by Jimmy Hughes and his wife and it was a sad day for many when the Fair was abolished by proclamation in 1874.

Although the Fair itself was abolished, Lydd Club Day, held annually in June has revived many of the activities and continues to be an extremely popular festival and where most things are free!

CHAPTER 4

The Marsh Villages

"Brenzett, Snargate, Snave, surely
the most resounding phrase in the English language"
The late Archbishop Fisher on his first visit to Snave church

It would be hard to find anywhere else in Kent with so many mediaeval churches within comparatively short distances of each other as there are in Romney Marsh, and each with its intensely interesting and individual characteristics.

In alphabetical order the village of BRENZETT comes first. It lies north westward of New Romney towards Appledore. Just after passing the Brenzett crossroads, on the right will be seen the Inn, The Fleur de Lys, which has an attractive signboard. After the battle of Crecy in 1346, the Kings of England styled themselves — "King of France, Duke of Aquitaine and Angouleme". All claims to this anachronistic title were given up only at the Peace of Amiens in 1801. On the opposite side of the road, in the lane that leads to Brookland, are some attractive 18th century white weatherboarded cottages.

The church has the particularly Kentish dedication to Saint Eanswyth (A.D. 640) shared with only one other church in the Diocese, that of the parish church at Folkestone. She was the daughter of Eadbald, King of Kent, grand-daughter of King Ethelbert, the first Christian King of Kent and Abbess of the Folkestone Nunnery. The chief features of the church are the 12th century chancel arch with roll and chevron moulding on the pillars, the north aisle dates from the 13th century, the work in the nave and Fagge chapel dates from 1639 to 1696. The tomb of John Fagge and his son is colourful and decorative with their painted heraldic shields. The inlaid sounding board of the old Georgian three-decker pulpit has been preserved as a table top in the vestry. Above the west tower is a small timber belfry with a spire, these are frequently seen in the south-east of England, where timber is more plentiful. There are three bells, in a reconstructed mediaeval frame.

In September 1971, in the recently ploughed "Big Field" the owner, Mr Harry Finn, found a small piece of metal 2½" × 2 2/5th" which the mediaeval department of the British Museum suggested was of copper and was all that remained of a *champlevé* enamel, probably made in England at the end of the 12th century.

Tile-hung Fleur-de-Lys, Brenzett.

The Fagge Monument commemorating John Fagge, Esq., son of John Fagge of Rye, who married one of ye daughters and heirs of Clement Cobb, of Canterbury by whom he had issue two sonnes and four daughters he departed this life the 22nd day of June A.D. 1639.

Harriet Cottages, XVIIIth century, at Brenzett.

St. Eanswyth's Church, Brenzett.

Plaque of copper found by Mr. Harry Finn at Brenzett, with slight traces of a red vitreous substance which suggests it was the remains originally of a champlevée enamel. It is English work of the 12th century. Drawing by Kenneth Gravett.

The figure represents Christ, with the right hand upraised in blessing and in the left is depicted, what might be a ladder or possibly a book.

Before leaving Brenzett it is worth paying a visit to the Aeronautical Museum, situated on the Ivychurch road. An immense amount of research has gone into the discovery of crashed aircraft in Romney Marsh, and in some cases has led to the finding of the body of the pilot still strapped in his seat, which has ultimately been returned to his native land for burial. The Museum itself contains many interesting relics of air combats, machines, documents etc., relating to the last war.

Brookland

One of the delights of exploring the hinterland of Romney Marsh, is the unexpected pleasure with which one comes upon an attractive village and its timbered cottages clustered round its mediaeval church. Alas, the charming old timbered shop at Brookland, which stood facing up the street, at right angles to the Church, sadly has been demolished. It was customary in Georgian times for houses to face up the street rather than on to the street, so that they would more readily see the approach of unwelcome strangers. To the east of the Church stands the Village School. The Church has been closely associated with education from early days, when the first village school was held in the porch with the Vicar as the Schoolmaster. Later it was held in what is now the vestry chapel. In 1800 there were fifty pupils. The present school was not opened until

July 14th 1873, as an Infants' School. The first mistress was Mrs. Sophia Anne Hort, who was engaged at a salary of £30 per annum. On the opening day there were seventeen scholars, only three of whom were able to read mono-syllables, and none able to form a letter properly. In less than a year the numbers had increased to sixty-one. The Log Book now in the care of the National Society, makes interesting reading. . . . "The Reverend Baldock visited the school and heard a lesson on the Ball-Frame" . . . "Two children absent through harvesting" . . . "Not so large a school this week, as many of the children are at work cutting wurzels" . . . "Three children kept away to gather wool" . . . "A days holiday to prepare the room for 'Penny Readings' " . . . "Several children away hop-picking".

The summer holidays from August 14th until October 2nd were called "Harvest Holidays", and it is obvious that children of seven were expected to take part. The School Treat for which they joined the Brenzett school children, was an annual happy occasion.

In accordance with the new Education Act of 1944, on August 1st 1949 the school was classified as a Church of England Controlled Primary School, the ages of the children are now from five to eleven years and the average number of pupils is fifty.

Continuing further along the street in the direction of Brenzett are several houses of interest. On the left hand side is Pear Tree House, a double fronted house, where the village Doctor, George Hougham lived from 1813 to 1859. He was frequently called out to help wounded Blockade Officers and smugglers alike. On the opposite side of the road is Mulberry House, which has been refronted in brick, but at the back of the house, the mediaeval black and white timber framing is visible. Next to this is the Manor House, another house of great interest and character, and timber framed. Beyond the Manor House, is a new development of glass houses for the cultivation, mainly of tomatoes. On the same side, is another house of special interest, called "The Filberts", here Doctor Hougham's son, Ralph Papworth Hougham lived, and which is closely associated with the tragedy of the maid of Kipling's poem "I met a maid on the Brookland road". It is believed that Kipling was referring not to a maid in person, but the phantom wraith coming out of the mist from a Marsh dyke. On the outskirts of the Village on the road to Fairfield, is Poplar Hall, where a delightful Queen Anne house once stood. This has been demolished and in its place is an impressive red brick house built in Tudor style, overlooking a paved courtyard.

Brookland boasts of two Inns, "The Royal Oak" which is next to the Church and "The Alliance" which is a little further away on the Rye road. The "Royal Oak" commemorates the escape of Charles the First from the Cromwellian soldiers by hiding in the Boscobel Oak near Worcester. "The Alliance" commemorated the Alliance with Scotland in Queen Anne's reign.

One must retrace one's steps to visit the mediaeval church, dedicated to St.

Sedilia and Piscina, in Chancel of Brookland Church.

Augustine, the first Archbishop of Canterbury. Here little has changed structurally since the church was built in the mid-thirteenth century. Entering by a sixteenth century north porch, with interesting carved wooden spandrels, and then by way of a heavily studded door. To the left of the porch can be seen the shutters of a "Fives" window.

Inside the church the first thing one sees is the famous lead font, which is the most important of the thirty lead fonts remaining in England. The workmanship has been ascribed to Norman or Flemish craftsmen of the twelfth century. Here children have been baptised for over six hundred years and it retains its original drain. Under the projecting rim of the font are typical cable and saw-tooth mouldings. For the antiquary, its interest lies in the unique ornamental Norman arcading in two tiers round the bowl. Under the arches of the upper tier are the signs of the Zodiac and under the lower are depicted the Occupations of the Months. The combination of the signs and occupations reflects the influence of the calendars which were attached to early Psalters, the Zodiac sign was usually at the top of the page and the month's occupation at the foot. Signs of the Zodiac are to be seen round the arches of Norman doorways at Iffley in Oxfordshire and Brinsop in Herefordshire, on the ceiling at Waltham Abbey and in France in the porches at Autun and Vezeley, while the months appear on the twelfth century font at Burham,

St. Augustine's Church Brookland with its detached belfry.

The Norman Flemish lead font in Brookland Church.

A Pre-Reformation Brass of Master Thomas Leddes who died in 1504 — note, the mass vestments are very similar to those used in the Church of England today.

56

Deepdale, but the combination of the Zodiac and the Months is rare in England. This noteworthy circular font stands on a plinth of Caen stone. How or why it ever came to Brookland has been an abiding problem to ecclesiologists. Whatever its history, it is today a part of the parish's proud and precious heritage.

Another interesting feature of the church is the mediaeval wall-painting above the piscina in the South Aisle. This was discovered in 1971, until then it had been hidden by a wall tablet. It depicts the martyrdom of Saint Thomas Becket, the armour of the Knights is of special interest and dates the painting, declared Mr. Clive Rouse who superintended the delicate task of cleaning.

Over the South door will be seen the Royal Arms of George II, dated 1739.

It will be noticed that the Georgian pine box-pews are still in use, and on the back of the last pew on the south side there is an ancient wooden "Hatler", where male members of the congregation hung up their high hats.

Before leaving the church, at the west end, the set of Tithe Weights and Measures, including a brass ell measure for the ells of cloth, now protected in a wired glass case, should be noticed, here too, are the last three original sixteenth century pews.

There is an interesting history of the Advowson of this church, which was in the possession of the Abbot of St. Augustine's Abbey for many years.

In 1314 Abbot Ralph obtained for the Abbey the first Bull of Appropriation of the Church of Brookland, but because it was so conditional and likely to produce litigation, the Abbot was unwilling to put it into execution. Consequently in 1349 when the Abbey was "weighed down with divers expenses and burdens", another petition was made to Pope Clement V, for "the relief of the continual strain". The "remedy of useful help" was the final appropriation of the churches of Stone-in-Oxney and Brookland "to you and your monastery for ever", but "reserving from the incomes and rents of the same churches for one perpetual vicar to be canonically appointed a suitable portion "to support him".

Ten years later when Master Mason, the Rector died, and the living became vacant, the Abbey entered upon corporal possession of the church and presented Sir John de Hoghton to the perpetual vicarage. Sir John was permitted to have the greater tithes of the lands, "lying across the Re", tithes of sheaves "arising from gardens dug with the fork", all church offerings and "tithes of hay, calves, chickens, geese, hens, eggs, ducks, doves, bees, honey, wax, swans, wool, flax, hemp, ... fishing and fowling". He was also to find lights in the Chancel, bread and wine for the Mass, and be responsible for the washing of vestments and repair of books, all other expenses to be paid by the Abbot of St. Augustine's Abbey.

The Advowson remained with the Abbot and Convent of St. Augustine's until the Dissolution of the Religious Houses at the Reformation and passed finally to the Dean and Chapter of Canterbury. The value in 1587 was £60, the number of communicants 166, and in 1800 the value was still £60.

Lastly, the famous detached wooden belfry should not be missed. This dates from the thirteenth century, a date ascribed to it in 1968, by the expert on mediaeval timber-framed buildings, Kenneth Gravett, M.Sc., F.S.A. It was in making a detailed examination he discovered the notched lap joints where the lattice braces were fixed to the four upright posts, which indicated at the latest, a date in the thirteenth century or even earlier, thus making the belfry contemporary with the building of the church.

He states the whole structure is not unlike an electricity transmission tower, and serves the same purpose, the support of a heavy swinging load, the posts in compression and the braces in tension.

Quite contrary to the many and various theories and legends as to the reason for the belfry being detached from the church, the truth is, the water-table being such, the church could not have carried the weight of the bells.

The Church Commissioners in 1552 recorded "iiij small bells", together with "one warning bell, one hand bell and one sacringe bell". Of the mediaeval bells one of c. 1450 probably by William Chamerlain survives as the third of the present ring. John Hodson made the Treble, the Second and the Fourth and each is inscribed "John Hodson made mee 1685", to each of which the names of the Churchwardens are added. Today there is a ring of five bells.

When the belfry was first constructed the bell-ringers were not under cover, and the wooden upright posts show evidence of this. Not until the sixteenth century was the ringers' stage enclosed and later the bell-frame.

As one leaves the village and takes a last look at the unusual wooden belfry, it remains an unforgettable picture, with its dark cedar shingles, laid in 1936, its three distinct sections, placed one above the other, rather like three candle snuffers, and surmounted by the well-known weather-vane of a winged dragon with forked tail and tongue, dated 1797.

Burmarsh

Tucked away at the eastern end of Romney Marsh, peacefully apart from the rush and hustle of the modern age, lies the village of Burmarsh. The Cottages clustering round its ancient church, which is flanked on the left by the Old Rectory and on the right by the white-washed village Inn, significantly named "The Shepherd and Crook". The village population consists of about 200 people.

The parish is bounded on the north by the ancient course of the River Limen, which flowed into the sea at the foot of the Lympne hills, and on the south, by the parish of Dymchurch, where the seashore borders the English Channel.

All Saints Church, Burmarsh.

Burmarsh Church and the adjacent Shepherd and Crook Inn where services were held during restoration work.

59

This is one of the earliest settlements in Romney Marsh and its roots are deeply embedded in history. Until this century, its quiet story of village life had been unchanged and unchanging for over a thousand years. The name appears in several grants of land, and in various forms of spelling, Borewarme, Burwarmerck, Burware Mersce "the men of the burgh of the Marsh". One of the early and most interesting of references is in a Charter of the year 850 A.D., when Eadbald, King of Kent for the sum of 4,000 pence gave this land to his friend, Wynemund. Later Wynemund gave the land to the Abbey of St. Augustine at Canterbury, and as such it is recorded in the Domesday Book of 1086.

With the dissolution of the Monasteries in the reign of Henry VIII the lands passed to the Crown. The old association survives in the name Abbott's Court Farm, a manor which carries a Lordship of Romney Marsh. The above link with the monks of Canterbury in Saxon times suggests the probability of their being a small Saxon church here, in fact it has been thought that the chancel of the present church might have been the Saxon oratory or chapel.

The church is dedicated in honour of All Saints, a dedication shared with the "Cathedral of the Marsh" — Lydd, and the modern church built at St. Mary's Bay. What led to particular dedications is a fascinating and elusive subject, but there is something intensely sympathetic and universal in this commemoration.

The church is of Norman origin and the plan that of a typical small twelfth century church and much of the fabric is of that date. The little Norman work that remains may be seen in the north window and in the south doorway.

Crossing a small stream by a gated wooden bridge one is in the churchyard. The church is entered by a sunny south porch of stone, added in the sixteenth century. It shelters a good Norman doorcase, dating from 1140, which has columns with typical cushioned capitals. The round-headed arch is ornamented with three distinctive types of Norman mouldings, triple chevron, roll and billet, the outer order, a billet moulding, is interrupted at the crown of the arch with a sculptured human head, which is rather worn and off centre.

Inside, one is struck by the peace, the simplicity and serenity and the intimate smallness of this shrine of faith. The nave measures only thirty-one feet by nineteen feet and has no aisles.

The Chancel is separated from the nave by a good modern screen erected in 1923, as a memorial to two Burmarsh men, Albert Butcher and Simon Beale, who lost their lives in the First World War, 1914-18.

The reredos of carved wood panels was put up between 1897 and 1900 by the Rector, the Reverend Edmund Ibbotson, the beautifully carved angels were the work of a woodcarver of Oberammergau. On the rafters are stencilled paintings with various symbolic motifs, colourful and attractive. These were added by the Rector with the help of his churchwarden, Mr. Albert Checksfield, as were the painted inscriptions on the beams.

The south window of the chancel has been blocked up, but the window on the north wall is of exceptional interest and is the only one remaining of the original Norman church and has a semi-circular head cut from one piece of stone, and a deep splay.

In 1877, it was considered expedient alas, to "restore" the church, fortunately there is a photograph of 1876 showing the interior with its Georgian furnishings and fittings. Behind the altar was a painted reredos, set in a Georgian framework, a three decker pulpit in the nave, typical box pews with panelled doors and on the north wall a "Hatler" with its wooden pegs on which men hung their hats.

During the restoration services were held at "The Shepherd and Crook", until the Church was re-opened in 1879. A last relic of the Georgian fittings is the oval shaped blackboard text on the Tower Screen inscribed, "Let us not be weary in well doing, for in due season we shall reap if we faint not".

The nave windows are eighteenth century insertions, except the one near the porch, which dates from the fifteenth century, this wide splayed two-light window has graceful trefoiled headed arches. In the will of William Arminand of Orgarswick, dated 1508, he left two sheep to the reparation of this window.

One of the oldest farms in the Parish is mentioned, by name, in a Deed of 946 A.D. Gamelanyrthe — The Old Man's Farm, which survives today in Gammon's Farm and Gammon's Field. When Earl Godwin married for a second time in 1019, his bride's father, Byrhtric, granted the land at Burwara Mersce as a marriage settlement and also gave, 30 oxen, 20 cows, 10 horses and 10 serfs.

These two records bespeak the existence of a community here in Saxon times.

In contrast, it is interesting to recall that from this small remote marsh village, two families emigrated to America in 1828 — John Whitehead and his wife and John Hogbin, his wife and their eight children. In 1834 Onslow Sharpe also left Burmarsh to seek his fortune across the Atlantic in the New World. He was assisted with £60 and the two families received grants of £100 each.

In the eighteenth century Vestry Book, it is recorded that the Royal College of Physicians owned land valued at £46 in 1804. Burmarsh had an even closer association with the Royal Veterinary College, for it was in this parish that Edward Coleman was born on the 28th of June 1764. A tablet to his memory on the north wall tells its own story, a story of which Burmarsh is justly proud.

It reads:
"Sacred to the Memory of Edward Coleman, Esq.,
who was born in this parish 28th June 1764 and died at
The Royal Veterinary College, London
14th July 1830".

In early life after studying under the celebrated John Hunter he entered the Medical Profession and in 1794 was elected Professor of the Royal Veterinary College, an Institution which his Scientific Research and mental energies, attained a degree of usefulness and celebrity that exceeded the sanguine expectations of its distinguished founders.

Under his fostering auspices, the progress of the Veterinary Art was such as qualified its practitioners to hold Commissions in the Army, and in 1797 he had himself the honour to be appointed Veterinary Surgeon-General to the British Cavalry the duties of which responsible situation he faithfully discharged with credit to himself and advantage to the country.

His Physiological Investigations and the services he rendered the science caused him to be elected a Fellow of the Royal Society and a member of other British and Foreign Associations.

"This Tablet
is erected by his surviving children in whose
fondest and most grateful remembrance his
parental affections and undeviating kindness
will be for ever most dearly cherished
Requiescat in Pace"

Several other tablets commemorate members of the Coleman family, one to Richard "snatched away by the Hand of Providence", at the early age of sixteen years 1808, and another to another Edward Coleman, who held the post of Common Expenditor of Romney Marsh, he died in September 1811 at the age of 70. "The situation he had most honourably and disinterestedly held for 36 years at the expense of both his health and his property".

Rothschild's Farm brings to mind Baron Mayer de Rothschild, who with his brother, Lionel, fought long and hard to gain seats in Parliament, and to be the first Jews to do so. He was elected the Member for Hythe in 1847. At the same time that Lionel was elected for the City of London. On the first occasion when he presented himself in the House, he was unable to take the oath, unless, according to his faith, his head was covered, and was therefore unable to take his seat. It was eleven years before legislation was passed to allow a Jew to sit in the House, and it was only then his brother Baron Mayer Anschel Rothschild was able to take his seat as the member for Hythe.

Dymchurch

Situated between the Cinque Ports of New Romney and Hythe lies Dymchurch, which has a long and interesting history from early times. This is borne out by the discovery, by the notable nineteenth century engineer, James

Elliott, who when excavating, in preparation for repairs to the Dymchurch Wall discovered a quantity of Roman pottery. From the coarsest unbaked kind to the finest Samian ware, much of it in a perfect state of preservation, he also found beds of fine white clay and layers of clean sharp sand, and as the effects of fire were evident, he came to the conclusion it was a site where pottery had been made.

The name Dymchurch or Demechurch is interesting, but it is curious it is not mentioned in the great Domesday Survey. Although the neighbouring Manor of Eastbridge returned two churches and is known to have extended well into Dymchurch, it would seem probable that the church here was one of the two. Deme comes from old English, *Doema* or *Deme* and in middle English it meant a Judge or Arbiter. As the headquarters of the Lords, Bailiff and Jurats was at New Hall, immediately opposite the Church and it was in the Elizabethan Court room there that cases were tried, the name could have arisen from the association with the courts. The mediaeval Hall with its thatched roof was burnt down in Queen Elizabeths reign in 1574, but a New Hall was built on the site. Sadly, all the corporation's valuable mediaeval records perished in the fire.

After the granting of the Royal Charter by King Henry III in 1252, a later charter was granted by King Edward IV, this was a "Judicial charter", and contained tremendous privileges. It decreed that the Bailiff, twenty-four Jurats and the Commonalty "They shall be one body in deed and in name in Kent forever". Yearly at the feast of St. Michael, "Four of the most discreet and sufficient Jurats shall be elected as Keepers of the Peace and Justices of us and our heirs, to be coroners and to erect gallows". The Justice of the Peace Act of 1952, swept away not only this court but those of Lydd and New Romney. The Royal Arms still hang above the Bailiff's seat although he may no longer dispense justice. The small prison with its great padded door and iron barred window may still be seen adjoining New Hall, together with the small exercise yard.

The church is dedicated to St. Peter and St. Paul and retains good Norman features. The Chancel arch is noteworthy and on either side are two unusual arched recesses. The font is of an ancient Kentish type of uncommon design and possibly has been re-tooled. The Royal Arms of George III hang on the north wall and bear the date 1778.

Among the New Romney records in "The Book of Notte", written by the Common Clerk, mention is made of the watch-posts, prepared to give warning of the threatened Spanish invasion, these included one at Romney Helmes and the second at Broadhull, Dymchurch. It was at the Brodhull that the Courts of Brotherhood and Guestling of the Cinque Ports were held until 1443; which suggests there was some connection between Broadhull and Brodhull of the Cinque Ports, and reflects too the importance of Dymchurch in the Middle Ages.

St. Peter and St. Paul's Church Dymchurch.

Interior of the Dymchurch prison in use until 1860.

Entrance to Prison.

64

Martello Tower, Winter time.

There are no less than three Martello Towers in Dymchurch, one of which has been restored, by the Ministry of Works, and is open to the public. Originally there were seventy-four towers stretching from Folkestone to Eastbourne, and they provided the first line of defence during the Napoleonic threat. Each was manned by thirty-two men, and gun mounted, ready to fire on the horse-boats or the troop ships if a landing should be attempted. No shot was ever fired in anger, only for rejoicing.

It is believed that the Martello Towers, sometimes called Corsican or SaracenTowers originated in the Bay of Myrtles, where on Cap Mortello there was one of these towers which withstood a hot and concentrated bombardment by British ships and a simultaneous land attack in 1794. Lord Cornwallis, then Master of Ordnance, ordered a plan of it to be made, on his return to England a model was built and for many years stood in the Rotunda at Woolwich.

The towers each took seven thousand bricks set in Russian tallow, the bricks were brought from London by barge, to Hythe, local horses and carts were hired to convey the bricks to the sites. There was no ground floor entrance but a ladder was let down for the coming and goings of the garrison.

The second line of defence was the Royal Military Canal, which Defoe, dismissed contemptuously when he first came upon it "as if those great armies, which had crossed the Rhine and the Danube would be deterred by thirty feet of water".

From the Kentish Gazette of September 11th 1904:—

"During the Napoleonic threat, Mr Pitt accompanied by General Twiss and General Moore met the Lords and Bailiff of the Level of Romney Marsh at New Hall, to consider the best mode of inundating the marsh in case of invasion, when it was determined that on the appearance of the enemy on the coast the sluices should be opened to admit the sea so as to fill the dykes, which might be accomplished in one tide, and in case of actual invasion remain open another tide, which would be sufficient to inundate the whole level".

It is interesting to recall that it was not until the supply of shingle was cut off from this line of the coast, by the accumulation at Dungeness Point that Dymchurch seemed to be in danger, apparently none of the numerous commissions or anxious investigations dealing with the state of sea walls, from the reign of Henry III, refers to Dymchurch Wall. It was not until the reign of Henry VIII that the danger was appreciated and steps taken to prevent the sea from flooding this part of the marsh. This was effected by a system of brushwood piles of thorn and overlathes, so important were these piles that anyone found cutting down a thorn tree, the wood of which was thought to be impervious to salt water, had his ear cut off, and if the offence was repeated the other ear was cut off. The faggots were lashed together along the seashore and wet clay thrown over them, which baked hard in the sun, this system of sea defence was used until the gradual introduction of Kentish ragstone about 1825.

The Inns of Dymchurch have seen many changes. Coming from New Romney, the first inn on the right is now called "The Ocean", it was formerly the "Victoria". The "City of London", further along the High Street, has a signboard depicting the arms of the City of London which incorporate Wat Tyler's dagger. This inn is named after a barge, wrecked off Dymchurch in the eighteenth century. The other Inn with a long story to tell is opposite the Church, and called "The Ship Inn", this has many associations with the Lords of Romney Marsh and with notorious smugglers. Inside, the low beams, the attractive staircase, curious cupboards, all suggest the atmosphere of old exciting times and the nearness of the Inn to the little prison meant thrilling adventures in helping captured smugglers to escape. The prison was in use until 1866, when the Romney Marsh constables, whose painted staves may be seen in the Court Room at New Hall, were superseded by the County Police. At this Inn the Lords, Bailiff and Jurats of Romney Marsh still hold their annual luncheon after their Grand Lath at New Hall, always on the traditional day, the Thursday after Whitsuntide.

The Tudor vicarage stands in the High Street, near the Church. It has magnificent open fireplaces, and attractive beams.

At the Romney end of the High Street, is a right hand turning to Eastbridge, within two hundred yards, standing apart, is the eighteenth century Mill House. It is a fine tall, attractive brick building, with a plaque bearing the date

The Old Mill House, Dymchurch.

1736. Alas, the Mill itself has been demolished, but it gave its name to the road, Mill Road.

Among the notable inhabitants of Dymchurch was Richard Coleman, Bailiff of Romney Marsh for several years, in the eighteenth century, who was one of the signatories to an agreement between the town of Hythe and Romney Marsh, clearly defining the contested boundaries between the two places, the much faded document is dated 1816.

Richard Coleman's daughter, Caroline, married another well remembered Dymchurch figure, Walter Elliott Whittingham. He organised the first Non-Conformist school at Dymchurch and was himself the Headmaster. Later on he left Dymchurch for Walthamstow in Essex, where he established another

Non-Conformist school, and an Independent Congregational Church. He became an auctioneer and was the founder of the National Freehold Land Society. His son, Walter Basden Whittingham was employed by Harry S. King, Merchant Bankers, now Lloyds Bank Plc. He published and became the editor of no less than three weekly papers. Another son, William Elliott Whittingham, born at Dymchurch in January 1812, founded a Grammar School at Walthamstow, and was interested in, and became an active supporter of many local activities. It is said there were three thousand people at his funeral! The third son, W. E. Whittingham later became Bishop of Bury St. Edmunds and Ipswich.

Dymchurch with some delightful old cottages with their dormer windows, is a curious mixture of "ancient and modern". Every two years, the notorious smuggling gang, headed by Dr. Syn, is commemorated in the celebrated "Day of Syn". The writer Russell Thorndike, for many years had a house at Dymchurch, and here began his series of the well known "Dr. Syn" books, of which there are seven. These have given the name "Day of Syn" to these hilarious celebrations.

Much water has flowed under the bridge since the days when the Roman soldiers tramped dusty tracks to the modern brightly coloured lights of the present day Amusement Park and Hamburger "take-away"!

Fairfield

The parish of Fairfield lies completely in Wallend Marsh and comprises the mediaeval church and five main houses, Becket House, Becket Barn, Dean Court, Parsonage House, now Old Farm, and Fairfield Court and about eight cottages. The population for centuries has been sparse and has never reached three figures, and it was to the Church the small community turned for worship and secular activities.

This area of Wallend Marsh was one of the last to be inned the work carried out in the thirteenth century under the auspices of four successive Archbishops, their names are recalled in the Innings, Archbishop Boniface, Baldwin, Becket and Peckham. The surrounding land is still very low and in common with most of the Marsh Churches the Church was built on an artificial mound to lift it above flood water level. The churchyard is unlike any other for there is no defined boundary and sheep peacefully graze around the church walls, there are no tombstones, no memorials, no trees, no flowers and not even shrubs.

It is interesting to recall the Church was never dedicated because it was built of lathe and daub, yet the churchyard was dedicated, although no burials have taken place for many years.

Inside, the Church has many interesting and attractive features, eighteenth

St. Thomas Becket Church, Fairfield.

century white-painted box pews, with their original iron latches, a complete three-decker pulpit and at the east end a Laudian altar, behind which is the framed blackboard, with the Creed and Commandments. Between the arched panels at the top is painted a golden sun, underneath, in Hebrew the inscription "The Sun the Eye of God". At the west end there is a notable font of Kentish ragstone, unique in the diocese with its heptagonal bowl an extremely rare shape, the interest of which is increased by the circular stem and polygonal base and step.

Fairfield was one of the thirty manors of Romney Marsh, but only twenty-three carried the right of representation at the Grand Lath. The Church was built customarily by the Lord of the Manor for his tenants and he usually appointed the Chaplain.

Various changes have been made in the Church's external appearance, the south wall was reconstructed in the early thirteenth century and the west and north walls in about 1800, the porch was added in the eighteenth century.

In 1912, with dismay, it was seen that the whole church was in a deplorable condition and in danger of collapse. Eventually, the Church Commissioners agreed that the entire chancel, the north wall of the nave, the porch and the bell turret, together with the roof covering, should be taken down. It was found happily that the foundations were sound, and that enabled the building to be reconstructed. The Church was dismantled, every piece numbered and stacked on site, every scrap of material which could be used was re-used. The late Mr. Bedo Hobbs found some ancient timbers which were useful to replace defective ones. The porch was entirely rebuilt, the bell turret re-designed,

69

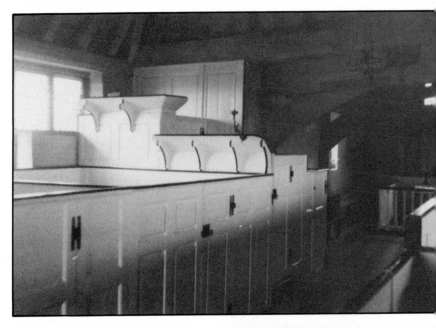

Three-decker Pulpit, Fairfield Church.
The only one remaining in Romney Marsh.

The rare seven-sided font bowl,
Fairfield Church.

cedar shingles replacing the weatherboarding. Originally the church possessed three mediaeval bells, one of these was cracked by 1887 and another had a piece missing, these bells were broken up and re-cast into the present three bells, the wording of the original bells was reproduced on the new bells and added to the waist of each is "Recast 1913". By Mears and Stainbank, London". The eighteenth century mounting block was replaced at the west end, a reminder of the days when parishioners came to church on horse-back.

Thus, the only church in the Canterbury Diocese dedicated to the martyred Archbishop St. Thomas Becket was restored to use for services and it is hoped preserved for many years to come.

During the course of centuries so many invaluable records have been lost, but happily among the archives of the Dean and Chapter of Canterbury there are some vellum rolls of the proceedings in the Court of the Commissary of the Priory of Christ Church. After Archbishop Peckham's death the See of Canterbury was vacant for more than two years. During this time the Prior and Chapter carried out almost all diocesan functions. One of these was the holding of visitations in the Parish Churches, possibly because of the fees which could be exacted. These rolls reveal much detailed information on the condition of Church life in the country parishes more than six hundred years ago. A visitation made at the Church of Feyrefeld, on Saturday next after the feast of Holy Trinity in 1294 by Simon Chaplain of the same, Will' Comffrey, Stephen le Longhe, Simon Clesy, Richard le Wolfe, and Lovekyn Brekebot, parishioners of the said Church.

"The frontal of the high altar is lacking and there is only a poor carpet before the same. A cloth is required for the lectern, because the one that is there is very dirty and in poor condition. They lack a psalter, manual, processional, ordinal, and martyrology. There is an antiphoner which is of no use or value. The oil had not been changed and the font has no lock as it ought to have".

A woman served mass occasionally but even in that sparsely populated parish the practise could not be permitted. Parish clerks were sometimes married but if so, were strictly forbidden to serve at the altar, or even to carry the holy water. Charges against the clergy were by no means uncommon and there is evidence to show "that the celibacy of the clergy did not ensure purity of life".

"It was stated Roger de Kenardintone, clerk of the church, is married and he carrieth the blessed water and it is believed that he married a widow". He appeared and swore that he would no longer serve about the altar.

"The present chaplain pastureth lambs in the churchyard". He appeared and swore that he would not pasture lambs in the churchyard except at gathering time *(Tempore collectionis)*.

"The rector does no good in the parish . . . . and the chaplain has so meagre a portion that he cannot live or sustain himself in a decent manner".

Greatstone

When one hears the name Greatstone, one thinks of the modern bungaloid development between Littlestone and Lydd-on-Sea. It has a far longer history and was connected with the smuggling trade, the great stretches of shallow sandy beaches made it ideal for landing small boats coming from France or Holland to exchange their cargo for Romney Marsh wool. There is a record of a boat coming to land at Greatstone and being seized by a vigilant Excise Officer in the seventeeth century.

The origin of the name Greatstone is derived from the larger pebbles scoured up channel in contrast to the smaller pebbles which came from the Dover direction and gave the name to Littlestone. Maps until 1908 show the Bay of Romney with to the east Littlestone Point and to the west Greatstone Point. The Bay extended north to the site of the old Southern Railway Station.

Before the outbreak of the Second World War in 1939, a developer decided to see what success he would have and as an inducement to purchasers he advertised "Five pounds deposit secures a plot". Soon the Local Authority became aware that small beach-type huts were being erected on the plots and used by the owners for weekends. There was neither water nor drainage available. A survey was taken and it was found there were no less than forty-two of these huts. No planning regulations were in force in those days. The then Mayor invited the late Mr. Ewart Culpin to address a public meeting at New Romney Town Hall on the subject of Town Planning, after an able and enthusiastic speech, Mr. Culpin convinced the Borough Council and his audience of the need to adopt a Town Planning Scheme. Greatstone was part of the Borough, and New Romney became one of the first towns in Kent to be town-planned.

Greatstone's claim to fame was the best kept secret of the last war, operation, P.L.U.T.O − Petrol Line Under The Ocean. The petrol came from the ports, underground, by pipes that had been laid to Greatstone and Dungeness, with filters installed at certain points. There were three pipelines of petrol, Airforce Petrol, Vehicle Petrol and the third as a reserve. Many of the bungalows had been taken over by the Army, some were gutted for the installation of centrifugal pumps. The enemy came over frequently to photograph the coastal area, so that extreme care was taken to ensure there was no visible change in the landscape. Great pipes were wound round enormous conumdrums, these were towed across the English Channel at night and the pipes unwound, they laid on the bed of the Channel. By the end of the War no less than seventeen pipes were carrying petrol to our troops, as General Montgomery advanced, until his army reached Berlin.

Before the War a commodious Holiday Camp had been built, which was extremely popular, but was taken over by the Army. The large Ballroom provided a splendid hall for entertainment of the troops, by visiting ENSA parties. Just before D-Day a personal visit was arranged for Miss Gracie Fields. The vociferous affectionate welcome by nearly a thousand soldiers, was unforgettable, as of course, was her programme, she was recalled again and again for an encore and eventually left laden with beautiful flowers.

After the War bungalows were de-requisitioned and gradually the owners returned, and in the course of the years many more bungalows and houses were built and a sense of security returned. An Anglican Church was erected, designed in the shape of a ship and dedicated to St. Peter.

A fine attractive new Inn was built and called "The Jolly Fisherman", which took the place of an ancient low black-tarred building of that name, that stood on the shingle between Greatstone and Lade.

For lovers of wild flowers there is a surprising variety even on the pebbly roadside verges, the pink and white Valerian, the wild Mignonette and yellow Sea Horned Poppy. It is astonishing that such plants can and do root in this shallow soil, great clumps of sea-kale are dotted along the shore, Sea pea and Sea thrift, Stone cross, tall elegant Foxgloves, Hawkbit and Marram grass, the latter, planted by the River Authority to help consolidate the sandhills. In July the beauty of the red-fanged Viper's bugloss attracts a number of visitors, especially artists.

Today Greatstone is a thriving modern seaside resort with a resident community, its Post office, Church, Supermarkets, fine Restaurant "The

The "Listening Ear" at Lade, used during the last War.

73

Romney Tavern", a popular rendezvous, and along the coast, great stretches of soft sand make an ideal safe playground for children and for bathing. Adult leisure pursuits include boating, sailing, water-ski-ing, wind-surfing and shrimping. The excellent fishing provides a means of livelihood for some of the residents. More and more bungalows are built and there is a thriving branch of the Ratepayers Association, which keeps a vigilant eye on modern regulations and developments.

At Lade, between Greatstone and Dungeness is the Number 2 Battery of the Napoleonic defence fortifications. The red brick building is in a good state but it is believed it was taken over for some time by the Coastguards.

Nearer to Dungeness far out on the desolate shingle is a "Listening Ear", erected before the Second World War, the purpose of this was to detect enemy aircraft flying over the area and to establish, if possible their nationality. Today they are called "Accoustic Mirrors". Conversations may be heard for eighteen miles.

Ivychurch

The name Ivychurch proclaims its island origin "The Church on the isle in the waters". Anciently it was written Ive Circe, and later Yve Church. Today the Village consists of a short straggling street with a mixture of weatherboarded cottages with lichened roofs, farmsteads and some modern council houses.

Adjoining the churchyard is a mellow tile-hung Inn, "The Bell", a name frequently used for an inn since Chaucer's day. Handel called England "The ringing island", because of its national fondness for bells but it was Fletcher, the Elizabethan dramatist, who wrote "Like as the Church and the Ale-house, God and the Devill they manie tymes dwell very neare together".

Ivychurch is one of seven mediaeval churches in Kent dedicated to St. George, soldier and martyr. It is interesting to recall that the Council of Oxford decreed in 1222, that April 23rd, Saint George's Feast Day, should be a national festival. It was not until the Order of the Garter was instituted in the reign of Edward III, that the date was recognised officially as England's national day and St. George her patron saint.

Ivychurch has one of the longest village churches in Kent, and is most interesting and attractive from an architectural point of view. It is considered one of the most complete examples of fourteenth century craftsmanship, the late Sir Reginald Blomfield, declared it the best example of fourteenth century church architecture in the whole district. The church dates fron c. 1360-70, when it was rebuilt. This date is supported by a record that in 1364-65 William de Appuldrefeld, gave half an acre of land to the rector of Ivychurch, Robert de Charwelton, to enable his dwelling place to be enlarged.

The Church with its magnificent embattled west tower dominates the Village and its plan is uncommon, and comprises chancel, nave, three parallel aisles, of equal length, which run from the tower to the east end without any structural divisions. The unusual length of the Church is 135 feet, which is enhanced by the absence of pews. In the Middle Ages the floor would have been strewn with rushes, gathered from the neighbouring dykes and borne in procession to the Church at the greater festivals; such as Christmas, Easter, Whitsuntide and St. George's Day, the latter is still honoured today, as the Church's patron. Against the east wall of the chancel may be seen a semi-circular ragstone base of a pillar, which only recently has come to light, and is exposed for the sake of record. This has the typical thirteenth century water-holding moulding and supports the existence of an Early English church; at the same time was found the top of a bronze censer, with unbroken loops and chains. Documentary evidence furnishes further proof, for the names of Rectors are recorded from 1286.

The east window of the chancel is an example of late Perpendicular work and has five unfoliated lights under one arch, contemporary with the east window at Brookland. Flanking the window are the blackboard Decalogue and the Lord's Prayer.

An interesting and important feature is the fifteenth century carved wood work of the screen and the stalls. Only the wainscott of the rood screen remains, a reminder of Richard Rogers, Bishop of Dover's enquiry at the Visitation of 1569, "Whether images and all other monuments of idolatry and superstition were abolished and destroyed and whether rood lofts had been taken down". Parclose screen of Chinese Chippendale design, reputed to have come from Old Romney when the livings were united, separate the chancel from the north and south aisles. Today Ivychurch is part of the benefice of St. Mary's Bay. The attractive altar rails are contemporary with the tower screen. The absence of a chancel arch adds greatly to the sense of spaciousness.

Ivychurch is fortunate in possessing that rare feature of a Village Church, a clerestory. On the north side of the nave is a fifteenth century font, on its original stone steps, which are porous and when rain is imminent they are damp. The font is of ragstone, octagonal and plainly moulded. In the Middle Ages witches used to steal the consecrated water from the fonts for their incantations. To prevent these constant thefts, Archbishop Edmund Rich, ordered that fonts were to have flat lids fitted, and were to be kept under lock and key. Part of the broken staple for the lock may still be seen in the rim of the font.

The curious sentry-box that stands nearby is a Hudd or Hood, a reminder that every parish, had to provide a "shade of wood for the Minister when he buryeth the corpse". The Hudd, was solemly carried out into the churchyard in wet weather, the Rector stood within it, to shelter from the rain and to keep his wig dry, while he conducted the funeral service. Above the north door will be seen the Royal Arms of George III.

St. George's Church, Ivychurch and The Bell Inn.

An Inventory of 1552, enumerates "The holy cloth" as a separate item from "the clothe for marriages to hold over the brid". The Church also possessed a parure of emeralds, which brides might hire for their weddings.

In the fourteenth century the chief family was the More family of More Court, of which no trace remains. It is recorded that a daughter of John Brenchley married William More of More Court in the twenty-first year of the reign of Henry VI, 1442.

From the church and the slender records of the parish, one gathers there has been village life in Ivychurch in the Middle Ages.

Littlestone

Littlestone is situated at the seaward end of New Romney and is in marked contrast to the resort of Greatstone. When the late Sir Robert Perks had completed the construction of the Hong Kong Shanghai Railway he was looking around for a new field of activity. On a visit to New Romney he came to the sea, and found only a sandy track that lead to Dungeness, where there were some old railway carriages on a pebbly beach. By chance he met the late Mr. Henry Tubbs, who was a surveyor, who was also surveying the scene; subsequently they planned to lay out a new seaside resort, they had built a terrace of dignified Victorian houses, four storeys, over looking the sea and a splendid "Grand Hotel" for visitors, and an attractive balconied house for Sir Robert himself. To add to the attraction they had laid out the Littlestone Golf Course in 1888 and used the house at the corner of Maderia Road as the Club House and it is interesting to recall that the present seventeenth tee was part of the coal wharf, where the coal for New Romney was delivered and the horses and carts came down to collect their sacks. Two of the grey stone houses on the front became the "Dormy House", which alas was burnt down in 1983. Posters at Charing Cross station invitingly advertised "Come to Bexhill and Littlestone-on-Sea the coming seaside resorts", a neighbouring poster countered with "Deal – Caesar's Choice". An avenue of elm trees was planted from New Romney to the sea, but in 1981-82 many were attacked with Dutch Elm disease and had to be felled. Flowering cherries and rowan trees have filled some of the gaps.

Sir Robert Perks was a devoted Methodist and as there was no such church at New Romney, he had one built at Littlestone and used to invite famous Methodist preachers as weekend guests, to take the services on Sundays, these services were very popular and people came from New Romney and even from Lydd. During the Second World War the hall was requisitioned and used by ENSA parties for the entertainment of the troops stationed in the area. After the war it was taken over by the Roman Catholic community, the Austin Friars from Hythe, and services are still held here every Sunday.

Going westwards to St. Mary's Bay, an outstanding solitary house was built on the coast and painted a vivid yellow, now painted white, it was called locally the "Mustard Pot". The architect was none other than the creator of the italianate Portmeirion in Wales, Sir Clough Williams-Ellis.

The outbreak of the Second World War changed Littlestone completely, from the venue of the many famous people who had houses here, distinguished members of the bar, the medical profession, who came year after year to enjoy the sea, the sands, the restfulness, the social round, the golf and the invigorating air. Mr. Gladstone, Lord Henry Gladstone, Lord Maugham the Lord Chancellor, Lord Justice Romer, to name but a few, had houses here, but in 1939 battalions of infantry arrived for training and later no less than five airfields were constructed in Romney Marsh, for the Second Tactical Airforce, who were to harass the French ports where flat bottomed boats were being built for the invasion of England and to destroy the new menace of "The Doodlebugs". Only civilians on essential duties were allowed to remain in the area.

In July 1931 a Roman brass coin was found near Littlestone Station, three feet below ground. On the obverse were the words:—

Imp. C. Maxentius P. F. Aug.

and on the reverse:—

AETERNITATI Aug. N.

77

Low tide at Littlestone showing the groins and on the horizon a section of Harbour Mulberry, which never got to Arromanches.

Many people who have come to reside in the New Romney coastal area in recent years are unaware that a Lifeboat was stationed at Littlestone many years before the R.N.L.I. decided that an "Inshore" lifeboat was necessary on this section of the coast. The Lifeboat played an important part in Littlestone's history. The first boat was moved from Dungeness to be stationed at Littlestone, owing to the increase of shipping in the channel, in 1858. This was replaced by a new and larger one, 32 feet long and 7½ feet wide, rowing ten oars double banked and supplied with a transporting carriage. For which a new and commodious house had been erected, on ground granted to the Institution at a nominal rent, by the Corporation of New Romney. The whole expense of the new Lifeboat establishment was

Coastguard Cottages at Littlestone now all in private ownership. Number One is still known as the Officer's House.

78

presented to the Institution by Mrs. Hatton in memory of her husband, after whom the boat was named, the "Dr. Hatton". In July 1871, the boat was conveyed by road, on its carriage, to Belvedere, in Kent, the residence of the donor and after being exhibited there, was sent to Ashford, by the South Eastern Railway, the Company granting it a free conveyance and bringing back the old boat and carriage on similar liberal terms. The first launch of the new Lifeboat at its new station took place on the 4th of August, on the occasion of the Annual Regatta. Before the launch, the Inspector of Lifeboats, Captain J. R. Ward, R.N., handed over the boat to the charge of the local committee. The gift being duly acknowledged, by the then Vicar of New Romney, who expressed the hearty thanks of the inhabitants to the Institution and the benevolent donor, Mrs. Hatton, for the fine boat committed to their charge. The Lifeboat was then named by Miss Cobb, who, having dashed a bottle of wine against the boats side, said "I name this boat Dr. Hatton and may God prosper her". Mr. A. Andersen the Government Superintendant of Lifeboats on the coasts of Denmark, had come to England especially for information on the Lifeboat work and the Rocket and Mortar life-saving apparatus, worked here by the Coastguards. It was not until 1904, that the first petrol driven Lifeboat came into service, its development enabled the number of Lifeboat Stations to be reduced, especially along the south coast and in 1928 the Littlestone lifeboat station was closed. Before the Littlestone Lifeboat was allowed to go on service in 1966, the crew which Mr. Ken Boardman had recruited were given a six weeks intensive training course by the R.N.L.I. One of those men was named White, but before training had started he had an appointment with Her Majesty's Government, which took priority. he was, as many will remember, notorious as a member of "The Train Robber Gang". He certainly had initative and was an experienced yachtsman, Mr. Boardman adds "I wonder what kind of a Lifeboatman he would have made"!

The lifeboat in early days was manned by the Coastguards who lived in the nine coastguard cottages in St. Andrews Road. The larger end house, was and still is called the Officers House. The coastguards had to sleep in the back bedrooms of their cottages. When the maroon went up, the "knocker-up" on duty immediately went to each of the cottages in turn and pulled the "knocker-up cord", to ensure that the coastguard was awake. This was a strong piece of cord with a loop at one end fastened to a cup hook and at the other a metal device was fixed to the sash window and when the cord was pulled the device tapped on the window to awaken the sleeping coastguard.

In Elizabethan times Littlestone was in the Hundred of St. Martin, which was bound to supply two watchmen for the Beacon at The Helmes, in fact, there were three ancient watch-posts for this stretch of the coast. Among the New Romney records is the Book of Notte, written by the Common Clerk, Arthur Bee, in 1571, and he puts on record, that in the reign of Edward III, the Watch at The Helmes was to consist of seven men of whom two were to come from the Hundred of St. Martin, two from that of Oxney, two from

Aloesbridge and one from Ham. In 1588 William Southland, a member of the John Southland family was Captain of our select band and had the oversight of the Romney Beacon and of the Helmes Beacon. The beacon was actually at Littlestone and today a house called "Romney Helmes" marks the site.

Another feature is the tall red brick Water Tower a well-known landmark and the last reminder of the Littlestone Water Company; the function of the Tower was to store thousands of gallons of water in an elevated position to supply the area in case of pump failure. During the Second World War it was used as a vantage point, today, it is an attactive and unusual dwelling.

Newchurch

Leaving the A259 at New Romney and turning to the left at The Plough Inn, one finds oneself on the way to St. Mary-in-the-Marsh and Newchurch, this is a straggling village, but one of great charm and interest. To come at Harvest time it may astonish the visitor to see the number of cars parked in the roadway, and closely packed in a field, but the attraction is not a particular church service, but the "Harvest Sunday", when going back to mediaeval times, when the parishioners gathered in the nave of their church for any special occasion, the nave belonged to the people and the chancel to the priest, hence the separation by a rood screen. There were no village halls nor assembly rooms but the church was the focal point for every secular activity. In the Middle Ages ale was brewed in the churchyard for the festival and a small hut in the corner of the churchyard was where the vessels and utensils were kept. Inventories of church goods often include those of "the Lord's Brewhouse". Today, the mediaeval atmosphere is recaptured on the occasions of the Buffet lunches, people come from far and near joining their friends or bringing visitors, suddenly the church comes to life with fun, laughter and good cheer. Various local crafts are displayed and there is always a well laden produce stall, with some home-made cakes, jams and pickles. These buffet lunches are always extremely popular and a rewarding effort for fund raising.

The church is dedicated to St. Peter and St. Paul, it is one of the few churches in Romney Marsh in which no trace of Norman work is found, although Newchurch is mentioned in Domesday Book, as the name of the Hundred. The crossed keys and the sword, symbols of the two Apostles appear on two of the font's fluted sides, the stem of the font is buttressed and stands upon steps. Over the west doorway of the Tower is a square-headed label, the returned ends culminating in the sculptured heads of St. Peter and St. Paul. The earliest features of the church are the the lancet windows in the chancel, which possibly date from the thirteenth century as do the arches north and south of the chancel. The chancels of both north and south aisles are separated from the aisles by fifteenth century screens. It is possible that these screens

St. Peter and St. Paul's Church, Newchurch.

formed part of the original rood-screen of the church. The pulpit is a fine example of linen-fold work, but it has a modern sounding board.

The north chapel is dedicated to the Blessed Virgin and it was here the Guild of Shepherds held their annual service.

The south chapel is dedicated to St. Michael and St. Thomas of Canterbury. The Will of John Cobbes, dated 1472, directed that he should be buried within that chapel and that in it during seven years a priest should sing masses for his soul. In 1483, Thomas Rowe by his Will, left £6 13s. 4d., to pay a priest who should during one year sing a Trental of masses for his soul, and £20 to be expended "in the purchase of a suit of vestments for use in this Church". The vestments were at one time kept in the beautifully carved sixteenth century chest, now in the vestry.

There has always been an enthusiastic musical tradition in this parish. A former rector, the late Rev. Canon Lampen, composed his own oratorios and taught the young shepherds to sing and play the violin.

Shortly before one of the Flower Festivals, at the south-east corner of the churchyard, the Sexton, who was a keen bell ringer, was digging a grave when suddenly the soil collapsed, revealing a hole in the outline of a bell mould. He realised he had come upon one of the small foundries of an itinerant bell maker. This aroused great excitement and the Whitechapel bell foundry sent

81

some of their experts down to see it, they were tremendously interested, and offered to provide a small exhibition illustrating the various stages of bell founding, this was gladly accepted and proved a great attraction at the Flower Festival.

In a record of 1340 it is related that the Dean of Lympne certified that two parishioners of Newchurch, had compounded for six floggings through the market place at Romney and as many round their parish church, by a payment of 26s. 8d. to the poor.

The local inn, "The Black Bull" is a real village inn, peacefully apart from the bustle of the village, where famous actors and actresses found a haven of peace when they could escape from their London commitments during the last war.

At the entrance of the lane leading to the Church, on the right will be seen a tall creeper covered house, which was originally the Schoolhouse, here during the last War, one of Glubb Pasha's officers lived *incognito,* for some time.

An eccentric old Newchurch character was Barney Cole, in his lifetime he was a "rock breaker". Traction engines brought rock from Aldington Quarry to be stacked in cords by the roadside then to be broken down, by men, who were past heavier and more active work. This was Barney's job and his equipment was simple. A sledge-hammer for the initial break, a smaller

Ploughman's Lunch held in the nave of Newchurch church.

hammer to finish, a bag of straw to sit on and a piece of leather to protect his fingertips, a refinement being a pair of wire-gauze goggles to protect his eyes, from flying chips of rock. His dress was remarkable, the head gear was a fur or astrakan effort like a woman's toque. Rumour had it he bought sixteen of these for 6d. when he was young. At the age of sixty he was wearing the second, number one only being used for rougher occasions. There were several layers of voluminous jackets and sleeved waistcoats, a narrow black and white plaid scarf and the outfit was completed by an enormous pair of corduroy trousers, supported below the knees by straps, known as "yorks". This remarkable man was born in 1835 and died at the age of 87. He is buried in Newchurch churchyard.

Old Romney

Before the Romans left Britain a small island existed where Old Romney now stands, which was destined to be the nucleus of the flourishing port of the eleventh century. Saxon grants of land, evidence, beyond doubt that large tracts existed above high water level. Skilful and ingenious embankments were carried out and massive earth walls raised to resist the tides. Gradually a drained and protected area came into existence.

Old Romney's earliest written reference is in a Saxon grant by King Offa of Aghene or Old Romney Court to Christ Church, Canterbury, this may have lead to the erection of a Saxon church, for the later lessees of Aghene Court, by their Lease, were bound to repair the chancel of the church.

The prefixes "old" and "new" had not yet been acquired, both places were more or less continuous on the shore of the estuary. The growing and flourishing town and port at the seaward end of the Quay, called the Langport, acquired the prefix "new" to distinguish it from the old haven, which gradually decayed as it became further inland and little was left save the church and a handful of shepherds' cottages, and the site of a moated manor.

The most important manuscript in the history of Old Romney came to light in 1978, in an interesting Cartulary of *L'Abbaye d'Arrouaise,* an Augustinian Abbey in the *Pas de Calais* which contains a grant of the church of St. Clement to the Canons of the Abbey of St. Nicholas of Arrouaise! The historical context points to a date of *c.* 1140.

The manuscript has been acquired by the *Bibliotheque Municipale* at Amiens, MS 1077. Roughly translated the grant reads:—

"Wimarch wife of Torgis of Abrincis Greetings to all the sons of the holy church, those of the present as much as those of the future. Let it be known that I have granted to the Canons of St. Nicholas of Arrouaise for the well-being of my soul and of my ancestors the Church of St. Clement of Old Romney with its appurtances in perpetuity."

The witnesses to this grant are Geoffrey de Bernulvilla and Adam his brother, Richard de Begevilla, Symon a clerk, Baldwin a clerk.

The history of the patronage of the benefice is especially interesting not only because it is one of the few churches in Romney Marsh in which the advowson remained in lay hands for many centuries, and in one family for nearly three hundred years, and particularly the families so renowned in history as the Badlesmeres, the de Roos, and the Scropes, Lords of Leeds Castle.

Aubreda de Romenal and heiress of the Norman landowner Robert de Romenal, held the advowson by special service or serjeantry of acting as Marshal of the King's Falcons. She married William de Jarpenville, and had one daughter, Alice, who married Thomas Fitz-Bernard. Aubreda survived her husband and her son-in-law, and died in 1225, when her widowed daughter, Alice, succeeded to the advowson and the manors. The second recorded rector of St. Clements was Robert Fitz-Bernard, presented by Alice's great-grandson, Ralph Fitz-Bernard in 1287. In the fourteenth century the advowson passed to the unfortunate Bartholomew de Badlesmere, a brother of Fitz-Bernard, during the upheavals of Edward II's reign, the King besieged Lord Badlesmere's castle of Leeds, near Maidstone, which surrendered to him on November 1st 1321. Lady Badlesmere and her children were sent to the Tower of London as prisoners. Her husband was beheaded and his head fixed over the Burgate at Canterbury. All his estates were forfeited. In 1338 the four sisters of young Giles de Badlesmere were allowed to succeed to the property. The advowson was usurped by King Edward III, until King Henry VIII transferred it to Archbishop Cranmer and it has remained in the Primate's gift until this day.

St. Clement's church stands in an attractive setting away from the busy main road that leads from New Romney to Appledore. Like all the churches on Romney Marsh, it was built on a mound to lift it above flood water level. In the churchyard is a great spreading Yew, which has had room to grow for some hundreds of years, the light, supple, and whippy nature of the Yew made it invaluable for the bowyers to make the bows for our famous archers in the Middle Ages. There are three other churches in Kent dedicated to St. Clement, a successor to St. Peter at Rome, who was martyred in A.D. 102, by being cast into the sea, with an anchor fastened to his neck. His festival on November 23rd is observed faithfully every year.

Sometime in the eleventh or twelfth century the small Saxon church was superseded by one of the early Norman type, an aisleless nave with a square-ended chancel. This was enlarged in the thirteenth century.

Today the church consists of nave and chancel, a transeptal chapel on the north leading from a small aisle and a chapel at the east end of the south aisle, a small tower built above the south-west corner of this aisle and a north porch. The nave roof is carried on moulded tie-beams with king posts, the rafters are mostly of chestnut.

St. Clement's Church, Old Romney.

The arch leading from the nave into the chancel is an interesting Norman arch, plain, low, of one order, without impost mouldings. The first three courses are original wrought stone but above, the arch has been rebuilt retaining its original shape.

When the writer first visited this church in 1927 the surround of the chancel arch and the walling as far as the walls of the north and south aisles were enclosed in eighteenth century panelling, erected about 1788. During the incumbency of the Rev. E. H. Lord, a scheme for putting the church into good repair and for many much needed improvements was prepared. The wainscotting was stripped and revealed the rood staircase doorway to the north of the archway, with the actual oak frame of the doorway *in situ,* several interesting worked stones were found in the recess and are still there. Two hagioscopes also came to light, the one to the north with a lancet head and the other a rectangular segmental headed opening. During the 1929 restoration the Sanctuary was extended by moving the alter rails two feet forward, the plaster ceiling of the chancel was removed revealing the fine old rafters. The Sanctuary otherwise is much as it was in the seventeeth century. Behind the altar are the painted wooden boards with the Lord's Prayer, the Creed and Commandments, set in their seventeenth century panelling — a reminder of Puritan austerity, when the altar was shorn of cross, candlesticks and frontal. Fairfield church too has its "blackboards" *in situ.* The twisted balusters of the

85

altar rail were turned in Queen Anne's reign. The east window is of two trefoiled lights and was probably inserted in the fourteenth century. It is set beneath a larger, earlier arch, which may have contained an Early English triple lancet window. In the middle of the chancel floor is a large polished stone slab to the memory of a former rector, John Deffray. He was born at Tours, took a degree at Samur and at Oxford University. After the Revocation of the Edict of Nantes which had given liberty of worship to French Protestants, they were outrageously treated, children dragged from their parents, priests taken from their wives and thrown into prison, so that many Huguenots sought refuge and security across the Channel in England. Many were craftsmen skilled in making pottery, silk weaving, dyeing and the weaving of textiles. John Deffray was one of the hundreds of priests forced to flee from France and settled in Old Romney. The registers record . . . . "he took possession of the Rectory on August 10th 1690, after reading prayers and The Thirty Nine Articles." The memorial ledger stone records that . . . . "he was a faithful and diligent rector of this parish for nearly forty-eight years. After much delight in doing good he departed this life September 4th 1738."

The church suffered a great deal of damage during the Second World War when labour was not available and building material was difficult to get. Rain dripped for many months on to the pews and then poured through broken roof tiles and still nothing could be done by way of repair, matters went from bad to worse so it was little wonder after the War, the Diocesan authorities were anxious to declare the Church redundant. It was reprieved through the efforts of the Archdeacon, and the well known Canterbury architect, Mr. Anthony Swaine, who was appointed to be in charge of the restoration. In 1959 he drew up a scheme at an estimated cost of £7,000, the tower was tackled first, the fissure was stitched through the whole length, the bulging stonework on the east face was rebuilt, the tower was re-shingled and the timbers made good. The walls of the sanctuary were strengthened, but the major task was the nave and the south aisle roof, the former had to be shored up temporarily on the north side as the ends of the tie-beams had decayed, this beam was strengthened with steel plates and re-faced with old timber. The repair of these roofs and the tower had completely exhausted all the money that was available, £2,700, so work had to stop, this was a bitter and grievious disappointment. Then a miracle happened, the Rank film organisation asked for the use of the church for certain scenes, in the "Doctor Syn" film, which they wished to make on location, they wished to bring the Minstrels' Gallery into use, and a new stairway was essential to replace the battered unsafe steps, for this Rank's very kindly paid. They stabled eighteen horses in the churchyard, when the company left, a generous cheque was sent to the Parish, which enabled more work to be tackled. A visit of "The Friends of Kent Churches", in 1965, resulted in the restoration of the Royal Arms. Meanwhile, the original estimate had soared to £10,500, repeated grants from the Friends of Kent Churches and the Historic Churches Trust helped the work along, as well as a broadcast appeal on the radio, by the Rector, who was now

The remains of the original Rood-loft doorway, uncovered when the 18th century panelling was removed.

An unusual stone Coffin Slab in the floor of the north chapel, no reference to this has been found in any records.

supervising the building. By 1967 the new west door was inserted, electric light installed and new curtains for the belfry and vestry entrances, and a new sanctuary carpet had been fitted.

From the chancel a few steps leads one into the north chapel here will be seen one of the most historic finds. During the very wet days of November, when the restoration work was being carried out, the constant coming and going of wheelbarrows through the porch and into the church, had worn the grass away, and one of the workmen noticed that a part of a flat stone had been revealed, which was believed to be a memorial slab. With the Rector's permission this was dug up and to everyone's astonishment it was found to be the pre-Reformation stone *mensa,* this was subsequently mounted on a wooden frame and set up under the east window of the north chapel, so that the Lady Chapel might be restored to its original purpose. St. Catherine's chapel was cleared of lumber, under which were found the Chinese Chippendale chancel gates, these were replaced in their original position. The high box pews were cut down so that the congregation all faced eastwards. There is an especially interesting coat of arms. When the peace of Amiens was declared and England gave up all claim to the French throne, the *fleur de lys* was removed from the Royal Arms of England. This present coat, dated 1800, is the last year in which the *fleur de lys* appeared in Royal Arms. On either side of the Royal Arms hang Georgian texts painted on wooden panels. What must

The Moat, which once surrounded a mediaeval Manor House at Old Romney.

surely be the simplest and most touching memorial of two world wars is a small oak tablet on the south wall of the nave inscribed "For their country" – and then in capital letters "God knows" and the four names, A. Grocott, A. Beeching, H. Masey and W. Stephen.

Another remarkable feature of this church is the interesting font, it dates from *c.* 1300, and is an unusual example of a font of the Decorated period, the plain bowl of Purbeck marble is square and stands upon a central octagonal stem, with chamfered edges and small roll stops. Some adze work visible on the stem suggests it may be re-used Norman stone. The bowl and supporting shafts stand upon an original square plinth of Caen stone, the upper edges of which are chamfered, the remarkable carved capitals of the supporting pillars are all different. Canon Scott Robertson, writing in the nineteenth century thought the figures unique as capitals of font shafts.

The original Queen Anne three-decker pulpit was divided into pulpit and reading desk, originally the rector read the prayers and the lessons from the middle section, preached from the topmost section and below at the desk, sat the clerk, who led the responses and on occasions prompted the rector on any local matter.

In the lane that leads to Ivychurch, is a moat surrounding rising ground, which is believed to be the site of the old manor house. In an adjoining field, on one occasion in the past, a tractor ploughed up various human bones, including skulls, which suggests that this might be the burial ground of the manorial chapel. The Kent Archaeological Local Excavating Unit, carried out

The original stone Mensa surmounted by a flower arrangement at a Three-day Flower Festival, Old Romney.

The Chinese Chippendale gates beneath the Norman chancel arch with the two hagioscopes, one with a pointed and the other a segmental head.

89

a detailed examination and amongst their finds was the complete skeleton of a woman with a child in each arm.

Today the village of Old Romney is divided in two by the main road, the A259. Turning into a lane on the opposite side of the road will be seen a close with bungalows specially designed for the elderly, on the other side of the lane, is the village inn "The Rose and Crown". When the writer knew this inn in 1927, it was a simple village inn, with sanded floors and spittoons. The name Rose and Crown reflected the end of the feud between the houses of Lancaster and York, after the Battle of Bosworth in 1485.

On the completion of the restoration of the Church in 1968, a four day flower festival of praise and thanksgiving was held, to offer up the immeasurable gratitude that this historic and ancient church, a shrine of faith for over eight hundred years, had been safe-guarded for future generations.

St. Mary-in-the-Marsh

St. Mary-in-the-Marsh stands peacefully apart from the hum and bustle of the modern age. There are a few cottages, the lovely old Haffenden Farm, the deeds of which go back to Queen Elizabeth's reign and the local inn opposite the Church "The Star". Since the Second World War a row of Council Houses has been built in what is now called Rectory Road. Farm work was the most sought after employment but with the coming of the Council Houses and the modern motor car the inhabitants were able to go much further afield for their work. Several were employed on the construction of the Littlestone sea wall in the 1930's, others have found employment on industrial estates at Ashford, in the last ten years. The village school was founded in 1871 when all the parishioners were asked to contribute to the cost of the building. Some were able to afford only 2d per week. It was closed after the outbreak of the Second World War and the children transferred daily by bus to New Romney.

The Church is attractively set on an artificial mound as most of the marsh churches were. From Saxon records there is evidence of an earlier church here, but the present grey stone building dates from Norman times. Much of the stonework is of Kentish Ragstone although in the tower and tower arch are traces of Caen stone brought from Normandy.

The oldest part of the Church is the twelfth century square tower, solid and squat, of three stages, ending in a shingled spire, which was added in the fifteenth century. This is surmounted by a weathervane and a large copper ball. In the lower stages are two deeply splayed Norman windows which should be looked at from the vestry in the tower. An interesting doorway with scalloped capitals leads into the nave, but the pointed arch above indicates the enlargement of the Church in the thirteenth century, when the nave walls were pierced with arches and on the north and south, narrow aisles were added. The small Norman square-ended chancel was extended eastwards, note on the

St. Mary-in-the-Marsh Church.

south wall the remarkable double *piscinae* and *sedilia*. The double *piscinae* one for washing of the celebrant's hands before consecrating the Elements at the Mass, the other for the ablution of the chalice after the service. The double *sedilia* or stone seats, all of which are of Caen stone, have interesting corbels, one the tonsured head of a monk and the other a grinning mask. This work dates from about 1220 and is a well preserved example of thirteenth century work. On the floor of the nave are two fine brasses set in stone slabs, one to the memory of Matilda Jamys who died in 1499, the other to her son, William Gregory a Jurat of Romney for several years. Matilda wears a beautiful "butterfly-winged" headdress and William the long civilian gown of Henry the Seventh's reign. In his Will he left the sum of £4, "for two stones to be upon me and my mother". St. Mary's had an unusual Elizabethan communion cup, round the bowl of which were engraved a grasshopper; an eagle and a snail. The grasshopper signified the Resurrection; the eagle the Ascension; and the snail "Verily thou art a God that hidest thyself". The original cup has been stolen but a good photograph of it enabled a new silver cup to be faithfully copied by a London silversmith. The original had the maker's mark, a windmill, which was the mark of a silversmith in "Chepeside".

In the tower hangs a pre-Reformation peal of bells. They bear the following inscriptions:—

WILLIAM GREGORY 1504

© St. Mary in the Marsh

MATILDA JAMYS 1499

© St. Mary in the Marsh

Floor brass commemorating William Gregory who died in 1504, St. Mary-in-the-Marsh.

Floor brass to Matilda Jamys who died in 1499 and was the mother of William Gregory, note the "Butterfly Wing" headdress.

(i) 30 ins. *Sancte Petre ora pro nobis.*
This is from the foundry of I. Danyell, who flourished about the middle of the fifteenth century, and whose bells frequently bore the impress of the Royal Arms, as does this treble bell.

(ii) 36⅛ ins. *Sit Nomen Domini Benedictum.*
Ascribed to William Burford, London, 1371-1392.

(iii) 40 ins. *In Multis Resonet Campana Iohannis.*
Ascribed to Robert Burford, who succeeded his father in 1392.

Outside on the thirteenth century priest's door is a Mass Dial or Scratch Dial, which has a number of grooves representing the hours of the day and a gnomen in the centre, which was turned to the groove that coincided with the hour of the next service.

Near this door lies the beloved childrens' author, E. Nesbit. Above her grave are two wooden posts and rail, lovingly carved by her husband, Captain Tucker, with on one side one word only "Resting".

The records of the parish are of some interest. The Registers date from 1675, the Churchwardens were the overseers of the poor and it would seem from their records they attended to every need of the poor.

92

.... "For corne and a seame of pease to fatt Goody Bunce's Hogg" ....
"For smoak money for ye widdow Sturge's hous".
.... "For futing Joan Marten's 3 payers of Stockons and for lethering and woods for a paier of pattens for her".
.... "I lett Sharp have two bythings to comfoft him". One overseer ...." craved to be allowed for selfe and mare fetching ye midwife, riding to severall places in ye bitter weather .... 5s."

After Henry VIII came to the throne images and pictures of Saints and a single picture or carving of the Kings Arms, "with texts of Scripture about" were set up, no doubt to emphasise the position of the Sovereign as "Supreme Head of The Church".

After the restoration of Charles II in 1660 it became compulsory to set up the Royal Arms as enjoined by the Great Counsel of England "that in all churches thorowout the Kingdom his Majesty's Arms shall be sett upp." St. Mary's complied and in 1664 the Churchwardens' accounts record "For the

The Priest's Door into the south wall of the chancel, St. Mary-in-the-Marsh. Note traces of Mass or Scratch Dial on western jamb.

making of the Royall Armes . . . . £2 11s." The present Georgian coat is dated 1775 and probably replaced the 1664 arms.

In the seventeenth century it became compulsory for everyone to be buried in woollen. An Act was passed "for the encouragement of the woollen manufacturers and the prevention of the exportation of monies for the injury and importing of linen." It enacted that after March 25th 1667 no person should be buried in any shirt, shift or sheet other than should be made of wool only and a second act of 1678 obliged the clergy to make an entry in the register that an affidavit had been taken before a Magistrate after the burial certifying the requirements of the law had been fulfilled.

Besides the customary baptisms recorded in the Registers many interesting and surprising subscription lists are to be found these were called "briefs" and were Royal Mandates for collections for disasters such as fires and floods. Some of St. Mary's briefs include . . . . "For ye redemption of captives in Turkish slavery. . . . . Given for ye reliefe of French Protestants driven away to ye Vaudois in Piedmont. . . . . Given for ye relief of Tignmouth, yt was burned by ye French. . . . . Given for ye suffers by ye fire of Warwick. . . . . Given for ye relief of Protestants driven out of the Principality of Orange, by Louis XIVth", then King of France, because they would not change their religion.

It is astonishing that the parishioners of so small and needy a parish felt called upon to contribute to the relief of such far away distress.

In the Overseers accounts is an interesting entry recording the repairs of the village "Stockes". The last reference is to the erection of a . . . . "new paire and fence and repairs" in 1727.

The churchyard and the bells were matters of considerable expense, a "newe clapper for the grett bell, which weyghed 34 punds and a halfe, cost £1 14s. 6d., and new framing and for timber and other stufe used about the bells amounted to £8 4s. 10d."

At the seaward end of the parish of St. Mary-in-the-Marsh is the ever growing community formerly known as Jefferstone, then abbreviated to Jesson and now called St. Mary's Bay.

In the 1914-18 War there was an emergency air landing ground here, with a hutted settlement, including photographic dark-rooms and printing hut. There was little more than one Farm called Jesson Farm, in the long lane leading from the main road and winding its way to St. Mary-in-the-Marsh.

After the First World War, seaside bungalows began to be built and these have so much increased and there is now a large residential development here.

In 1938 the foundation stone of a modern church was laid, for until then, services had been held in a garage, in use during the week for repairs and cleared for Sunday Services. The then Bishop of Dover, the Rt. Rev. Alfred Rose accompanied by the High Sheriff of Kent, Major Teichman Derville and neighbouring local government dignitaries were present in the large crowd that had assembled. The foundation ceremony was blessed with a lovely summer day.

Captain Allnatt who had presented the ground on which the church was built, had an office in Manchester, on one of his visits to the drawing office, much impressed by the drawings of a young man, he asked him if he would care to design a church incorporating the essential fittings, of necessity these had to be plain and simple because of the limited funds available. He agreed to try his prentice hand. The result was the church as it is today, with prayer desk and lectern incorporated in the south wall and a pulpit built in the same way on the north wall. These together with the steps to the altar give great dignity to the church. Although so modern in design, the church has an atmosphere of sanctity enhanced by the carefully tended garden that surrounds it, and is well worth a visit.

The population has and is still increasing, with the building of more houses, so rapidly that under the new Pastoral Re-organisation Scheme in 1983, this church has become the parish church and St. Mary's Bay created a parish with a resident vicar, for whom a Vicarage was built. The first Vicar was the Rev. Mark Roberts, St. Mary-in-the-Marsh church with its fine Norman Tower and mediaeval fittings, and the delightful Victorian Vicarage next door, after enjoying its own Rector for over seven hundred years was relegated to being a daughter church *"sic transit"*.

Jesson Farm still exists at St. Mary's Bay; there is now an Inn, "The Bailiff's Sargeant", with a portrait of the then Bailiff's Sargeant of Romney Marsh, who lived in the cottage next to New Hall at Dymchurch, the Headquarters of the Lords, Bailiff and Jurats of Romney Marsh. The Bailiff himself unveiled the sign.

Another landmark in the St. Mary's Bay story was the construction of what is now called The Romney, Hythe and Dymchurch Light Railway. This went originally from New Romney Station, where the engine sheds and turntables are, to Hythe, stopping at St. Mary's Bay, Dymchurch and Burmarsh. Later the line was built across the shingle, westwards, to Dungeness. Captain Howey and his friend Count Zoboroski were the instigators of this great venture.

Adjoining St. Mary's Bay Station is the road called Nesbit Road, commemorating E. Nesbit, who lived in the two air force huts with her second husband, Captain Tucker. The two were connected by a covered-in corridor, the one was called "The Long Boat" and the other "The Jolly Boat".

The safe and sandy seashore at St. Mary's Bay is a great attraction to visitors and especially to children. Together with the shops, restaurant and motel they make St. Mary's Bay an ideal family holiday centre.

Snargate

The origin of the village name Snargate is interesting, and may be traced to the River Limen which flowed from Appledore towards the harbour at Romney. It was essential for sluice-gates to be erected to maintain the waterway and it was the sluice that gave its name to Snergate, the gate to snare the water, later spelt Snargate, to conform with orthography. The change of the letter "e" into "a" occurs in many Kentish place-names, Beyfreystone, Berham, Chetham, Dertford, and in the Isle of Thanet Mergate and Remmesgate. Other towns in England have retained the old spelling, like Derby, Hertford and Berkely, but they retained the mediaeval pronounciation when the vowel "e" was pronounced as the modern "a".

Snargate Village consists of about twenty houses, the church and the Inn. There was a Manor to which the earliest reference dates from 1306, when Admiral Gervase Alard, held the Manor for the Archbishop and paid a quarter of a Knight's fee. A little further along the Appledore road is an eighteenth century house, built of brick. In the west wall facing the road was a single brick stamped with the word "DRAIN". A Tax was levied in England, in 1784, on bricks, the only bricks exempt from tax were those used for drainage purposes, used by builders and farmers and these bricks had to be stamped with the word "DRAIN". The tax was not abolished until 1850. This is the only brick marked in this way the writer has come across in a long life.

The Red Lion Inn probably originated in the early seventeenth century. The son of Mary, Queen of Scots, Queen Elizabeth's half sister, was then King James the 6th of Scotland and was the rightful heir to the English throne. He became King James I of England, on the 24th March 1603. Inn keepers

St. Dunstan's Church, Snargate with the old Union Cottages in the foreground, now converted to a modern dwelling.

96

The sluice at Snargate, built "to snare the waters" from Appledore to Romney. It gave its name to the Village.

The Arrow head sewer at Snargate which takes its name from the Arrow Head Plantain Illustrated here.

welcomed their sovereign from across the Border and adopted the Red Lion as an Inn sign, which was the distinguishing badge of Scotland and was now incorporated in the first quarter of the Royal Arms of England.

The church is dedicated to St. Dunstan, to whom there are only four other churches in Kent similarly dedicated. St. Dunstan was born near Glastonbury in 909 A.D., the son of a West Saxon nobleman, who encouraged a love of books in his son at an early age. When Prince Edmund succeeded to the throne after the death of Athelstan, in 939 A.D., he called Dunstan to his council and made him Abbot of Glastonbury. Dunstan did much to restore the Abbey and a year later it was he who introduced the Benedictine Order into England with much enforced ecclesiastical discipline. When King Edgar came to the throne in 959 A.D., Dunstan was made Archbishop of Canterbury. He died in May, 988 A.D.

Like many other marsh churches, Snargate church was built on an artificial mound. It was built in the thirteenth century, about 1220, in the Early English style. The church comprises chancel, nave, north and south aisles and a later tower at the west end, there is no chancel arch, but the two bays are upheld on slender octagonal shafts. The arcades north and south of the nave, each has four circular columns, with rounded capitals and square bases, dating from the thirteenth century. At the west end of the nave is a large embattled tower, of two stages, which was added in the fifteenth century. Evidence of its independent erection is clearly marked at its junction with the nave into which it opens by a lofty arch. There is a west window of three lights, and buttresses at the angles and a turret at the north east corner. The thirteenth century font, near the south door, is square, it retains its original lead lining. Near the font are two lead sheets taken from the roof when repairs were carried out in the late eighteenth century, one of the sheets commemorated the workmen:—

"J. Bourne, C. Warden; Warrington, Romney Plumber;
T. Apps, Carpenter; and all his jolly men   1780"

The flooring near the font still has some of the original encaustic tiles, these beautiful tiles were the customary flooring of the period. John Benett left five marcs towards the paving of the chancel in memory of his wife. There are other fifteenth century tiles in the church, but the nave and chancel flooring was completely retiled in 1871. At the same time the old pews were removed and the present ones installed together with a manually operated reed organ, made in Canada, by W. Bell & Company. The electric lighting was installed in 1958, as a gift, from a former rector, the Rev. A. B. Cole, in memory of his wife, Lucy, who died in February 1953.

The nave roofing consists of sixteenth century tie-beams. In 1967, one was found to be badly decayed and unsafe. By chance, a twenty-two foot replacement beam was purchased for £22. It came from the Quakers' old Meeting House in Harbour Way, Folkestone, which was also being repaired, and provides an interesting ecumenical link between the two places of worship.

On the north wall opposite the south entrance is a painting of a Tudor galleon, in a terra-cotta colour, local legend believes that the ship was a signal to the smugglers entering the church, that it was a safe hide for their goods, which were often concealed under the altar or in the Tower, until it was opportune to share them with the members of the gang.

The bells are interesting, there are three in the tower in addition to a "warnying bell, one hand bell and one sacryng bell". Of the three bells in the tower, two date from pre-Reformation times, one is 36 inches long, a long waisted tenor bell weighing 7½ cwt and inscribed *"sancte dunstane"*, which dates from the end of the thirteenth century. The other, a 30 inch treble bell is stamped *"Ave Maria"* and dates possibly from 1310 and probably came from the same foundry. The third bell, was replaced in the seventeenth century and is inscribed "John Hodson made me – 1673 Richard Hall Churchwarden". The Hodsons often set coins into their inscriptions, the Snargate bell has a Crown of Charles II dated 1671, and several Half-Crowns and Shillings of the period. In 1958 the three bells were overhauled and are now sounded by a swing-chiming mechanism, similar to the mechanism at St. Mary-in-the-Marsh. The bell frame dates from the middle of the seventeenth century.

There is a George III silver chalice engraved with the monogram "I.H.S.", it was fashioned by a London silversmith, William Bateman. Matching this chalice is an oval silver credence dish on four legs with the same monogram in the centre, also made in London but by Peter and Ann Bateman and bears the date letter "q" for the year 1791-92.

The church registers begin in 1552. Among the records there are many interesting of the Poor Law administration, for the Churchwardens were the overseers of the Poor. One bill was paid to a Miss Smith "for nursing the smallpox victims at Snargate workhouse for three nights and three days and a half, 6s. 6d." The workhouse is now a delightful cottage.

Snargate's most famous rector was Richard Harris Barham, who was born in Canterbury, in December 1778. He was sent to St. Paul's School in London at the age of eight, where for two years he was elected Captain. At nineteen he entered Brasenose College, Oxford, where he studied Law. It was after a severe illness, his thoughts turned to becoming a candidate for Holy Orders. He passed the necessary examinations, and was appointed to a curacy at Ashford. He later went to Westwell, where he married Caroline Smart in 1814. In 1817, he was moved to Snargate, but preferred to live at Warehorne. In 1819 he met with another serious accident when the gig in which he was travelling overturned. He had fractured one leg and sprained the other, and so, was confined to bed, during this enforced rest he wrote his novel, entitled "Baldwin". In 1821, he was elected a Minor Canon of St. Pauls Cathedral. Finding he had a considerable amount of leisure on his hands he began writing for Gorton's Biographical Dictionary, Blackwoods Magazine and Bentley's Miscellany. He is probably best remembered for his "Ingoldsby Legends", some of which were obviously inspired by his time at Snargate, such as, The

Lay of St. Dunstan, The Lay of St. Nicholas and the Lay of St. Thomas Becket, reflecting the dedications of the churches at Snargate, New Romney and Fairfield.

Snave

Snave is one of the smallest villages on Romney Marsh, but in mediaeval times it was a Village of some importance and possessed two Manors, Snave itself, of which the Manor House is a reminder and Snave Wick which occupied the land on the opposite side of the main road, but no buildings remain.

Today, Snave consists of the Manor House, the Glebe House and a splendid Colt built bungalow called *Phragmites,* the latin name for the marsh rush, which abounds in the dykes here. Two old cottages at the fork where the Rye road branches to the right, have been converted very skilfully into an attractive house of character. On the right of the Rye road the first farm one comes to is Walnut Tree Farm, which has a row of walnut trees edging the roadside. A little further on is Hangman's Toll Bridge, but more of this anon.

The Manor House and Glebe House stand on either side of the entrance to the pleasant grass track flanked with elm trees, which leads to the Church. Dedicated to St. Augustine, the first Archbishop of Canterbury, the only other marsh church which shares this dedication is that of Brookland.

In springtime, this Avenue is a . . . . "host of golden daffodils". Some years ago, a visitor to the church felt it was lonely and needed some happiness to enfold it, he generously sent nearly five hundred daffodil bulbs to be planted here, which has given Snave the name of − The Daffodil Church, just as Hinxhill is the − Snowdrop Church. Snave is well worth a visit in springtime just to see the carpet of daffodils.

Like most thirteenth century Marsh churches, Snave is small as befits a small population. According to the Census of 1801, the population numbered only fifty-nine, twenty years later it was a hundred and eight. After that date it was united with Brenzett and Snargate.

The church is entered by way of the west tower and the lower half of the tower is of thirteenth century date, it is square, with a large squat buttress writes the Rev. David Cawley, A.K.C. F.S.A. (Scot), in his delightful guide to the Church. The upper part of the tower dates from the fifteenth century and has plain square headed windows, it has a timber turret at its north-east corner, ending in a nineteenth century weathervane, capped with a ball.

The nave has two-light windows of the thirteenth century and between them there is the outline of a blocked-up north doorway, probably blocked with bricks early in the eighteenth century, before the Brick Tax was imposed in 1784. Opposite the north doorway is the south entrance by way of a south porch. It was customary for north and south doors to be built opposite each

St. Augustine's Church, Snave, in daffodil time, showing the south porch and fine battlemented West Tower.

other, and were known as processional doors, which were to enable the processions at the great festivals to leave the church by one door and come in at the other. The porch is Victorian, and is now in a sad state of ruin. The north side of the nave leads by way of a screen into a chapel, this was the Lady Chapel, in the south east corner is a trefoiled *piscina,* alas the bowl is broken. The Chapel was later in use as a schoolroom, which explains the fireplace, it is now the church vestry. The chancel is most probably late thirteenth century work, in the south wall is a *piscina,* but the bowl is broken, next to it is a *sedilia,* or seat, with an unusual carved embattled top, and a cinq-foiled arch, there are arms to the seat. The chancel floor was raised in Victorian days, which alas has spoiled the proportions of the seat. On the walls of the chancel are the early nineteenth century painted commandments, creed and Lord's Prayer. These were restored by Flight Lieut. Parker, M.B.E., who also restored the Royal Arms, which are dated 1735, George II's reign. Unusual in that the first quarter has the lions of England impaled with the lion of Scotland, the second is the quartering of France, not until the Peace of Amiens in 1801, did the King of England surrender all claims to the throne of France, as they had done from the Hundred Years War, the third quarter has the Harp of Ireland, with the Mermaid, and the fourth quarter, the Hanoverian arms. The font is Victorian, but the remains of the original octagonal bowl of the thirteenth century font are to be found on the back pew on the north side of the Church. This was rescued from use as a rain water butt!

There is a noteworthy silver chalice, which bears the inscription "William Gootli of Snave". The date letter indicates this was made 1554-55. It was given in the reign of the Roman Catholic Queen Mary. The remaining plate is of pewter and comprises an eighteenth century Alms dish, a small plate dating from about 1700 marked "Snave", two other plates of the eighteenth century and two spout lamps also of pewter. None of the plate is kept in the church.

There are three bells in the Tower, the largest and the smallest were cast at the Whitechapel foundry, by Thomas Mears in 1795, the middle bell, probably the most valuable possession of the church, is one of only three known survivors from the foundry of Stephen Norton of Maidstone c. 1380, and is inscribed:—

"STEPHANUS NORTONE DE KENT ME FECIT"
(Stephen Norton of Maidstone made me)

The church registers are kept in the Kent Archives Office at County Hall, Maidstone. The earliest record of a presentation to the living is 1219, when the Advowson was given by the De Snaves family to Saint Augustine's Abbey at Canterbury.

In 1981 the Church was declared redundant, by an Order in Council which means that only one service may be held here a year. But the church has been well restored and is kept clean, as befits a place of worship. In September 1983, the first service was held, a Harvest Service of Thanksgiving, the church was full and the retiring collection amounted to over £100.

Snave-Wick

Snave-Wick, "Wick" a word of Saxon origin, means a dwelling, would seem to suggest it was the original home of the De Snaves family, of which there are no remains of any buildings today. Snave was one of the twenty-three Manors of Romney Marsh, one of its privileges was the right to erect its own gallows. Hangman's Toll Bridge to which reference has already been made,

Tombstones rescued from the dyke in Hangman's Field at Snave Wick.

although not necessarily connected with the gallows, refers to men who were hanged, probably at Maidstone, and the bodies were brought here for burial. The Hangman having to pay a Toll to cross the bridge to enter the field, it is not known how many people were actually buried here, but two tombstones still exist, giving the names. These were found, slightly damaged, in one of the dykes that border the field. They have now been recovered, but bear no date. The letters S.U.R. are on both tombstones and probably represent SUR – Above, i.e. Above the body, or marking the place where the body was buried.

CHAPTER 5

The Lost Villages

Although there are seventeen villages in Romney Marsh today there are reminders of several communities which have completely disappeared. Fortunately there are some visible vestiges of these parishes, sometimes the ruins of the church itself, or perhaps a stone cross to mark the site of the church. These churches were built by the Lords of the Manors for their tenants, and they usually appointed the *capellanus* or chaplain.

One of these Saxon Manors was that of Blackmanstone, adjoining the parish of Newchurch. Stones of the ruined church have been incorporated into a small farm building, a looker's hut, and some were used in the repair of Blackmanstone bridge, which is marked on the ordnance survey maps. The plough still turns up mediaeval stones of the church.

This important Saxon Manor was granted at the Conquest to Hugh de Montfort. In 1541 it came by marriage to Sir Thomas Wyatt, who exchanged it with the King, in 1587 Queen Elizabeth granted it to Roger Parker who sold it to William Hall, in 1630 it was alienated to Sir Edward Hales, in whose family it descended for over one hundred years. The Lord of the Manor in 1815 was Samuel Finn, the Captain of Dungeness Fort. In 1848 it came to Sir Edward Knatchbull Bt., and in 1888 Sir Edward Knatchbull-Hugesson, the first Lord Brabourne. In more recent times it came into the late Arthur Finn's hands, and then to his nephew, the late G. Frank Finn, a well-known Marsh farming family.

From a Visitation Roll of 1292 it is recorded . . . . "mass was wont to be celebrated in the said church of Blackmanstone every day, but in the time of the present parish priest it is not always said. The chaplain . . . . appeareth and was enjoined to serve the said Church regularly and in seemly fashion, as far as his strength allowed under pain of severe penalty if he should be negligent in the future".

"Henry Tuke, farmer of the mill, hath not paid the tenth seam of wheat for tithe of the mill, although he payeth to the lord of the mill ten seams yearly, he saith that he gives to the said Nicholas Barrok for the farm of the mill only eight seams a year. He must pay to the Rector of Blackmanstone two bushells of wheat for the arrears of half a year under pain of excommunication".

The population in 1377 was recorded as twelve.

Although not strictly a lost village, the name of the Manor of Craythorne lives on in a house in Cannon Street, New Romney. Craythorne is one of the twenty-three Manors of Romney Marsh and in addition to the Manor House there was a manorial chapel. In the thirteenth century there appears not to have been a Lord of Craythorne but a Lady of Craythorne, who was presented at the visitation of 1292 because . . . . "she doth not come to church as she ought, and is bound to do, nor does she contribute either to the work of the church, to the Pascall candle, or the blessed bread, because she hath a chapel in which her chaplains use a bucket for a font *(Faciunt sibi fontem in uno buketta).* The Missal is in bad condition *(debilis)* and through the poverty of the parishioners it is not possible to get it repaired or renovated because the men of Romney possess almost all the lands in the said parish." "Adjourned until the Lord shall come to Romney".

The Manor is in the parish of Hope All Saints and lies wholly within the Marsh. Until recently the site of the manor house was indicated by the moat, in a large field on the right of the Ashford Road, it eventually dried up and has now been levelled and is part of an extremely productive "pick-your-own" fruit centre.

The most important of the lost villages was probably Eastbridge, where there was originally a small Saxon church. Today travelling from Dymchurch to Bilsington one passes all that is left of Eastbridge Church, a section of the West wall of the west tower of the mediaeval church; originally it was a fine tower with pinnacles.

In the great Domesday survey of 1087 the entry relating to Eastbridge may be translated thus:—

"Hugh himselfe holds ESTBRIGE in demesne AELSI held it of Earl Godwin it is assessed at 1 suling. There is land for six ploughs. On the demesne are three ploughs, and two villeins with thirty-six bordars have four ploughs. There are eight salt-pans with a third of a ninth worth 20 shillings, a moiety of a fishery worth 8 pence, woodland yielding three swine from pannage dues and two churches. In the time of King Edward it was worth ten pounds it is now worth fifteen pounds." The second church was that at Dymchurch.

This reflects the importance of the Manor, which was a well known landmark in this part of the Marsh, for it stood up well on a hillock.

An extract from the 1292 Visitation Roll for Romney Marsh reads as follows:—

"The Rector did not appear to receive the Lord's visitation nor has he ever been in residence there nor was a chaplain found therein at the time of the visitation, and the parishioners asked that a fit priest may be provided for them. Wherefore it was decreed that the fruits of the benefice should be sequestrated until other order be taken. The Rector doth not appear and therefore he is suspended from celebrating divine service. And an inhibition was issued that no one should presume to violate this sequestration on pain of excommunication, also the Rector is cited to appear at Braburn on Thursday, after the feast of All Saints, to answer to the premises and to the charge. On the day, he did not appear nor did any proctor appear in his name, the case standeth over."

The remains of the West Tower, Eastbridge.

The cross marking the site of Fawkenhurst Church.

"Edward, Vicar of Westhethe hath the said church to farm and hath held it a long time. He was suspended and deprived of his vicarage."

Eastbridge was originally a Manor of Godwin, Earl of Kent but in 1086 it was held by Hugh de Montfort, in 1229 it passed to Hubert de Burgh, who gave the revenues to the building of the *Maison Dieu* at Dover. This "House of God" was erected to accommodate the Pilgrims coming from Europe to St. Thomas Becket's shrine in Canterbury Cathedral. Pilgrims came from as far afield as Iceland. Hubert held it by the petty serjeanty of a Sparrowhawk at Lammas each year. At the Dissolution, the Manor passed to the King, in 1563 it was granted to Cuthbert Vaughan and together with Honeychild Manor passed later to the Twysden family and then, by marriage, to the Derings. In 1920 it was sold to J. Constantine, in 1928 Major Teichman Derville, O.B.E., D.L., F.S.A., purchased it. He bequeathed it to Anne Roper on his death in 1963.

The manor was known as the "sea-girt manor of Eastbridge," and the Homage in the seventeenth century presented "that the royalty and claim of wrecks at sea belong to this Manor and extend along the sea coast from Brockman's Barn Wall to Romney Warren Post." This is recorded in the volume of proceedings of the Court Baron of Eastbridge, 1650-1802.

In the census of 1801 the population was given as twenty-one.

107

Returning to the Aldington Road, the road continues to Sherlock's Bridge where one crosses the Canal, turning to the right, following the pathway takes one along the canal and then turns left up the slope to the top of the hill to Fawkenhurst, marked on maps frequently as "Hurst". The site of the church dedicated to St. Leonard is marked with a stone cross on a stepped plinth. Every year in June a service is held here, two bales of straw provide the altar and the farm lorries bring up wooden benches for the congregation. On a peaceful summer evening this setting is a perfect background for this annual service of Evensong.

The house called Fawkenhurst near the site of St. Leonards Church, was in all probability the seventeenth century manor house. In the eighteenth century the Marsh lands amounted to 105 acres. This Manor was one of the fees of Dover granted to Fulbert of Dover. Henry II granted the Manor to William son of Balderic, to hold by the grand serjeanty of keeping one falcon for the King's pleasure. His descendant Godfrey le Huton took the name of Le Falconer and his family held it under this name until 1394, they had free warren, view of frankpledge, and assize of Bread and Ale.

Another of the lost communities of the Marsh centred around the church of Hope All Saints, all that remains today are the ruins one sees about half a mile from New Romney on the road to Ivychurch. The church has been a ruin since the eighteenth century, it was actually in use in 1541. In 1573 at Archbishop Parker's visitation the church was in decay for lack of repairs. It consisted of a nave without aisles with an irregular twelfth century chancel, and was dedicated to All Saints.

From the Visitation Roll of 1292 (Roll X) it is learned that . . . . "The Rector does not reside because he is at school *(stat in scolis)* by licence of the Lord Archbishop and Master Nicholas, master of the schools of Canterbury, keepeth the fruits of the same church and answereth for the same. The Vicar of Romene doth wrong to the church of All Saints in that he taketh a moiety of the tithe of the milk of beasts which are milked in the parish of the same Vicar".

Midley mid-way between Lydd and Old Romney, is another of the lost villages of the Marsh, with only the ruins of the church today to indicate its existence. It stands in the midst of fields with vestiges of various foot paths leading to it and is plainly visible from the road that leads to Rye, as it was built on rising ground. In fact Professor Montague Burrows' map in his book on the Cinque Ports suggests that the Church once stood on the banks of the old course of the Rother.

After the great storm of 1287 when the harbour of Romney became choked with debris, Midley gradually formed "the middle island", between the two larger ones of Romney and Lydd. From the Domesday Book it is clear there was a Church here then and it is recorded that in 1377 the population was sixty-five. In 1801 the census gives the number as twenty-three.

108

The ruins of Hope All Saints.

Remains of the West Tower, Midley.

109

*The cross marking the site of
Orgarswick Church.*

At Archbishop Parker's visitation in 1573 the church was described as "decayed". Today only the arched west wall with fragments of the north and south walls stand above the ground. The interior of the church was plastered and above the gabled weather mould on the wall "seemed to indicate a bell-cote". Petrie's sketch of 1806 shows the whole of the south wall standing. In the jambs of the west doorway it was interesting to find "the draw-bar hole and stop" for securing the door, although much worn from constant use.

On the road from Dymchurch to Bilsington, just beyond the Royal Oak, now an attractive private house, there stands beside the dyke, a cross of stone collected from the ruins of Orgarswick church, erected presumably on the site of the church. It is impossible to envisage what the church looked like as there are no walls standing. Behind the cross is Chapel Cottage Farm with fine modern buildings. Not only is this the site of the lost village but it would appear to have been a deserted village for over a century, for the census of 1801 gives the population as six.

The inscription at the foot of the cross reads:—

A. M. D. G.
THIS CROSS WAS
ERECTED ON THE
SITE OF THE
ANCIENT CHURCH
OF ORGARSWICK
1938.

110

CHAPTER 6

Dungeness

Dungeness is a place of unknown age and infinite mystery. One cannot imagine anywhere comparable in the country, there are so many fascinating aspects that it merits a chapter to itself.

An extraordinarily interesting story can be gleaned from two leaves of parchment bound up in a cartulary of St. Leonards, York, now in the Cotton Manuscripts at the British Museum, they appear to be a statement of the claim of the Abbot of Battle to a share of whales and other royal fish stranded on the shores of Dungeness.

The statement reads, that . . . . "William the Conqueror founded Battle Abbey in memory of his victory on that spot and gave it to the Manor of Wye in Kent, with all its customs and liberties, as a royal manor. This included the whole of any "craspeis" coming ashore on any of the land of the Manor, and the tongue and two thirds of the body of any such fish stranded within the boundaries of "Horsmede", Blakewase and Brudelle" as far as "Witheburne" whoever might own the land. Before the manor left the King's hands, while Richard of Dover was reeve, a fish was thus stranded on land held by Hugh de Montfort of the Archbishop. Richard claimed the King's share but was forcibly repulsed, and so, when making his account as reeve before the treasury at Winchester, claimed an allowance of £30 for the loss of this advantage. Hugh was compelled to make good the loss and fined £100. This right was expressly transferred to Battle in the Charter which gave Wye, as also the King's right to two-pence apiece on all forfeitures and pleas pertaining to the summons of Wye."

In the thirteenth century Romney Marsh comprised Romney Marsh proper, Walland Marsh, (to the end of the old Appledore wall) then Denge Marsh and Guldeford Level, Denge Marsh became Dengeness and later Dungeness.

There is a movement up channel known as the eastward drift which is a combination of wind and tide. In severe storms the shingle on the seabed is scoured up and hits the promontory at Dungeness, whereby some seven feet of shingle is added each year, thus the Point continually gets nearer to France. When Napoleon threatened to invade this country, General Moore ordered four forts to be constructed, one of which was to be at Dungeness. Captain Samuel Finn of Lydd was appointed first Captain of the Lydd Volunteers, and in 1794 Barrack Master at Dungeness. Other steps were taken to deter the enemy from landing. Chief of the defences was the construction along the coast, of Martello Towers, seventy-three in number from Folkestone to Seaford. Their purpose was to bring concentrated fire on an enemy who might attempt a landing. So sure was Napoleon of succeeding in invading these shores, he had had a medal struck "Frappé à Londres", for his brave officers. Although there is no Martello Tower at Dungeness, tower number 24 at Dymchurch may be inspected, as it is open to the public.

The promontory stood out as a natural bastion to the defence of Romney Marsh. It was protected during the French Wars by a redoubt sited near the point and four four-gun batteries, substantial remains of number one Battery may be seen near the Pilot Inn; although Dungeness seemed an unlikely spot for a major enemy landing, the miles of loose shingle provided an obstacle to movement, the promontory did provide shelter on either side and a safe anchorage from which the French might land troops.

In addition to the remains of the fort there are two other gun emplacements with brick facings and the rails, *in situ,* for the traverse of the guns, these are interesting remains. They are practically opposite the turning to the right of the Lydd road. At one time there was the ammunition store, the doorway of which had oak posts and lintel. A rectangular well stood in the grounds. It would be a pity if this relic of the defences against the Napoleonic invasion was destroyed.

Long after the dissolution of the monasteries there was no light at Dungeness, and each winter, shipwrecks, to an enormous extent, happened, in one year over a thousand lifeless bodies of shipwrecked victims were collected at and near the Ness, and merchandise to the value of £100,000 perished there. In the early years of the seventeenth century building began as a financial speculation. The speculators decided Dungeness was a spot at which a Lighthouse was necessary and expedient. In the year 1615, Sir Edward Howard one of the King's Cup Bearers, built a lighthouse at Dungeness and petitioned for leave to collect Toll for its support. Trinity House offered an uncompromising proposition, nevertheless James I gave Sir Edward the licence he sought. Sir Edward found the dues were paid reluctantly and eventually was glad to part with his interest to one William Lamplough, Clerk of the King's Royal Kitchen on whose behalf the Crown, by its Customs Officers, directed that the Tolls should be paid. This was too much for the ship owners at Trinity House. In 1621 they were prompting eagerly a Bill in Parliament for the suppression of the lighthouse, describing it as "a nuisance to navigation", but Parliament would not interfere with the King's grantee and the end was that Lamplough was told by the Crown that he must keep a better light at Dungeness than he had done. Candles had replaced the original coal fire, possibly from the difficulty of getting coal to such an out of way point.

As time passed by, the sea had receded even further and seamen complained of the distance of the Lighthouse from the water's edge, so in 1635 the patentee, pulled down the existing tower and built an altogether more

112

Dungeness Fort built as a coastal defence when Napoleon threatened to invade these shores.

The gun traverse of one of the Napoleonic batteries.

113

The First Lighthouse at Dungeness lit by a coal brazier.

substantial one, nearer the Point, with a coal fire on top. The coal fire continued to light Dungeness until 1746, but the position of the Lighthouse was again complained of as being misleading. The sea receded leaving the tower once again far from the waters edge.

In 1792 Samuel Wyatt built a tower about 116 feet high, of the same design as Smeaton's lighthouse on Eddystone, which lasted for over a hundred years. Eighteen sperm-oil lamps then took the place of the coal fire. Robert Stevenson, the father of Robert Louis Stevenson, when inspecting the Lighthouse in 1818, found parabolic reflectors which had been obtained from Howards in Old Street, London, in 1802, a rival of George Robinson, then chief suppliers of parabolic reflectors to Trinity House.

During a violent storm on Christmas Day in 1822 lightning struck the tower and made a rent in the masonry on the north side. The tower however was so well constructed the damage sustained was not serious, but an alarming experience for the Lighthouse Keeper.

In 1862 an electric light was installed and Dungeness became one of the first Lighthouses in England to be lit by this means. Subsquently this form of lighting was superseded by a huge oil lamp of 850 candle power, surrounded

Wyatt's Lighthouse in 1792 surrounded by the Officers' quarters, which are still in use.

The Lighthouse completed in 1904.

The newest Lighthouse, opened by His Royal Highness The Duke of Gloucester, in 1961.

by glass prisms, which increased the illuminating power by a hundredfold. In addition, the outer wall of the tower was painted black with a white band to render it more easily visible to mariners in daylight. Today, the Officers' Quarters which were built round the base of Wyatt's tower are still in use. It is recorded in the 1890's they were some five hundred yards from the high water mark, but now they are very much further, this increased distance became somewhat misleading, so Trinity House placed a small revolving light nearer the sea, which is called the "Low Light" and, with it, a siren fog-horn, the latter a present from America.

The next Lighthouse, begun in 1901, was completed in 1904, standing some 136 feet high and 38 feet in diameter at the base, and was in continual use until 1960, it still stands today, although no longer operational, and it is now in private ownership and the public may visit.

The present Lighthouse which was the first to be built by Trinity House for fifty years, was opened by H.R.H. The Duke of Gloucester, the former Master of Trinity House, in 1961. It stands on the site of the old fog signal and the low light structure and rises a 140 feet from a white concrete base, which is in the form of a spiral ramp and contains the main machine apparatus and control rooms. The Tower of revolutionary design, pencil slim, and constructed of precast concrete rings 5 feet high, 6 inches thick and 12 feet in diameter are fitted one above the other, the black and white bands are impregnated into the concrete. It is fitted with a rotating AGA Gearless Pedestal light whose intensity is equivalent to 4 million candela and has a range of 27 miles, its characteristic is a white flashing light every ten seconds.

In the perforations below the top of the tower are incorporated sixty hundred watt loudspeaker type units constituting the electric fog signal, this is automatically set in action by a fog detector on top of the spiral ramp, as visibility demands, and was invented by the Trinity House Research staff. It is interesting to note that every Lighthouse has its own colour banding and its own frequency of flashes.

Another point of interest is that since May 1962 the whole Tower has been floodlit to assist identification from the sea, this floodlighting has reduced the bird mortality rate at this Lighthouse considerably during the migration season.

The most recent of modern developments is the erection of a Nuclear Power Station. The "A" Station (Magnox Reactor) was opened formally by Lord Hinton of Bankside on May 26th, 1966. Both reactors had in fact been commissioned earlier, reactor one in September 1965 and reactor two in December 1965, ... "and after nineteen years in service the Station continues to perform consistently well". Dungeness "A" Nuclear Power Station is the fifth station in the first Nuclear Power Programme and already it has been possible to improve the design and efficiency of the plant. Dungeness has a capacity of 550 megawatts linked to the National Grid by 400,000 volt lines, supplying the South Coast and London via the Canterbury-Northfleet connection. Extensive investigations showed this site to be the best in South-eastern England, particularly as it was close to deep water for cooling purposes and utilised land which was of minimal value to agriculture.

The first reactor (21) of Dungeness "B" (Advanced Gas Cooled Reactor) was commissioned in December 1982 and electricity supplied to the National Grid from April 3rd 1983. This reactor/turbo alternator unit has also performed well, until shut down in March of this year (1984) for statutory overhaul. It is expected that the second reactor (22) will be commissioned before the end of the year, with both units (21 and 22) supplying electricity to the National Grid. Dungeness "B" was the first Power Station to be ordered under the Government's second Nuclear Power Programme. The Power Station may be visited on Wednesdays.

The rich fishing grounds of Dungeness have been a source of great attraction to fishermen for some centuries. Today, on an average the fishermen catch each day about thirty stone, or 3¾ cwt, of fish. Looking back over the years, the number of fishermen has increased but not the number of fish. The usual fish caught are Flounders, Dabs, Plaice, Huss and a few Whiting, Skate and Mackerel, but on the east range Plaice are the main catch. The summer fishing is on the south and south-east, but there is no shelter here and it is not suitable to fish in the winter. Sometimes they go nearly half way to France, some six or seven miles into the Bay and fish the Grand Bars. Most of the boats are twenty-eight to thirty feet long, all with diesel engines and with the most modern equipment. There are some thirty fishing boats at Dungeness, although some of them are used only seasonally. Most of the Dungeness fishing boats have the Folkestone registration "FE", the first and last letters, others are registered at Rye, "RX".

Mr. Richardson, a former Fishery Protection Officer, recalls, that at the outbreak of the last War all the fishermen were called up for the Navy and sent out to the Mediterranean, some to Malta, some to Sicily. It always amused them seeing so many nanny goats in the streets with bells round their necks, and on Sundays their tintinnabulations vieing with the ringing of the church bells.

An interesting reminder of bygone fishing days, is on the left edge of the road leading to the Lighthouse, a small brick built boiler with a copper within the brickwork and a brick chimney, this is a "Kutch boiler" or familiarly known as a "Tan copper". Mrs Tart, née Oiller, of Ocean View, who lives in the house in which she was born, recalls that this was the boiler used by her grandfather, and father, in earlier days, for when the fishing nets were bought, they were white, and were always boiled in the copper with kutch, before they were used and then taken out and dried on the shingle, this was to colour and preserve them and gave them the tan look with which one is familiar today. Kutch is a substance which comes from Malaya and is amber in colour and looks like translucent coarse pebbles.

117

Before there was a road from Lydd to Dungeness there was only a shingle track and normal walking was very difficult and slow. The residents took to what they called "backstays", this was a rectangular flat piece of wood with a leather strap into which the foot slipped. Almost everyone wore them to facilitate their progress across the shingle. When there was a school at Dungeness all the children, of course, wore backstays to go to school, their initials were carved underneath the sole, which each day were lined up outside the classroom. Today, now that there are tarred roads, the backstays are not essential, but some of the older residents are still glad to wear them.

Outside Mrs. Tart's house, like so many of the older houses is a wide outside ladder leading up to a door which opens into a loft, here the fishermen stored their nets in winter. Garden Cottage is the oldest cottage at Dungeness, it is over a hundred years old.

The story of the Life-boat at Dungeness goes back a long way and the present boat is called "The Alice Upjohn", after the generous donor Miss Upjohn who lives in Sussex, and gave it in memory of her mother.

On the corner, where the road divides, coming from Lydd, there is a substantial red brick house, called "Watering House", this is where small boats came ashore to collect casks of fresh drinking water.

The "Watering House", Dungeness.

Air view from the South of the new Nuclear Power Stations 'A' and 'B' at Dungeness.

Dungeness 'B' Power Station.

Fishing boat on the beach, with the nets being dried.

The "Tan Copper" or "Kutch Boiler".

120

Another building, which has been recently demolished, alas, and may possibly have been the last example in the country, was the "Earth House". When the Coastguard Cottages were built, they had no indoor sanitation, only the usual earth closets, but Dungeness was devoid of earth, so it was necessary for regular supplies to be brought to the Earth House. This was brought in carts from Lydd, the inhabitants of the Coastguard Cottages then came with their pails to fill them as and when necessary.

Further along the road, past the Lifeboat house, on the opposite side, will be seen a house with an outside staircase, this was known locally as the "Dutch Consulate", so called, because the occupier of the house spent a good deal of time watching the shipping in the channel, logging the details and if it were a Dutch ship, he reported it to the Dutch Consulate in London, this happens no longer.

Still further along, taking a shingle track to the right, by a signboard, which says, "The Sanctuary – R.A.O.B. – William Fagg Lodge", one comes to a small church, this started life in 1943 as a "PLUTO" building, and housed a large fuel tank, ten years later it came to life in quite another guise, for it was

The "Earth House", Dungeness now demolished.

121

The Sanctuary, formerly part of the P.L.U.T.O. buildings.

dedicated by His Grace the Lord Archbishop of Canterbury, Dr. Geoffrey Fisher. On the wall is a tablet which reads:—

The First Sanctuary
at Dungeness
Given in memory
of Mildred Parnell
Wife of the Lightship Secretary
of the Mission to Seamen
Dedicated by the
Lord Archbishop of Canterbury
for the celebration
of Holy Communion
11th April 1954.

Owing to the dwindling congregations and the vandalism, even the brass bell, in the bell-cote, given by Trinity House, was stolen, the nave of the church is now used by the William Fagg Lodge of the Royal and Ancient Order of Buffaloes for their meetings. William Fagg lived at Lydd and was a devoted worker for the Order. On entering one is immediately struck by the contrast of the rather stark exterior of the building, and the warmth and comfort of the transformed nave, all due to the hard work and generosity of the Buffaloes. Two services are still held in the church annually, Harvest Festival and a Carol Service at Christmas time, both joyous occasions.

Dungeness is a paradise for bird lovers, there has been a Royal Society for

Sea-Kale at Dungeness.

Pink Valerian.

Vipers' Bugloss.

White Valerian.

the Protection of Birds Warden there since 1907, it is the society's oldest reserve. Before the Power Station was built the Board took special measures to minimise any disturbance to the natural life and surface features. This is one of the major crossroads of bird migration routes. In conjunction with the R.S.P.B. a local warden was appointed to protect these interests and close liaison with the Board's resident engineer was established even before any construction work was started. Birds are trapped, ringed and released to aid the studies of migration.

In 1952 an independent committee set up the Dungeness Bird Observatory which not only welcomes visitors from overseas, but trains bird ringers.

This is one of the largest areas of its kind in Europe and the co-operation of the Gravel Extraction company has resulted in the great open lakes of fresh water, which together with the islands, undisturbed, provide ideal nesting and breeding grounds for the birds. At migration time the bushes are alive with birds, over 270 species have been recorded in recent years.

Dungeness is equally a paradise for botanists and entomologists, three species of moth, found only at Dungeness, are the Eyed Hawk Moth, the White Spot Moth, and an immigrant species, the Silver "Y". There are many unusual mosses and lichens to be found, of special interest is the reindeer moss, "reinemusse", which grows extensively in North Norway, and on which the reindeer live. In June the shingle is a sea of great clumps of silver-green sea kale, with splashes of pink and white valerian, – the latter called by the older residents "May" – and the golden gorse. Also, for the eager searcher will be found the Yellow Horned Poppy, Vipers' Bugloss, Sea Lavender and Sea Milkwort, to name but a few.

Very few people know of or have visited the other Dungeness, which is in another continent, South America. When Darwin made his voyage to the Straits of Magellan, before the "Beagle" turned into the Straits, Darwin noticed a rocky promontory, which he said at once reminded him of Dungeness in Kent. The writer was so intrigued by this and made enquiries about it and found that it also had a Lighthouse. The Lighthouses in Chile are under the control of the Navy and permission had to be sought from the Naval Authorities to visit, this was readily given and an appointment made. It was reached after travelling over a vast desolate area of scrub, where there were many wild ostriches, and at the approach was the exciting board, with one word "Dungeness". Driving across the forecourt to the Lighthouse, the Lighthouse Keeper, his wife and all the children were waiting to receive us. The only other house in the vicinity being a small wooden shepherd's bungalow. We were shown the Lighthouse, which is still in use, and recently had been fitted with a new Swedish lantern, of which the Keeper was very proud. He was tremendously interested to learn there was another Dungeness, in England, which was described to him in detail. It was an unforgettable pleasure to come face to face with another Dungeness, across the Atlantic, in Chile.

CHAPTER 7

The Marsh Countryside

Between the little range of hills, which formed the original coastline, and the waters of the English Channel, lie some miles of farm land interwoven with drainage dykes, which have called for a special administration. Since the appointment of Justices of Laws and Sewers from 1288 onwards, the Commissioners were appointed annually. In 1290 Stephen de Pencestre and Apuldrefeld were called to settle a dispute between the master of *Domus Dei* and his tenants at Eastbridge about the repairs of walls in the marsh. During the thirteenth and fourteenth centuries, in conjunction with the Justices of the Sewers, experiments had been made so that in 1531 when the land drainage of the kingdom became the subject of statutory enactment Commissioners of Sewers were established by Act of Parliament, Romney Marsh was always exempted from their rulings, and so retained its unique organisation. Laths or Lasts were fully established towards the end of the thirteenth century. By 1600 procedure had become fixed and the annual meeting of Lathe was followed by a feast or "dinner" provided by the corporation out of common funds. In 1654 a total cost of the dinner was limited to forty pounds.

"Paid for fetching a loade of water at Hythe against the Lathe for dressing the dinner — 18s.
John Martin for turning the spit at the general Lathe — 6d.
William Clarke for fetching wood into the Kitchen for the cooke — 6d.
Widow Hobdaye helping — 8d.
Reynold Witherlay drawing beers — 12d.
Henry Warney working in the kitchen and turning spits — 12d.
Goodwife Clarke helping at New Hall 2 days, 9d. a day — 18d.
2 Cooks attendance at New Hall dressing the dinner 3 days — 20s.
Paid Elizabeth Merriman scouring the spits and dripping pans belonging to the Country (i.e. Liberty) against the Lathe — 12d."

The dykes flowed into the sewers and the sewers carried the water to the outfalls. Through the outfalls the water flowed into the sea, at low tide, but at high tide the water is controlled automatically by steel doors, as at the Littlestone Outfall.

When the sea receded from Romney Marsh it left behind what became rich pasture land and over the years the rearing of sheep has been an integral part of the farming here. There is in existence a well-known long letter, written about

125

Typical bridges across the Marsh dykes.

126

◄ *Looker's Hut –*
St. Mary-in-the-Marsh.

Looker's Hut –
Old Romney. ►

Looker's Hut –
Cutler's Bridge. ◄

127

1786, from the Rev. Daniel Jones of New Romney to his brother at Llanio near Lampeter, describing sheep husbandry at this time. How the land was divided, fields and enclosures each with its own pond or watering-place. The rents in general were from 20s. to 35s. per acre, with prime fatting pieces as high as 40s. to 50s. and the tenant paying all water Scots for the public sewers up to 2s. 6d. per acre. The Scots were levied on all land-owners for the maintenance of the walls from "the wash and rage of the sea".

They employed a man called a looker to look after their stock when they themselves could not attend to them. He was paid 8d. per acre per annum, in addition he usually had a house, the keep of a cow, the privilege of keeping a horse and was paid for doing any other work on the land. He also was allowed the fat of any dead sheep, which he skins and takes off as much of the fat as possible, stews it in a large copper, and then takes the scum to melt down with other tallow, this he sells, at 4d. or 4½d. per pound.

The land is divided into two degrees of goodness, the breeding land which is the general quality of the marsh and is supposed to be not sufficiently good to fatten, and the fatting land, which comprises the prime pieces and is very rich. From September the lambs were sent to the upland farms, where they were put on turnips and kept there until the beginning of April. The ewes began to lamb in mid-April.

Some of the sheep were sent to the London market and took nearly a week, travelling at a rate of 14 miles a day, some were sent to the lower markets, Tonbridge, Rochester and Maidstone. The Drovers acted as Agents and also Salesmen.

They also kept a meticulous record of all the stock, noting down the number of the whole, and in what fields – the numbers of ewes and lambs in each field – when removed – when taken out – how many of each had died – what their skins sold for – when any were sold – and to whom. The number of bullocks they took in from the farmers and what charge per head per week. The price they sold their Packs of wool for and the number of Packs, a Pack was 244 lbs or 4 draughts of 61 lbs, and 1 lb being an allowance for the pitch marks.

This letter was ". . . . never sent on account of the extraordinary length and the expense for its postage."

Nearer our own time, at the beginning of the last War, plans were made for the evacuation of the Marsh. The importance of the sheep was paramount, for they were evacuated, by train, before any plans were made for the women and children to leave.

In the 1880's before the railway came to Lydd, there were some hundreds of Looker's Huts on the marsh. It was here that the Lookers spent many long hours at lambing time, they had an open fire on the hearth over which a kettle or cauldron hung on a pot-hook, for his own cooking and for heating the milk for weak and sickly lambs; his family came at weekends and spent the day with him, bringing with them his supplies for the whole week. Today, sadly, there

128

Romney Marsh Sheep.

Sheep shearing.

129

are a mere handful of huts remaining and unhappily for the farmers, most of these have been a target for vandals.

It was during the last War when so many good Romney pastures had to be ploughed up, to grow more food, the late Lord Cornwallis, then Chairman of the Kent War Agricultural Committee, once told the writer, how the hardest task he had during the War, as Chairman, was to go to so many of his personal friends and tell them that they had to plough up a third of their land, and to have to go back a second time and tell them they had to plough up *"even more."*

Today, the crops grown on the Marsh include corn, potatoes, cabbages, peas, including vining peas and the recent new-comer "oil seed rape," which makes great splashes of golden colour on the marsh landscape in the Spring.

Travelling along some of the little known by-ways of Romney Marsh in springtime, rounding a quiet corner, one is likely to come across a devoted Moorhen with her brood of adorable little black chicks. On the banks of the dykes one might see a patient Heron watching quietly, on one leg, for an unsuspecting fish. On St. Valentine's Day the first thing one does it to drive to the Heronry near the Royal Military Canal to see whether the Herons have returned to their same nests, or, alternatively, to the garden of The Grange at Lydd where there is an old established Heronry.

Whereas today the swans are virtually wild birds, in the fourteenth and fifteenth centuries they belonged to a number of private owners. With a single exception, no record appears to be in existence of the names of any of them nor of the marks they used, but a few names may be found in the archives of New Romney and Lydd. Although neither town owned any, they frequently purchased swans in considerable numbers for the mayoral banquets, or still more, as gifts to persons in exalted positions from whom it was desired to win friendship or support. The swans were usually delivered alive, by the Common Sergeant, who was able to include in his charges the cost of oats for feeding them on the journey.

From Lydd records:—

"1445   Itm paid for three couple of cignets whereof two couple were sent to the Lieutenant of Dover and another couple sent to the Steward of Dover for their friendship to be had to the Town   12s.
(Richard Alayn was the Common Sergeant of Lydd at this time)

1446   Itm to Henry Alayn for a cignet bought of him   3s.
Itm paid for a couple of franked swans sent to our Lord Archbishop of Canterbury when he was and lay at Maidstone, to secure his friendship for the whole Town   8s.
Itm paid for ledyng of the same couple and for another couple sent up to him   3s. 4d.

A typical Marsh dyke.

Swans and cygnets.

131

A "franked" swan was one that had been fattened-up in a frank or pen, hence the increased cost.

In some of the dykes, particularly in the neighbourhood of New Romney eels can still be found, these are regarded as a great delicacy. Having made the long journey right across the Atlantic to get here, after a few years they set about making the return journey to their old breeding ground.

Although not a native of the Marsh, the Marsh frog, *Rana ridibunda,* as this large water loving creature is best known, inhabits Central Europe. It occurs in large numbers in marshes and slow-flowing rivers. It was introduced to the Marsh in 1935 by Mr. Edward Percy Smith, the dramatist, who released twelve in his garden at Stone-in-Oxney. They formed part of a consignment sent from Debrecen in Hungary, for scientific research at University College, London, only two of them were thought to be females, but that spring they bred in the pond, after which they all moved down the stream that supplies the pond and occupied a dyke on the Marsh, about half-a-mile away. Next spring they bred in this dyke and so began their rapid colonisation of Romney Marsh, nowadays they occupy an area of well over 100 square miles, and still seem to be colonising new waterways although the rate of spread appears to have slowed down in recent years. The Latin name *"ridibunda"* means "laughing", hence its alternative name "Laughing Frog". It is much larger than the common frog, with a voracious appetite and will eat almost anything, including young mice and voles, it has little trouble in similarly despatching common frogs and their tadpoles. In 1937 they were so vocal in the spring that the Villagers complained to the Ministry of Health and to the local Member of Parliament.

The marsh dykes are full of interest not only for the wildlife but for the wild flowers too. Near Snargate will be found the Arrow Head Plantain, giving its name to the Arrow Head Sewer, which runs parallel to the road past Snargate Church. The marsh Mallow grows in hedgerow profusion near Fairfield Church, in springtime the Blackthorn blossom adorns the hedgerows, Phragmites, the Reed Mace, the Yellow Iris, will be found in the dykes. In the meadows, Birds' Foot Trefoil, and the Silvered Leaf Potentilla flowers along the roadside.

For the keen botanist who is prepared to walk and search, wild orchids grow in certain places, although there are some fifty species growing in Great Britain, it takes many years for seedlings to grow and many years for the flowers to appear. Some of the varieties which have been found include the Early Purple Orchid, Marsh Helleborine, Fragrant Orchid, Green Winged Orchid *(Orchis Morio)* and the Pyramidal Orchid.

Some years ago, an old lady of the Marsh, aged 93, told the writer, how as a child they had never tasted tea, it was far too expensive, but at breakfast time her mother had made them Toast Tea, when freshly made toast slightly burnt was put in a large jug and boiling water poured over it. At other times they had

Herb Teas, such as Peppermint Tea and Lime Blossom Tea, the latter a popular French beverage, as is Camomile Tea.

In the Middle Ages the wild herbs provided the basis for many culinary dishes, Lamb's Lettuce, Sorrell and Salad Burnet for salads, Jack-by-the-Hedge made an appetising sauce, Stinging Nettles were used as a vegetable, as they are often today. Sea-Kale gathered from the pebbly beaches at Dungeness still is used as a Vegetable. The growing of a House Leek on a home was thought to protect a house from fire, lightning and witches, while Yarrow, tied to a cradle, protected the baby from evil spirits and it was believed that Chicory could even open locked boxes.

About the turn of the century it was customary for the Hythe fishermen to come in their small boats along the dykes to Romney Marsh to fish, for fresh water fish and eels. One of the dreaded perils was catching the Marsh Ague, this happened frequently, and the fishermen had to go straight to bed on their return, shivering with ague cold.

The Romney Marsh Harriers no longer exist as a pack, but the hunting of hares is an even older sport than chasing the fox. It is known that Xenophon (435 B.C. – 354 B.C.) used some form of harrier with nets for catching hares.

One of the earliest mentions of harriers in the Marsh is in 1844 when the late Albert Cock of Court Lodge, Appledore, went to The Bush, Brenzett, at that

Phragmites – The Marsh Rush.

time there was a scratch pack of trencher-fed harriers there, he took this pack in hand, greatly assisted by the late Thomas Finn, and after a few years the pack became established under him as Master. When he went to Appledore in 1853 he took the hounds with him and established the pack in the Kennels there. He died aged 39, in 1863, and was succeeded by Alured Denne and he, by William Walker of St. Mary-in-the-Marsh in 1868, who was the third Master. Mr. Walker's mastership did not terminate until 1892, so that he was in office for twenty-four years. In 1924 the hounds consisted of dwarf foxhounds though still with a strain of harrier blood and there were about seventeen couples. Both New Romney and Rye were considered good centres.

The other great sport of Romney Marsh is another hare hunting sport, the activities of the John Jones Coursing Club. In the Bull Inn at Newchurch is a framed photograph of the members of the John Jones Coursing Club with their founder, John Jones himself, this was presented by the members to him in 1893, as a mark of their respect and esteem. In contrast to today, the members are entirely a male assembly. The Club still meets, usually on Mondays, at various villages in the Marsh, the members bring their own coursing dogs. Unfortunately this year, 1984, there have been fewer hares to hunt which has been a great disappointment to them.

Hawthorn trees in blossom, a tree of the utmost importance in Romney marsh.

The ancient and curious game of Bat and Trap is still played in Romney Marsh, although Canterbury is considered the home of the game. Played on a pitch between seventeen and twenty-one yards in length, the object of the game is for the bowler to bowl the solid rubber ball to knock down the flap of the trap, which the batsman defends and aims to hit the ball through the goal posts. This game is still played at Lydd and at the Cinque Ports Inn, New Romney.

This chapter may end fittingly with two traditional Romney Marsh recipes: —

Looker's Pie
The traditional shepherds pie.
1 lb lamb cutlets
½ lb onions
1 lb potatoes
Salt and pepper
Mutton stock
½ lb suet crust.

Put a layer of lamb cutlets, a layer of onions and a layer of potatoes in a deep pie dish and cover with a layer of suet crust; repeat the layers, pour the mutton stock before adding the final suet crust layer.

Bake for 1½ – 2 hours in a moderate oven.

Gas mark 4, 360 F, 180 C.

Lamb Pie
The traditional lambs tail pie which used to be made at lambing time when the new lambs had their tails cut short.
1½ lbs lamb's tails
1 lb new fresh peas
6 hardboiled eggs
1 lb short crust pastry made from pure lard
Seasoning.

Scald, skin and joint the tails, put them in a large pie dish with the peas and hardboiled eggs. Roll out the pastry to ¼ inch thickness and cover the pie. Glaze with beaten egg. Bake in a hot oven at gas mark 7, 425 F, 200 C for 40 minutes, lower the heat and cook a further 20 minutes at gas mark 4, 350 F, 180 C.

CHAPTER 8

Mediaeval Plays

The mention of Passion Plays today immediately brings to mind, the greatest of them all, the Oberammagau Play, played every tenth year when the whole Village is involved. In this country some of the larger towns, such as Chester, Coventry and Wakefield held cycles of these scriptural dramas, which covered the whole of Christian history from the deluge and the Creation to the Day of Judgment. Chester records give details of twenty-four different dramas being acted from Whitmonday to Whit-wednesday; at Coventry forty-two dramas were represented annually at the Corpus Christi Festival and at Wakefield another series of thirty-two. Here, on Romney Marsh the Romney and Lydd records give interesting details of the plays performed locally.

The Passion Plays, Interludes, Miracle Plays or Mysteries, have a long history which can be traced back to the fourth century and followed until they reached their peak in the Middle Ages, when the spirit of the Elizabethan dramatists was reflected in the Arts and Drama, after which the plays gradually declined.

Fourth century records tell of the Church forbidding Priests to attend any theatrical performances and even those taking place on Christian festivals, by a curious paradox the drama which the Church tried to abolish was to come to the fore over the years, as part of the ritual of the most solemn festivals, when priests sang certain parts of the liturgy they accompanied their words with actions, to make them more easily understood, gradually the Plays developed, the mediaeval plays being acted in both chancel and nave. At this time, when few, except scholars, could read or write, these Plays were a method of instructing the people on the historical facts of the Bible, they brought it to life; generation after generation had gone to Church, and stood, listened and repeated the words, the Plays brought a new meaning to them and played an important part in their lives, and their faith.

The Plays were preceded by the "Bann Criers" who went ahead into the neighbouring villages to "cry the banns of the play", they were the mediaeval counterpart of bill-posters. Apart from proclaiming the Play they had to proclaim the meaning of each scene to the audience, as there was very little scenery, if any, some were little more than a tableau, the ban cryer would then shout out what the figures were supposed to say, in some instances the Players would hold cards depicting their parts. As time progressed these became a series of scenes, often given on a platform which was erected on a cart. The cart was

137

dragged through the Town and from village to village, no doubt, by the unfortunate Players.

It is recorded that each Player was required to bind himself, under a penalty of forty shillings, that he would persevere in performing the Play or else surrender his part.

In spite of the limited population and limited funds which prevented elaborate representations, Romney and Lydd indulged in less ambitious affairs and here Interludes or Miracle Plays were performed regularly at the churches' important festivals, a Nativity Play at Christmas, a play on Christ's Passion at Easter and at Whitsuntide it was the great May Day play. Even these small plays required a good deal of organisation, Wardens of the Play were appointed and among the New Romney records, as early as 1456, John Crays and Thomas a Nasshe were mentioned by name, as the two Wardens of the Play of the Resurrection. They were evidently very strict and rounded up all the actors who conveniently forgot to pay for the clothes or any who returned them torn or muddy. In fact, they actually brought an action for debt and damage against one poor young man, John Lyle, and recovered four shillings from him.

At Romney there were six Guilds to provide actors, but the most popular fraternity was that of St. George, for whom they had special plays or pageants. In 1480 there was a great celebration when an image of the Saint was put up. The men of Lydd were sent for to come and join in the ceremonies and were entertained at the expense of the town of Romney. Even today in Kent, this drama of St. George is roughly performed during Christmastide, by seven men who impersonate St. George, the Dragon, Father Christmas, the Doctor, The King of Egypt, a Turkish Knight and the Giant Turpin or the Hooden Horse.

The first mention of the manuscript of the play is in June 1516, when it is recorded . . . . "Le Playboke was delivered to Henry Robyn, to keep for the use of the Town". Later on it was handed to Robert May, the Town Clerk, ... "safely and securely to be kept for the behalf of the said town".

By 1517, the Romney play had become more important. First, Wardens were chosen by the Jurats and Commons. Richard Stuppeny, whose tomb is still in Romney Church, Robert Paris and John Bunting, who afterwards became Mayor of Lydd, William Bedell and Christopher Hensfield, ... "in order that the town might have the play of the Lord's Passion as from olden time they were wont to have it."

In 1518, there was opposition to the Plays for . . . . "The Lord Warden of the Five Ports sent, to the Barons of New Romney, a mandate that they ought not to play the Play of the Passion of Christ, until they had the King's leave."

Fabulous sums were spent on the Romney Passion Plays in the Middle Ages. The costumes and all needful paraphernalia were obtained and preserved by the Wardens. The Clergy sometimes lent their vestments. The Romney Council often paid for the carriage of the goods from London, one such record reads . . . . "of John Baptist's painted coat, the cotton coat of Judas,

138

and twelve sheepskins for "godhalls coats". Beards and wigs were hired for four "ban cryers." and a beard for the Fool. Three wayne-loads of bows; escutcheons costing 20s; dozens of gold-skins, and sheets of goldfoil; pounds of glue, brimstone, red lead, red ochre, verdigris, rosset, florrey, and nails; a gross of points; ells of buckram; a paschal lamb, which was "drest"; a shoe, set on the centurion's horse; a wayte, a drummer, and minstrels; were provided for these four performances at Romney in the reign of good Queen Bess, A.D. 1560." The Town Clerk that year, wrote out the play book on parchment and the parts on fourteen quires of paper for two pounds. The Wardens received thirteen shillings and four pence each as a reward for their trouble and expense upon the Play, to say nothing of the item . . . . "for wine delivered at the play — seven pence." From the performance of the magnificent play given at Whitsuntide . . . . "twelve pounds, five shillings and sixpence was collected from the spectators at the first performance on Whit-Tuesday."

It is well known that few records in the whole of Kent furnish us with so plain a proof of the perseverance, even in small parishes, of these Passion Plays or Interludes, as do the records of Romney and Lydd. They tell that parishes such as Stone, Ruckinge, St. Mary's, Brookland and Appledore vied with Romney and Lydd in getting up these popular scenes of scriptured history. No fewer than fourteen villages came to a performance on Le Crokehill, situated in the parish of St. Lawrence near the banks of the harbour. This was written "Crockley Green" in 1600, and thus we can identify today where it was. Players also came from further afield to perform. The Wittersham players came to Romney in 1426 and again in 1441, to Lydd in 1440; the Folkestone players in 1474 and 1478; from Chart in 1489; Wye in 1491; from Rye in 1489, 1493 and 1518; from Halden in 1499 and 1511; from Bethersden in 1508 and from Herne to Romney and Lydd in 1438. The troops of players were entertained at the town's expense in addition to the average fee of 6s. 8d. for each play.

Items in the Lydd archives, record:—

"1429 First given to the Players from Romney to show their Play here on the Sunday aforesaid, the day of the account . . . . . 6s. 8d.
Item paid for the expenses of their Players and others with them viz for bread, wine and beer . . . . 2s. 8d.
Item given to the Players from Rockinge for showing their Play here, viz on Saturday next before the Feast of Relics (Sept 15) . . . . 6s. 8d.
1436 Item paid for expenses incurred over the men of Romney when they showed here one sport (show) at St. Matthews day . . . . 14d.
1439 Item given the Players of Wytesham for showing their Play here in the month of June . . . . 6s. 8d.

	Item given the Players of Herne for showing their Play here	7d.
	Item paid for bread and ale given the Players of Romney in Richard Glover's house	6d.
	Item given the same Players in courtesy for showing their Play here the same time............................	6s. 8d.
1455	Item given the Players of Hamme showing their Play here on the day of the Translation of St. Thomas of Canterbury	3s. 4d.
1456	Item paid for bread and beer given the Players from Romney for showing their Play here the day of the dedication of the church	2s.
	Item given the same players the same day in courtesy	10s.
1465	Item paid for expenses of the Players of Hethe (Hythe) here on dedication day	8s. 10d.
	Item given to them the same time.....................	6s. 8d.
	Item paid for four Watchmen the first Sunday at the Play of Romney	16d.
1466	Item paid in expenses of our Bane Cryars *(sic)* of our Play	20d.
1467	Item paid unto the schewoars (showers) of the Play of Apuldore	3s. 8d.
1468	Item paid to the Players of Stone crying the Banns here ..	3s. 4d.

1466-7 the Play was performed on a Sunday during which day the town of Lydd employed four watchmen to "keep a good look-out at home," probably from the steeple of the church.

As the plays grew the churches were not large enough to hold the great crowds of spectators and the churchyard or Village Green was chosen. These Passion plays were not all serious. They brought in comic relief, amusing scenes and a "Devil", whose lines were impromptu, as were his sallies into the audience.

CHAPTER 9

The Marsh in Literature

As I went down to Dymchurch Wall,
I heard the south sing o'er the land;
I saw the yellow sunlight fall
On knolls where Norman Churches stand.

Davidson

Romney Marsh, so rich in literature with its peculiar development and its curious characteristics, is a delight alike to antiquary and to novelist. For those who would delve seriously into the secrets of the past, there is no richer storehouse than the volumes published annually by the Kent Archaeological Society since 1858, *Archaeologia Cantiana*.

The Elizabethan topographer, William Lambarde, in his *Perambulation of Kent,* described Romney Marsh as "famous throughout the realme, as well for the fertilitie and qualitie of the soile and levell, as also for the auncient and wholesome ordinances there used for the preservation and maintenance of the bankes and walles against the rage of the sea". Later however, he warns his reader, "If a man minding to passe through Kent towards London, should arrive and make his first step on land in Romney Marshe, he shall rather finde good grasse under foote, than wholesome Aire above the head". Such was the reputation of the Marsh in the sixteenth century, that even when Queen Elizabeth journeyed through the Weald to Rye, she could not face travelling to Romney 'through the dreaded Rumney Marshe', but re-traced her steps to stay with Mr. Baker at Sissinghurst.

In 1609 Shakespeare visited Dover with his company, "The Queen's Players". A raging storm during his stay is said to have provided much of the background for The Tempest, while his journey through the Weald to the old weaving towns of Cranbrook and Goudhurst suggested his setting for the Forest of Arden and his town of Athens. Mr. Halliwell Philips declared that Shakespeare's company performed plays at Hythe and Romney, basing his contention on the details in the Chamberlains' Accounts of that time of the fees paid to companies of strolling players by an hospitable Corporation, who entertained them with "wine an sugar cakes".

It is to a former Rector of Snargate and Warehorne, the Rev. Richard Harris Barham, one must turn to enjoy the real romantic atmosphere of the Marsh. He

141

immortalised this "Fifth Quarter" with its notorious witches and night-riders in his famous "Ingoldsby Legends", and steeping himself in the old tales of hags and smugglers, has transmuted them with the fun and frolic that were essentially such a part of himself. In 1817 he was appointed to the Rectory of Snargate, but even then preferred to live at Warehorne rather than in the dread malarious marsh. But it was chance that brought to the world his literary gifts. While living at Warehorne, he broke his leg in a gig accident, and the weariness of being confined to bed bored him so much that he was driven to writing! One has only to think of his view from Warehorne Rectory in the depths of winter across the mist laden Marsh, eerily peeping out between gloomy churchyard yews, to imagine the freakish delight with which he wrote his "Leech of Folkestone" or the stories of smugglers whom he knew so well, and whom he had met frequently coming home late at night, or of the witches, weathering Dungeness Point in eggshells, or careering over Dymchurch Wall, "a cow may yet be seen galloping like mad, with tail erect, and an old pair of breeches on her horns, an unerring guide to the door of the crone whose magic arts have drained her udder". Here is all the bleak desolation of the Marsh on windy nights, the thrill of adventure, the utter fearlessness that spurred on the nightriders, all excitingly told.

Two late nineteenth century novelists have described, so faithfully the Marsh landscape, Mrs. Hadden Parkes in *Ermengarde* and a writer "C.R.G." in *"Across the Marsh, a tale of the Kentish Levels"*, the old carrier Moses, "I be Kentish born and bred", says "I dessay now you think a mixen is a middling disagreeable place."

"Rather!"

"Ah! that shows you want larning about it," said Moses, superciliously. "Now I've got a mixen at the bottom of my garden, and a sweeter smelling place it 'ud be hard to find no-hows-de-wurreld. It has been topped with ammut-castes as I pecked up in the field, and all over one side is a vegeble marrer, real good seed that Miss Ina there give me, and a beth-wine, and some marygurls. You see, sir, my missus she is partial to her bit of gay-ground, and the seeds blowed across I rackon."

H. G. Wells in his youth was destined to be a linen-draper and was apprenticed to a draper at Southsea in 1881. In later years he lived at Sandgate, first at Beach Cottage and then at Arnold House. In November 1900 he came to Spade House, a house designed for him by C. F. A. Voysey, and lived there until 1909. His vivid recollections of Romney Marsh provided much of the background for his well-known and well-loved Kipps, and Dymchurch beach provided the opening scenes of *"War in the Air"*.

G. P. R. James has painted unforgettable pictures of the days of Free Trade in the Marsh in *"The Smuggler"*, and H. S. Garnett in *"The Infamous John Friend."*

Ford Madox Hueffer lived at Appledore and learned to love the open windswept Marsh the more intimately he knew it. He wrote many poems, and

142

also a book on the Cinque Ports. His pedlar leaving the Bar Parlour at Dymchurch offers a cheering word to the weary traveller.

"But the Marsh ain'd so lone if you've heered a good song,
And you hum it aloud as you cater along,
Nor the stiles half so high, nor the pack so like lead,
If you've heered a good tale and it runs in your head,
Good-night we'd best be jogging-on,
The moon's been up a while,
We've got to get to Bonnington,
Nigh seven mile."

The children's writer E. Nesbit (Mrs. Bland Tucker), loved Romney Marsh where she had spent so many happy holidays with her children. One of her ghost stories concerns the curious marble tomb of Sir John Fagg at Brenzett Church. Her engaging *"Railway Children"*, following the *"Phoenix and the Carpet,"* was written in her happiest vein. It was made into a film and serialised for television. She spent the last years of her life, with her second husband, Captain Tucker (The Skipper), at The Long Boat, at St. Mary's Bay, where she looked out "between the marsh and sky, upon the lovely little hills of Kent". She died in 1924 and was buried at St. Mary-in-the-Marsh. In 1958 a tablet to her memory, was erected near the font in the church, inscribed "I will dwell among my children".

The Thorndikes were frequently visitors to the Tuckers, and for some years Russell Thorndike had a house at Dymchurch, where he wrote his exciting not-to-be-put-down Dr. Syn novels. The stories centre round the village, the church,

E. Nesbit — The Children's writer.

143

the doings of the Rector and the smugglers, and is full of local colour. This has been filmed more than once, and actually in Romney Marsh in colour.

But of all the writers who have set their stories in Romney Marsh, it is Sheila Kaye-Smith, with her robust, vigorous style, so suited to life on the Kent and Sussex borders, who has caught the tang of the sea, who has entered into the farmers' problems, to make or break a pasture, who has enjoyed the thrills, the colour, the bustle, the gaiety of market days, and "the Ordinary" at the New Inn at New Romney. She enjoyed equally the quiet contentment of common, unchanging things. In *Joanna Godden* she portrays with stark realism the hopelessness of throwing to the winds the ancient farming traditions of the Marsh, where Joanna defied the counsel of the old farmers, only to eat the bitter bread of disillusionment. This book too was filmed in Romney Marsh and contained some enchantingly lovely scenes. *Green Apple Harvest* and *Sussex Gorse* may have more appeal to those who live on the Sussex side of the Kent Ditch, while *The End of the House of Alard* tells the story of the Alard family of Winchelsea, whose ancient thirteenth century tombs were salvaged from Old Wincheslsea Church, swept away by the sea, and are now in the present Wincheslsea Parish Church.

More recent publications, one breathlessly exciting and rumbustious, and which has now been filmed, is Howard Clewes' *Green Grow the Rushes O,* and the other, rich in traditions and the familiar background of the Marsh, is Catherine Gaskin's *Blake's Reach,* a novel that will have appeal far beyond the Kentish border.

Of all the poets who have sung in praise of Romney Marsh, from Ruskin, Meredith, and in our own times John Davidson, above them towers Rudyard Kipling.

Many of the Marsh villages are recalled by delightful references in *Puck of Pook's Hill,* the locally-known ghost story of Brookland is veiled in "I met a maid on the Brookland Road", and surely Edda the Priest might have mistaken Snave for Manhood End on a dark December night. Lonely Fairfield is not forgotten, nor its flooded winter waters.

> *"Oh Fairfield church is waterbound*
> *From Autumn till the Spring."*

In the enchanting story Dymchurch Flit, the blind and dumb boatman rowed away the last of the fairies, Widow Whitgift, the mother of the "men-grown but not wage-earnin" boatmen, had that uncanny second sight of old Marsh folk. She felt "trouble on the Marsh same as eels feel thunder, she was a wise woman". How Kipling loved the sleepy hamlets, the age-old farms, and how he understood the Marsh and Marshmen. "The Marsh is just riddled with diks an' sluices an' tidegates an' waterlets, you can hear them bubblin' and grummelin' when the tide works in 'em, then you hear the sea raging all up along the wall". He blamed the "diks" for the puzzling winding roads. "They twists the roads about as ravelly as witchyard on the spindles, so ye get all turned round in broad daylight". But he found peace in the whispering rushes,

"O Romney level and Brenzett reeds,
I reckon you know all my mind needs".

Perhaps this chapter may not unfittingly close with an extract from some lines written at the age of eighty-two by the late Bailiff of Romney Marsh.

"Behind me stretch the Levels of the Marsh,
Eastward, the sea-girt cliffs of Dover rise
Dim in the distance over Romney Bay.
While to the west, the lighthouse of Dungeness
Looks out across an ever-changing sea.
A dweller am I in a storied land,
Of Cinque Port Liberties and Level Lords,
Of feudal manors and historic towns,
And all the wide expanse of Romney Marsh,
That former outpost of the Saxon shore
Reclaimed by countless innings from the sea,
Mysterious Fifth Quarter of the Globe,
Whence from afar can oft be faintly seen
The dunes of Calais and the cliffs of France,
And old Martello towers their vigil keep,
And Dymchurch wall defies the Channel tide . . ."

CHAPTER 10

The Illicit Trade

"I like a smuggler," wrote Charles Lamb, "he is the only honest thief". For centuries in Romney Marsh the friendly smugglers in every town and village were more thought of than the Revenue Men, and herein lies the secret of the thrilling adventures of the Free Traders, or Owlers, as they were called, for like owls they worked at night. They were regarded as romantic heroes rather than wretches who were defying the law of the land with their illicit trade, and who received all the help possible from young and old, rich and poor, and even from the priests themselves.

The origin of smuggling – the word is derived from the saxon *smugan,* meaning "to creep about with secrecy", goes back to the reign of the thriftless, shiftless, Ethelred the Unready. When he was desperately short of money he conceived the idea of imposing a tax on every Tun of wine that entered the country. Men living near the coast were quick to find means of evading this import duty, and under cover of darkness at night the little boats came in from France and Holland, and discharged their tubs of brandy or casks of good "Hollands".

When Edward III set up his Wool Staple, to encourage the woollen manufacturers, he imposed an export tax on every fleece of wool leaving the country, this delightful friendly arrangement increased a hundredfold and became a basis for exchange of smuggled goods. The shallow beaches of Romney Marsh were conveniently near to France, the large churches provided commodious store houses, horses were borrowed at night from farmers' stables and returned later with mysterious packages, left behind as a reward for their owners. Woolpacks are not easily secreted, but so bold were the smugglers and so helpful their friends that a "run" was usually accomplished without mishap. Occasionally, when there was a rumour that the Revenue men were in the neighbourhood it was not unknown for the whole sheep to be put on board the French vessels.

Not until the Cromwellian régime in the seventeenth century was any attempt made "to prevent" the trade. Hitherto all monies paid in taxation went into the King's pocket. Cromwell passed an Act which ordered all Customs Duties to be paid to the Lord High Treasurer. To avoid any leakage of revenue from such duties he appointed Riding Officers, or Preventive Men, to supervise the coastal districts from The Wash to Lands End. The Officer appointed for Romney

147

Marsh had a very unpleasant time, he was no match, with his heavy cumbersome uniform which singled him out, for the wily marshmen who knew every inch of the treacherous marsh, where the dykes could or could not easily be crossed and they readily outwitted the unfortunate Riding Officer, in his efforts to apprehend them.

It is recorded in 1720, a treasury warrant for the sum of £200, for supplying the regiment with new boots and stockings, their usual allowances being "worn out in the pursuit of smugglers". Another reference to the hardship experienced by the members of the Collectors' staff in 1791 . . . . "Eleaxer Moule, Sitter of the boat at Dungeness, complained that his accommodation had been taken away, he and his crew were living in tents. By December he found it impossible to stay any longer as they were ill with colds having no fireplace to dry themselves and their clothes were nearly rotten with being so wet, for so long." Many are the stories told of the Excise cutters, on one occasion in 1805 two cutters "The Tarter" and "The Lively" chased a lugger, which ran ground into Dungeness Bay, the smugglers escaped. Boarding the lugger, the Revenue Officers found . . . . "665 casks of brandy, 237 casks of Geneva, 118 casks of rum, 119 bags of tobacco, 6 packages of wine and 43 pounds of tea." A "rescue attempt" by a party from Lydd and Dungeness was foiled by the militia.

In the eighteenth century, the smuggling had increased to such an extent that it had become alarming and the whole of the marsh area was committed to Mr. Collier, the Surveyor General of Riding Officers for Kent, appointed in 1733, and the following are extracts from his reports:—

1st October 1734. Mr Samuel Grey, Secretary to the Commissioners of Excise, to the Commissioners of Customs or their Secretary.

Sir,

The Comm^{rs} of Excise have received a Letter from Mr Dodd their Officer at Romney in Kent, giving an acco^t that since an additional number of Off^{rs} for the Customs have been sent to Dymchurch, the chief place now for running of Goods is Lydd, the wch the Smugglers pass and repass to and from the Sea Side forty and fifty in a Gang in the day time, loaded with Tea, Brandy, and dry Goods; that above two hundred Smugglers mounted were seen one night upon the Sea Beach there, waiting for the loading of six Boats, & above one hundred were seen to go off, all loaded with Goods. That they march in a Body from the Beach about four Miles into the Country, and there separate into small paties (sic), & that on the 19th past twenty-one Horses loaded passed from Lydd a little from New Romney between twelve and one o'Clock in the Day Time, and the Smugglers, who were armed with blunderbusses, &c., waited above half an hour at the Warren House in sight of the hole Town and declared they would be opposed by no Body. You are therefore desired to lay this before the Comm^{rs} of the Customs for their Information.

22nd January 1736. The Commissioners of Customs to Mr Collier referring to

148

the landing of large quantities of tea at Dungeness, which they attribute to remissness on the part of the Custom-House Officers, and they direct Mr Collier to examine into the journals of the Riding Officers and the Officers appointed for the water guard, and report to the Commissioners whether it appears by these journals that each officer was on duty.

They mention in the course of their letter, that the smugglers generally lodge their goods, at least for a night or two, within a few miles of the coast, so that the officers, had they been active, might have seized these goods where they were first lodged.

3rd February 1736. Draft of Mr Collier's reply, in which he says that in obedience to the Commissioners' commands, he has examined the journals of the Customs Officers, and that it appears they were all on duty both days and nights (the 13th and 14th), mentioned in the Commissioners' letter, that the Revenue cutter (though without the captain) was cruising in Rye Bay on the night of the 13th, and anchored under Dungeness Point on the night of the 14th, and that the Riding Officers seem positive that no such cargoes of tea were there on those nights.

1740. Affidavits of John Darby, Freebody Dray, Francis Riggs, and Richard Lake, Custom-House Officers, relative to violent assaults upon them by smugglers near Lydd, on the 16th and 18th December, and a draft of an advertisement offering a reward for the apprehension of any of the offenders, and a free pardon to any of the offenders who will discover their accomplices so that two at least shall be convicted. The reward offered is £50 for each offender convicted.

Under the year 1741 will be found a memorial to the Commissioners from Riggs, praying for their consideration on account of the damage done to his mare, which was rendered unfit for further service, and on account of the loss of one of his pistols, which was beaten out of his hand, and carried off by one of the smugglers.

22nd January 1740. Mr Clare, Supervisor of Hythe, to Mr Collier.

I was on the 20th Instant at Lydd, and then I was acquainted with the Complaints of the Officers – how the Smuglers who repulsed Riggs and Lake have sent them word they would soon be upon their Coast, and that if they can meet with Riggs they will assurredly kill him. They have been on the Coast two or three times since.

16th July 1743. Letter from the Custom-House at Dover about the running of some goods at Brockman's Barn (near Folkestone), and the forcible detention of the Custom-House Officers.

The smugglers in this case seem to have belonged to "Peak's Gang of

Outlaws". On the Custom-House Officers approaching the smugglers' boat, "the Smuglers called and bid them keep off, but "Mr Cadman pushing on in order to see who they were, the Smuglers.

20th July 1743. Mr Clare (Supervisor at Hythe) to Mr Collier.

. . . . Being every day in full expectation of seeing you on your Survey, has prevented me laying before you the dayly complaints of the Officers: that they dare not doe their duty, because they are Obstructed by such formidable Gangs of Smuglers all armed with fire Arms, in such numbers as were never heard of before. It was but last week fourscore of them loaded their Horses with Tea at Brockman's Barn. We hear there are Dragoons come into Sussex. I hope some are design'd for Kent likewise, for nothing will alter the property of this but a Millitary power.

1743

In his Report for this year, which commenced 8th August and ended 2nd September, Mr Collier says in reference to Riggs and Polhill, the Riding Officers at Lydd: "I am humbly of opinion that "unless a military force is sent to their assistance, these Officers "are almost rendered useless" – the large and formidable gangs "of arm'd Smuglers being frequently 50 or 60 men and horses at Lydd, publickly in the daytime loaded with tea, and their men all arm'd with blunderbusses and other fire arms".

17th October 1743. Mr Clare, from Hythe, to Mr Collier.

. . . . On the 13th Instant I went to Lydd, Surveyed the Officers and Examined their Journal Books there, when they told me there were a large Gang of Smuglers then in their Parish. I therefore thought it more safe for me to return to Romney and lye there. I came to Romney about six a clock in the evening, and went to the Rose & Crown, the house I allways use – When I came there, to my surprise I found the Stables were filled with Smuglers Horse, so that my Mare was carried to a private Stable. I went to my Chamber, sent for the Romney Officers, who came with their books, which I examined and sign'd. We lamented our condition, that such quantitys of Goods must be suffered to be run before our faces, and we not able to prevent or take any of it. The Boat came that night and worked for Goods at Romney Warren post in the morning. About eight a clock the same morning the Smuglers to the number of 18 men (armed with brass muskatoons, brass ffuzees, and pistols) and one boy, all with brazen faces, came into Romney Town with 60 Horses all loaded with dry Goods, Tea I took it to be, and as near as I can guess there was 3 half hundred upon a Horse. They took possession of the two Inns, vizt, the Dolphin and the Rose and Crown where breakfasted, and baited their Horses about two hours, then went into a long string, or train, out of Town, to make themselves or shew to the Inhabitants, that they were such fellows as dare bid Defiance to all Laws and Government. I cannot say but that I was very much concernd at the sight, which nothing but a military power can prevent.

30th April 1744. Report of the officers at New Romney as to the proceedings of the smugglers within their districts between the 1st April 1743 and the 1st April 1744.

It appears that on thirty-one days during the above period, armed smugglers (in one case to the number of fifty-five) were observed in Romney or passing through the town with their goods, and it would seem that on one occasion a number of them described as "a great company", remained in the town for five days.

30th April 1744. Report of the Dymchurch officers, Solomon Sparkes and Richard Lake headed "An Account abstracted from our Journal "Books of the sev^{ll} times meeting or seeing the Great Gangs in our "District by Order of our Surveyor General and Supervisor, from Ap-"ril ye 1st 1743 April ye 1st 1744.

1744. Account by Romney officers of seizures made by them, and of gangs of smugglers in the neighbourhood. They say:

May the 7th – saw 26 men armed and 53 horses go loaded through the Town.

July the 7th 8th & 9th several armed Smuglers in Town, supposed to be Trip's and Gray's Company.

The 10th saw 50 armed Smuglers and 135 horses loaded go through the Town.

The 30th several armed Smuglers in Town.

August the 13th several armed Smuglers in Town.

The 14th a Company of armed Smuglers in Town.

The 15th saw a great Company of armed Smuglers loaded go through the Town.

The 28th several armed Smuglers in Town.

September the 10th several armed Smuglers in Town.

Solomon Sparks and Richard Lake report as follows from Dymchurch.

1743.

November 19th. Out on duty in their Station in the evening met a Gang of Smuglers of 55 on horseback all Arm'd, & Threatned to blow the Off^{rs} brains out, & oblig'd them to return home.

December 12th. In the evening met a great number on horseback Arm'd, who threatned the Off^{rs} & oblig'd them to return home from Duty, tho they saw a large Smugling Cutter off near the Shore.

January 10th. A Gang at least 50 Arm'd Smuglers seiz'd upon Sparks at Brockman's barn & deteyn'd him several hours. Lake happened to escape them, but oblig'd to return home, tho expected Goods to be run.

Tom Tripp and Gray were members of the Hawkhurst Gang and are mentioned in this extract, as is Francis Rigg, who was Thomas Miller, the Diarist's son-in-law.

Brandy, tea, tobacco, silks, laces, fine gloves and many other goods were brought in illicitly and many are the stories told of hazardous adventures on dark winter nights of brushes with Revenue Men, who tried to seize the spoil. The churches at Ivychurch, Snargate, Appledore and isolated Fairfield all made good "hides" until the cargo could be distributed. Obliging sextons would open up convenient vaults and remove their contents in order to store French brandy or good Hollands, and usually received a jug of the precious spirit in return for their help. One Sunday morning the Rector of Ivychurch arrived to take the service and was met at the door by the Sexton, who warned him, "Bain't be no service s'morning parson, Westry be full wi' baccy and pulpit full o'brandy." The church door was carefully locked and there were no services that day. Another church where the font was used as the hide, the rector on arrival was told, "Goose be nesting in font s'morning parson." The smugglers were admired not only for their courage but for bringing such necessities as tea, salt and tobacco to the villagers at reasonable prices, for owing to the heavy tax on them, they were really the perquisite of the rich.

The late Dr. Cock of Appledore, a well known Kentish Antiquary, used to tell a charming story of the days when he spent his holidays with his Grandmother at Rye. One night there was a great disturbance in the stables and at breakfast next morning, he asked his Grandmother, was there something wrong with the horses, she replied, "they had been called out to carry out business on the Marsh". A few days later, on the doorstep was left a small cask of brandy, some of the finest French gloves, some lace and some large French walnuts, inside of which were French gloves for the staff. He remarked that his Grandmother never wore any other but the finest French Gloves.

As many as two hundred men might deal with a cargo, some rode down to the coast to deal with the "run", some were there already waiting to bring it ashore, others ready to load it on the pack-ponies and many others armed with staves, stood by to protect the smugglers and be on the alert for the Preventive Men.

Many of the churches were involved with the trade, in Dymchurch churchyard will be seen tombstones to Preventive men and Riding Officers, including one to Richard Lake, "who was 24 years a Riding Officer of His Majesty's Customs and died December 8th 1764, aged 53 years." Another to Edward Blake, junior, a Chief Officer in the Preventive Service, he was drowned by the upturning of a boat on the North River near Yarmouth in 1820.

At Snargate there is a painted galleon on the wall opposite the south doorway, which told the smugglers that the church was a safe hiding place. At Snave there are two tombstones, rescued from a dyke at "Hangmans Field" and these are believed to be of smugglers. Lydd has the grave of George Walker a well known smuggler, who was shot while escaping on his way to the Court-room, his epitaph reads:—

"Let it be known that I am clay,
    A bace man took my life away,
Yet freely do I him forgive,
    And hope in Heaven we both shall live,
Wife and children I've left behind,
    And to the Lord I them resign,
I hope He will their steps attend,
    And guide them to a happy end."

Another interesting tombstone, at Lydd, is that of Francis (Frank) Sisley, buried in 1808. He was a grazier and later actively engaged in smuggling. He was born at Rye in 1748 and married in 1770 at Ivychurch to Anna Chowning and lived at Lydd. He was described as a daring and desperate smuggler and was involved in the "Guinea-trade". During the Napoleonic wars gold was in great demand in France and had an enviable purchasing power, although Francis specialised in silks which were smuggled into England. His son Thomas born in 1772, was sent by his father to Dunkirk to supervise his part of the smuggling enterprise on that side of the Channel, he discovered his father's agent was not conducting affairs in a satisfactory manner. Thomas continued to live in France, he married two French sisters in turn and became a respected trader, dealing in silks and Paisley shawls, no doubt helped by his father's trading connections. One son Guillaume, became the father of Alfred Sisley, the Painter, who was born in 1839. He was a friend of Charles Monet and his work was much influenced by him, there is a painting by Monet of Alfred Sisley and his family – "Supper at the Sisleys" – dated 1872. Alfred Sisley lived at Moret, where, after his death, a statue was erected to his memory, in the Village square. To go back to Francis Sisley, his daughter Elizabeth married William Sell, a saddler at Lydd, who was also involved in smuggling, he was arrested, tried and imprisoned in Dover Castle. When he was released he obtained employment in the prison and finally was appointed "Boder" of Dover Castle. This meant that he was the Keeper of the Debtors' prison in the Castle.

153

In a Tudor timber-framed house at Lydd, there is an interesting but unobtrusive hearth-stone, which is removable, quite small, although large enough for a man to let himself down on to a ladder which is attached below to the wall, below the shaft then leads into a sizeable chamber, where no doubt, smuggled goods were concealed.

A celebrated Doctor at Brookland, a Dr. Hougham, was not involved with the smuggling trade, but was often used by the smugglers as well as the Preventive Men, when someone or even a horse had been wounded. He was called out so frequently that he had a special case made for his ointments and instruments, of red tooled leather, which was made to fit inside his greatcoat pocket. He lived at The Filberts, Brookland.

New Romney was not without its smuggling connexions, for centuries the cellars at the New Inn were full of good French wine. At the corner of the cross roads in the High Street opposite the Old Priory, stood the Rose and Crown, until recent times there was a grating in the pavement, which when lifted led to the cellar and was used for deliveries, it is believed that there was an underground passage from this cellar to New Romney church.

One of the most inhuman and unparallelled murders committed involving smugglers, was that of Galley and Chater, Daniel Chater, a shoemaker, who it is understood originated from Snave, Galley was a Customs Officer from the port of Southampton. A party of smugglers had arranged to go to Guernsey to collect a cargo of tea, which they did, and put it into the Customs' warehouse at Poole, subsequently they broke into the warehouse and took out the tea, the next day on their way through Fordingbridge, Diamond, one of the smugglers recognised Chater in the crowd, shook him by the hand and threw him a bag of tea. By this time His Majesty's proclamation had been issued, with a promise of a reward for apprehending those who were concerned in breaking open the Customs House at Poole. Diamond was taken into custody at Chichester on suspicion of being one of them. It came to the knowledge of the Collector of the Customs at Southampton that Chater knew Diamond, they had worked together in harvest-time, he sent William Galley with Chater with a letter to Major Battin, a Justice of the Peace for the County of Sussex, desiring him to take an examination of Chater and whether he could prove the identity of Diamond's person. On their journey they stopped at The White Hart at Rowlands Castle, kept by one Elizabeth Paine, a widow, who had two sons, Blacksmiths and reputed smugglers, Mrs. Paine being suspicious of Galley and Chater sent one of her sons to collect other members of the gang and detained Galley and Chater until they arrived, to decide what action they should take. On their arrival they put on a "Pot of Hot" and in due course when Galley and Chater were fuddled they were persuaded to go to the next room where there was a bed for them to rest, they promptly went to sleep and the letter to Major Battin was taken from their pockets. In the kitchen, it was read and the contents being plainly a design to promote "an information against some of their gang", they immediately entered into a consultation what course to

154

take on this occasion. All agreed that the letter should be first destroyed and then they would consider what to do with the men, in order to prevent their giving the intended information. Jackson started the cruelty by putting on his spurs, then got upon the bed and spurred their foreheads to wake them and then horsewhipped them. When they entered the kitchen Chater was as bloody as Galley, more and more barbaric atrocities were committed, at one time they were set on a horse, their four legs tied underneath the horse, and they were whipped continuously, occasionally slipping under the horse, only to be set upright and start again. They were whipped until they came to Woods Ash, some used long whips, some short whips, they lashed them over the head, wherever they could injure them most. Galley and Chater were then separated and set upon horses behind members of the gang and taken to Harris's Well near Lady-Holt Park, where they swore they would murder Galley. Galley eventually fell from the horse and they all thought he had broken his neck, after another heavy drinking session they set forth and buried him. Poor Chater was kept alive for another two days, they then decided to murder him, but not without two more days of barbaric cruelty, they then led him to the Well at Lady-Holt Park, forced him to climb the fence around it, tied a cord around his neck and to the fence and forced him into the well, but the rope was not long enough and his body would not hang lower than knee deep in it, so that the rest of his body appeared above the top of the well. This method not being successful they dropped him head first into the well and then threw heavy boulders down to keep the body down. The members of the gang were finally rounded up, tried and hanged, all except Jackson. He escaped the just punishment for his part in the murders. When he was being measured for his chains the night before, he died of fright.

The main gang of smugglers operating on the Marsh, for many years, was the Ransley gang, whose headquarters were at Aldington, After one run some of them were captured and sent to Maidstone prison, from which most of them escaped, were re-captured and incarcerated in Chichester prison. A Mr. Jackson of Aldingbourne, a grandson of William Jackson, relates that although the prisoners were all sentenced to death at the Assizes, by hanging, "Me Grandfer was not hanged – the night before, when they came to measure him for his chains, he died of fright!'". This is recalled on the Memorial Stone at the cross roads outside the Town where the gang were buried.

When the Government became alarmed at the increase in smuggled goods and the inability of the appointed officers to effect captures of goods, or of the smugglers themselves, a number of Revenue Cutters were released from the Navy to patrol the Channel. Their commanders were given authority to intercept, board and search any suspected vessel, even this scheme failed, there was no co-ordination between land and sea Revenue men and those in the Cutters were easily bribed with a cask of brandy or other spoils.

The most vigilant of these officers would have found it difficult to discover contraband in many of the smugglers' boats, the bows and rigging were often

155

hollowed out, the former to secrete ankers of spirit and the latter strands of tobacco. False bottoms were attached to the whole length of boats and filled with tea, silk, lace and other light goods. Buoys were secretly filled with the finest French gloves and silks, and when the boat came ashore, an Owler was ready to cut the false buoy and deal with it. Ballast of lime or stinking fish often hid casks of liquor and what purported to be cargo of hams, was an ingenious method of smuggling silk, the meat had been carefully cut out leaving just a little round the knuckle bone, the skin lined with water-proof material, was then stuffed with the finest silks to the shape of the ham, stitched up and covered with sawdust and sand, and completely deceived any suspicious officer.

When the tax on wool was reduced, the gang organisations which had originated at Hawkhurst and Aldington, were armed and smuggling became a dangerous livelihood. Like gangsters, the gangs were armed, and bound by an oath of loyalty to their leader to defend their goods to the bitter end. Wanted people with prices on their heads, convicts, highwaymen, unscrupulous villains who would stop at nothing, were recruited to the gangs and carried out their runs with brutal ruthlessness. Preventive Officers who had "wind" of an organised run one night, rode down to the coast, surprised the smugglers as they were unloading their cargoes and valiantly tried to sieze the goods. All three Officers were quickly overpowered, bound, and taken back to the gangs headquarters. Unfortunately two of the Officers were recognised as former members of the gang who had "ratted" and gone over to the Government, they were tied to trees and whipped merciliessly, almost to death, they were then taken back to the coast, lashed to the French tub boats and shipped back to France and were never seen again.

The following is reproduced from a document – "As to the felonious assembly on the 16th March 1826":—

This document is reproduced with the minimum of alteration and of additional punctuation.

As to the felonious assembly on the 16th March 1826

Edward Horn states that a few days after the Run at Hythe which was on the 11th March another Run was effected near 27 Tower at the West End of Dymchurch wall at the Herring Hang near Romney Warren. On this occasion he recollects there were present George Ransley, Samuel Bailey, Thomas Gillham, Thomas Denard, Edward Punteny, Thomas Winder, William Smeed, James Smeed, James Wilson, Richard Higgens, Paul Pierce, several men from Dymchurch amongst them were Flisher Waddle and Bourn, all armed and a great Body of the working party between three and four score. They met on the Evening as usual at Ransley's and under his lead. At between 9 and 10 they proceeded over Bonnington Bridge across the Military Canal by the Royal Oak kept by one, Huckstead, to Sutton Barn belonging to Mr. Tilby on the Road leading to Dymchurch and after resting in the yard about half an

156

hour they went on to a Horse Bridge across the Sewer called Tatnam Bridge into the main Road leading to Saint Marys to a Barn called Tatnam where they rested about two Hours. Here the Party from Dymchurch joined them. They then proceeded across the Marsh to a Farm House of one Sutherland called Jesson Farm then into a field on the right hand and across the Road leading to Romney. They then crossed by the back of the Coal Wharf. They were then within 80 or 100 yards of the Beach and there they laid down on the Turf for concealment while Ransley went forward to the Beach to look out for the Boat. In about half an hour he halloe'd to them as a signal and they then got up and went to the Boat and run the Cargo. The armed men were divided into two Parties; examinant was on the East side and so were Edward Punteny, Thomas Denard, Thomas Winder, Paul Pierce and William Smeed, he does not recollect who else. The Dymchurch armed men were stationed to the westward. A firing commenced to the westward. Immediately after they had got over the Beach towards the boat he saw a man whom he took to be a Blockade man about 10 or a dozen roods off. This man snapped his Pistol but it was only a flash and there was no firing by the armed men stationed on the Examinant's side, all the firing took place on the west side. Several shots, 6 or 7 Pieces might be fired on that side. The two divisions of armed men might be about 14 roods assunder so that Examinant could not discern what passed on the west side. The firing lasted about 5 minutes just while they were working the Boat. They secured the Tubs but lost the Boat. One or two of the Crew accompanied them part of the way home. He understood from the talk of the Party as they returned that some of the Blockade men were wounded. The goods are always worked at High Water and it might be between 3 or 4 o'clock when the Boat was worked. He believes they were not pursued by the Blockade Party for the firing ceased as soon as they crossed the full of the Beach. While they were running their Tubs across the Warren to the Turnpike Road he observed a light like a Rocket in the air. Ransley frequently carried Rockets with him as signals, but by whom the light was thrown up or for what purpose he does not know. They returned across the Marsh to Sutherland's Farm house and along the Beach Road and about a quarter of a mile or more from that House they turned into a field on the right where they laid down their Tubs and counted them. He does not know how many there were but he believes about 100. They then proceeded to Tatnam Barn where they again rested and the men from Dymchurch then took their share of the Tubs and carried them home. They then made their way behind Sutton Barn and on to East Bridge near the chapel and got into the main road leading from Dymchurch to Aldington. They then proceeded on their way home to the Royal Oak, Huckstead's, where they procured what is called their allowance, viz. Bread and Cheese and Beer. It was then about sun rise. They drew up near the House, sat in a circle round the Tubs and Ransley went into the House and brought out their provisions, the Bread and Cheese and Beer, the latter in pails. The party here might be about 50 or 60. Huckstead the Landlord came to the door, but he does nor recollect seeing any of the Family. They remained there about half an hour and then proceeded on towards Aldington and deposited the Tubs in a wood near Ransley's house, who afterwards paid him 40s. for this Job and that of the 11th March. There were several men from Ashford of this Party and amongst them Wright a Chimney Sweeper. The company met at Ransley's and got liquor. In going to the Beach, Ransley left his Cart at Tatnam Barn, he does not recollect seeing any one belonging to that or Sutton or Tatnam Barns, they are lone Buildings, there was a light in the Warren Gate House.

On their return they did not stop at Sutherland's. On the road near Tatnam Bridge they fell in with Ransley's cart and put about a score of Tubs into it and they left their Fire Arms at Tatnam Bridge which the Dymchurch People took possession of, except James Smeed's Gun which Ransley's Boy carried home in the Cart. Ransley himself accompanied the Party with the remainder of the Tubs. After leaving the Royal Oak about ten rods they passed Mr. Coleman's Farm where two men and one or two women came out and apparently welcomed them. They then turned to the left, out of the road into the Marsh to Bonnington Bridge and to the best of his recollection Ransley gave the Soldier at the Bridge half-a-crown. The object of giving the Money was to induce the Soldier not to let anyone know they had passed – Ransley's words were, 'you hav'nt seen any body, have you?' They then passed on, up the Horse Road to the Freight and laid the Tubs in a Dyke in the wood by Ransley's order, who was present.

There are many interesting details of "runs" over the years, the following gives an authentic account of a journey made to the Marsh by Dog-cart:—

"A curious circumstance once gave me such an awful fright that I have never forgotten it. It was the first journey I ever had 'down below,' that is to say to the coast. I could not have been more than twelve or thirteen years of age. I had been despatched in great haste to take a letter to 'Some One,' who would ask me for it at a certain house *on the Marsh,* where the dogs would take me. I took our dog-cart – I mean a real dog-cart with a splendid pair of large, strong dogs, who had made the journey many times before. They knew the way perfectly. There never was any fear of going wrong, so long as you trusted to them. To further our system of signs we retained one dog whose home was on the Marsh to run with ours. They on the Marsh retained one of ours whose home was Wrotham Heath. Each dog, as soon as put to the dog-cart and you had taken your seat, would start direct for home, whether it was Romney Marsh or Wrotham Heath. A perfect stranger could take his seat in the cart, and trust to his canine carrier to take him direct to his destination, and that in a comparatively short space of time. Some of the old stage-coaches, were overtaken and left behind by these dog-carts.

"After a journey of 70 miles to the Marsh – it took me best part of a night and a day – I came to the old thatched house where I had been sent and found

158

'Some One' to whom I delivered the letter from my father. A conversation took place between him and others, whom I thought were shepherds, there being so many sheep about. Some of them started off to look after other shepherds.

"As soon as evening came on I was told to 'turn into bed,' as I should most likely be wanted to return again soon. Along the sides of the room — a sort of kitchen — there were several rough benches made up one over the other, like berths on board ship, with hay thrown in for bed. I crept into the lowest one of these, and soon fell sound asleep. I don't know how long I had been so, but I somehow gradually awoke, through the sound of many footsteps outside. I had heard so many tales of the Free Traders that I did not much like this. In a few moments my surprise was turned into fear, so much that my little heart seemed to stand still. This was caused by a clamour of voices, and I heard disjointed sentences outside.

"The first words I distinctly heard were: 'Bring him this way and cut his throat; hold him tight — knife! That will so; can manage him now.'

"Still a great trampling of feet, and I thought I heard a groan or two and smothered cry. Then a silence that seemed so intense I dared not breathe. Presently the door opened, and some men, I could just discern, were dragging in a body between them into the room.

"'Where shall we put him; down here?'

"'No, chuck him up there over the youngster till somebody comes.'

"Then came a dull, heavy thud right into the berth over my head, of a heavy body thrown in. The men left the place to me and my dead companion overhead. In a few moments after I felt something warm falling on my hands and face like warm water, or blood; it came from the bed over me, and by the faint light I could see it was blood.

"I must have fainted, for the next thing I remember was a strong smell of cooking; and, opening my eyes, I saw at the fire a lad of about my own age, very busy frying meat, and close beside him was the body of a sheep that was not there when I entered the hut the night before. I looked at my hands. Yes, sure enough I had not had a dream; there was the blood there, also over my head. I could see where it had oozed through the hay. What could be the meaning of this? At last I ventured to put a question to my companion. I said: 'May I get up?'

"'Of course you can, if you like; I wonder you've been there so long, with this mutton frying close under your nose.'

"'Where did the sheep come from? Who brought it? Was it caught last night, killed, and put up there? etc.,' were questions I put in rapid succession.

"'Yes, somebody got it last night, and killed it, most likely. It was put up there; it looks like it. I'm left here to cook a lot of it in case somebody comes back for something to eat, which they are sure to do. I dare say some of the blood did fall through on you, but that don't matter.'

159

Substantial rewards were offered to any persons who would give information and in 1830 Robert Peel issued the following public notice:—

Two Hundred Pounds Reward.

WHITEHALL, 6TH APRIL, 1830

W HEREAS it has been humbly represented to the King, that about two o'clock in the morning of Wednesday, the 31st ultimo, a large party of armed Smugglers feloniously assembled on the Sea Shore, near Dymchurch, in the county of Kent, and were aiding and assisting in the illegal landing, running, and carrying away of uncustomed Goods; and that in opposing this felonious act, and in seizing part of the said Goods, Lieutenant Gustavus Spicker Baker, and Martin Donovan, seamen, both of His Majesty's ship "Talavera", were attacked, violently beaten with clubs, and severely bruised.

His Majesty, for the better discovering the persons who have been guilty of this felony, is hereby pleased to promise his most gracious Pardon to any one or more of the persons so assembled (except those who actually committed violence on the said Lieutenant and Seaman on this occasion) who shall discover his accomplices, so that they may be apprehended and brought to justice.

ROBERT PEEL.

And the Lords Commissioners of the Admiralty hereby offer a Reward of Two Hundred Pounds, to be paid to, or distributed amongst, any person or persons (except as aforesaid) who shall give information to Captain Pigot, of the "Talavera", or to any of the Officers of the said ship, as shall lead to the discovery, apprehension, and conviction of the said offenders: such Reward to be payable by Mr. CHARLES JONES, the Solicitor of the Admiralty and Navy, on the conviction of the said offenders, or any of them.

J. W. CROKER.

Nearly every house in the Marsh and in the Weald had its place of concealment, which accommodated kegs of spirit, bales of tobacco or even human beings, if necessary. Houses near the coast had secret passages leading one to another to outwit capture. "All trade's honest, except the Pickeroons", this was the nickname for the Revenue Men, who occasionally filched the smugglers' goods, for which, being honest, they had paid. The brutal gang organisation after terrorising the Marsh for many years was eventually wiped out, with long sentences or deportation for life took its toll of the defiant leaders and gradually broke up the gangs.

Even as late as 1932 when a new Revenue Officer was appointed to Littlestone, he reported that after a fortnight's investigation, he found that the coast "between Dymchurch and Dungeness positively reeked with smuggling, and he considered New Romney and Lydd nothing more than a nest of contraband runners; that he had been shadowed continually wherever he went, and that with the exception of the old coastguards and a few others, he considered that there were few residents who were not directly or indirectly connected with the smuggling activities.

From his investigations, he considered the four new Preventive Officers stationed in the district totally inadequate to cope with the large amount of smuggling that was continually being carried on, and has been carried on since the removal of the efficient Coastguard Control. In his opinion the contraband running would never be stopped until there was a patrol of armed motorcars patrolling the coast roads throughout the night. He understood the goods when landed, were quickly removed by car from the coastline to the centre of the Marsh, or some other lonely spot, where they were transferred to a lorry and taken at once to London. He and his fellow Preventive Officers were also convinced that the larger smuggling was run by a gang, with Headquarters in London, operating by means of fishing boats on the coasts of Suffolk, Essex, Kent and Sussex.

Today, in spite of heavy penalties, the thrill of smuggling attracts some people, methods do not vary much, there are suitcases with false bottoms, cars with false fascia boards and petrol tanks, as well as many other ingenious devices, all concealing hundreds of pounds worth of drugs, cocaine, canabis, hashish and many other items. The only difference is that the ingenuity of the smugglers is no match for the vigilance of the water guards and one can scarcely agree with Kipling in calling them "The Gentlemen".

The Parson no longer enjoys his contraband brandy nor the Sexton his jug of Hollands, the Squire who puffed his free trade cigars and his Lady who loved her rich silks and French brocades no longer graces the villages of the Marsh, ...

But,

"If you wake at midnight and hear the horses' feet,
Don't go drawing back the blinds and looking down the street,
Them that asks no questions isn't told a lie,
Watch the wall, my darling, while the Gentlemen ride by".

CHAPTER 11

Thomas Miller's Diary

These extracts from the Diary of Thomas Miller a school master of the Free School New Romney, from October 2nd 1732 until March 27th 1755, give a fascinating insight to life some two hundred and fifty years ago. Although he left the school in 1755, he obviously continued to live in the neighbourhood, for it is recorded . . . . "Thomas Miller was buried in woollen as appears by affidavit October 9th 1774 at New Romney".

During this period he faithfully recorded details of his wife, often referred to as "E.M.", and family, the births of his children and with obvious pride the career of his son Charles, and the delight of receiving his letters and parcels. He also records details of births, marriages and deaths in Romney and the surrounding parishes, as well as other local events of interest.

Thomas Miller played the violin, for there are references to his playing at local weddings as well as for the Yuletide "Waits".

There are details of visits to surrounding villages and further afield, journeys which today take only an hour or so, entailed Miller and his family staying overnight.

Possibly some of the most remarkable entries are those recording, not local, but events of national and historical importance, remarkable not only because of the length of time it took for news to travel, about three days from London to Romney, but that he considered them to be of sufficient importance to record, but perhaps, as a school master, his enthusiasm was all the greater.

It is not possible to include the whole Diary, because of the sheer volume of entries, also, as in life today, many entries are repetitive.

The extracts are reproduced exactly as they were written, and although the spelling of place names may vary from that of today, they will easily be recognised for the most part, although "Sanders" for Sandhurst may not be quite so obvious.

The early school at New Romney. This may have been Thomas Miller's school.

1732

Octo. 2 I began school att New Romney.

8 I was chose a member of Ye Society.

11 Mr. Greenland of Lydd died of ye smallpox.

29 My bro: Charles came to Romney, stayed until Nov-4 & made me a great coate, bought Jno Edwards cloth, buttons and all other Trimmings cost me £1. 10s. 4½d.

Jan. 17 I bought a Hogg of Mr. Geo Greene of Bellyvow Wgt 10s 16lb · 5s 2 £14.

Feb. 5 Wye Men was here a ringing

6 My Daughter Ann Dyed (born Aug ye 3rd 1732)

14 Dydimus Pettus Dyed drunk att Mr. Wm Gray's.

Mar. 14 Sir Robt Furnese Dyed

April 19 I bought a clock of Mr. Ansell, cost £1. 5s my clock

29 John Eastland (of Hope) was married to Eliz. Condit

May 2 Our Steeple was finished plastering over by Jno Gray cost £50

24 I carried my Wife and son Chas as far as Hythe and they went to Folkestone being Thursday, and Satt: ye 26 I went on foot there and Sunday we came as far as Hythe, stayed at Mr. Jackson's Swan Inn. Home on Monday

July 22 Jo. Gibson and Ann Coo was asked

31 Sarah Pratt swore a Bastard unto Anthony Hickmott

Aug, 22 I began learn Chas. O'Neale on ye Violin

Sept. 21 Jo Pain and I went to Warehorn Fair   Home at night

Oct. 4 Jo- Gibson & Ann Coo was married at Romney

5 I carried my wife up to see Jno Culverhouse at Lymn we had a dance, came home next day on Mr. Weldon's horse

Nov. 28 Began teach Mrs Jane and Susan Bachelor to write and sum

Feby 1 Jon Pain and I went to Dimchurch to dancing ye 2 to Wye and home on Sunday ye 3   I bought Watson's copy book 2s. 6d. of James Kenam

Mar 2 Mr. Poison was drowned in Rye Harbour

Mar 14 The Prince of Orange was married to Ye Princess Royall

May 15.16

17. The election for the county of Kent and ye Candidates, and ye poll stood thus   Sir Edwd Deering   4441

Lord Viscount Vane 4252

Lord Middlesex   3569

Sir Geo. Oxenden   3450

20 Lord Viscount Vane Parliment man Dyed

June 6 Being Dimchurch Lath Day my wife and I walked to Thos Brooks at Burmarsh to dinner, had a dance in the Evening at the Dimchurch Bakers

8 I bought 2 pair Gloves of John Godfrey of Lydd in all 1s. 10d

28 I cut my son Thos hair off ye first Time & shaved but one side

July 13 It being Wet wether none of us went to Fair (being Saturday) but on Monday Charles went in ye morning. I went in ye aft-noon & played to dancing of Servts at ye George in Lydd. Charles and ye Sadler man & I home together.

Aug. 9 Being Fryday My brother and Sister came to Romney (on foot) and stayed untill Tuesday 13th we had no other company at ye Fair. We had nobody with us at Fair Day but my brother & sister. We had roast of Lamb, French Beans, a Fowle Pye & Stufft Leg of Pork. We had no mild Beer, neither did I make any Punch.

Oct 1 My son Chas & I Walked to Warehorne Fair. Mr. Dodd Brt him home

21 Jno Gipson's daugh- (Ann) was born ye first child of Ann Coo

Dec. 5 The Tobacco Wrack was in ye West Bay

1735

Jan. 8 The tereble High Wind was of a Wednesday

Feb 1 My Father came to Romney (with J. Law & T. Pain) went away again (being Saty) Chas and I went to Newchurch with him

Ap: 6 I was chosen President of the Society for ye year 1735

May 3 Esqr: Furness carried the cause for Mayorship for Romney. Mr. Wightwick, Mr. Edwards, Mr. Darby went of their side. Mr. Finch, Mr. Mascall and Mr. Lofty went of the other side, Came home 9th inst with great rejoicing for the victory Drum foremost. Edwd Sandls and I with Violins. Mr. Gray with Couler (i.e. flag) and ye gent, all 2 by 2 after Mr. Mascall in the Coach. A Hogshead of Beer set out at the Dolphin.

26 Mr. Winters mare won ye Plate ye 1st day   Mr. Brooks ye cup ye 2nd day.   H. Wightwicks ye Sadle

June 2 My son Chas Miller began sum.

6 Went to Wye bought my Duroy of Mr. Hudson cost £2. 12s. Home ye 8th.

16 Chas bought 2 Rabbits of Mr. Jeremy Smith for 1/6d.

July 2 Mr. Benj: Cobb, Mr. Bartholow: Tookey, Mr. Robt: Langdon was sworn jurats by Mr. Ellis.

26 I went to Wye alone on Foot for my Duroy clothes and ye 28th I was at Troy town and chose Mr. Robt: Tabraham Mayor, and dance at Spring Grove home ye 29th.

Oct. 15 My son Isaac was born just ¼ after 1 o'c of a Wednesday noon.

Nov. 20 I went to Hythe Fair with Jon Atwell. Home at night, dined at J. Terry's.

1736

Jan. 17 Satturday Mr. Sanders and I first had ye Canterbury Post and News and J. Walk and Mr. S. Turner.

Mar	13	Three men put in Jail on suspicion of robing Mr. Roberts and Esqre: Teddeman.
	16	Put out of Jail
	23	My son Chas began play on the Violin, ye day my Father was 60 yrs old.
	27	Mr. E. Sanders drawed me a tooth.
	29	Wye ringers rung 5040 Grandsir Tripples in 3½ hours being ye only set yt rung it in ye County without ye Assistance of Londers or others. By Mr. Ths: Hudson 1st, Chas: Baker 2, Ths: Jarman 3, Robt: Baker 4, Chs: Miller 5, Ths: Tabraham 6, Lawrence Austen 7, Edwd: Pickenden & John Sharpe 8.
Apr.	10	The Right Honbl: Lewis Earl and Baron of Rockingham Viscount Sondes and Baron of Throwley was Mar'd to Miss Ann Furnese.
Apr.	28	Walked to Folkestone with Ric'd Wicks home again ye 30th.
May	8	Serg't Finch with ye Dragoons went away. Foot soldiery came in their room.
July	22	Mr. James Bannewell was chosen Bailiff of Lydd ye 3rd time.
Aug.	24	Mr. Thos. Pierce cleaned and mended my Clock, new line 9d. in all 3s.
	26	We had a new bottom put to our Warming Pan 4s. a pudden dish 2s.5d.
	28	I caught an Eel with my Shear in Slinches coarse weight 3lb 14oz. Just 3ftt 10 inches long.
Sept.	2	Jno. Pain brought us 5 Handkerchiefs from France 4 at 8s. 1 at 10s.
	29	I and Chas was at Dimchurch at (Mr. Rolfe's) the Bailiff's Feast.
Oct.	12	Began my grat book with Decimals.
Dec.	4	My Mother Brown moved out of ye Alms House into ye Hospital.
	27	I went to Wye came home Jan 2. Brt Harris's Hist'y with me.

1737

Feb.	5	I Brown turned my great Coat from a Book sleeve to a slash sleeve.
Mar.	22	Our market cross was begun pulled down and Sep'r ye 1st begun again.
Apr.	2	My daught. Mary had ye measles. Robt. and Chas. had ym at Lydd in 1730.
	14	My son Isaac had ye measles.
May	25	Wm. Ansell went again to sea, he went away in Capt. Harvey's Hoy, he come to Romney again April 29 1743.
June	6	Wm. Vindall fell with ye smallpox & carried to ye Warren House.
July	1	E. Miller found a swarm of bees in our great Garden.
Aug.	1	I left off Teaching school till Mr. Elles & Mr. John Coates presuyaded me to stay & go with ye Ch:Wardens about Town & make a gathering.

Nov.	6	Tho. Batcheler put in Jail for stealing Mr. Goddard's Mare.
Nov	20	QUEEN CAROLINE dyed aged 55yrs 8mo 13ds. born March ye 1st 1682 & married to His Majesty at Hanover Aug ye 23rd 1705. Had 4 sons 5 daughters.
Dec	21	I was allowed £5. 4s. 0. a year from Monday December ye 6th 1737 untill Sept. ye 2nd 1739.

1738

Jan	10	I put my Tom and Bett both to writing for Good.
Feb	1	Mr. Freebody had a sale of all his goods at ye Old George
Apr	28	Mr. Dan Yeoman was married at Fairfield to Mrs. Mary Godfrey
May	2	I played at Westbrook they kept wedding th:
	21	Being Whit monday E.M. Chas and I went a foot to Wye, home ye 27th.
	22	My father cut off Chas' Hair and gave him a Wigg, cost 2s 6d. of Mr. Estzberge.
	30	Sir Robt Austin was married to Mrs. Dashwood a fortune of £35,000.
July	10	Mr. Hoad hath put ye School house out to Mr. Gray and Mr. Wood to rebuild.
Aug.	11	Tho Wood was married to ye Wido Russell being his 4th wife.
	19	I remov'd to Mrs. Ward's to live till Michls. To ye Church to teach.
	24	(Barthow Day) The Foundation of my school was furst begun.
Sep	4	The Rev Mr. Jon Deffray dyed. Born Aug 17 1661. Mrs Deffray died 13th July 1761 Born Sep 18th 1671.
	9	Mr. Deffray was carried in a Hearst and 2 Mourning Coaches to Old Romney to be bury'd. His Paul was supported by 6 Ministers Mr. Pain, Mr. Sockledge, Mr. Cobb, Mr. Hoad, Mr. Brown and Mr. Bunce, and Mr. Wentworth and Mr. Potter walked before. Mr. Potter read prayers and buried him. Mr. Pain preached ye Sermon, ye tex 13 ch Hebrews and ye 7 ver. He was Buried in ye Middle of ye Middle Chancel.
Nov.	7	"Leaden Heels" run from Folkestone to Lydd in just 53 mins & 10 sec rode by Stumps.

1739

Mar.	31	I remov'd from ye Geo. yard to ye new School House.
May	20	John Rogers run away. Ye first time.
	24	Hythe Steeple fell.
	31	My son J. Deward Baptized. Rd: Wicks, Ed: Godfrey and Eliz: Morton stood.
June	2	Stephen Gibbon went on board ye Norwich man of War.
	9	Eliz: Crayfoot's leg cut off at St. Thos. Hospital

	12	A man flew from our steeple with his head in a sack.
Oct.	10	Bought our oval Table of Thos. Wood for 5/s.
	29	War was proclaimed (against Spain) at Romney.
Nov.	8	Thos Hoar whip'd at Dimchurch.

1740

Jan.	9	Fast ye 1st for ye War for Spain
Mar.	31	Step: Allen apprenticed to Eli Terry till Lady Day '47
Apr.	8	Bought a new tea kettle at Folkestone cost 8s.
	21	Mr. Mellen drop't down dead at Dimchurch, Ridg. offr.
	21	Mr. Hobby riding officer Lydd died.
May	19	Made John Mill's Will
June	4	Mr. Linnit's Play came to Town
	29	Isaac Miller breecht
Sep.	2	E.M. and I and Chas to Folkestone, home ye 3rd, all rode.
	4	Hugh Jennings dyed with smallpox Dimchurch
Oct.	9	Avery Cheston and I went up after Mersham school
Nov.	6	Ewd: Sanders arrested by ye Boarder & for £12.12.9.
	15	Our Stove built in my Parlow
Dec.	27	First time J. Atwell and I plaid about Romney for Christmas
Nov.	4	Jon Deward Died, born May 13th 1739

1741

Jany	12	Jon: Whitfield broke at ye Dolphin
	15	Jno: Parton took ye Dolphin
	25	Wm. Brisenden (ye Butcher) died
Mar	28	Chas and Mark Walk went to Beakesbourne
	30	E.M. and I went to Wye on foot, home Ap. 3
Apr.	6	Ld. Johnson fined £100 for Keeping alehouse &c.
	24	Bett Miller went afoot to Folkestone with Jane Basit &c.
July	4	I rode to Sandwich and home at night on Mr. Philpot's horse
	14	I went up after Ashford School
Aug	4	I first begun Keep the Warehouse books for Mr. Vavozer.
Sept	23	John Miller born Wednesday 7o
Oct	5	Avery Cheston begun teach school at Mersham
	13	I rode to Chilham for Mr. Sanders things, home 14th. I had a coat, wig, 1 pair of stockings, 1 cap, 2 knives, Money 10s
Dec	13	Chas to live with Mr. Lofty come away 16 inst.

1742

Jan	1	Shelly put in our Jail to ye 4th.
	2	Wm Pullen put in Maidstone Jail
	5	Jas Love put in Maidstone Jail
	19	Wm Macket carried to Maidstone Jail (of Dimchurch)

Feb	4	Wm Macket died in Maidstone Jail
	6	Wm Stace put in Dinchurch Jail. Beating Jas Lee
Apr.	1	Wm Pullen the Cricketer hanged at Maidstone
May	6	Chas Drawed Mrs Gray a sign for her back way of ye Rose & Crown had a piece of gold value 9s. for it
July	12	My Father Thos Miller died at Wye. He was born at Hythe Mar ye 23rd 1675
	20	Dolphin sign hung up drawn by Humph: Selly
Aug	2	Chas rode to Gallyromp Fair ye first Monday in August
	6	The old Warren house pulled down.
	11	Jno Siveyer was killed with Mr. Cobbs waggon
	19	Chas Miller went to live with David Pappillon Esqre at Lee, out of a Thursday evening, on Mr. Wightwick's Mare, car'd 11s. 3d. with him.
Sep	7	I had a tooth drawed by Sanders.
	22	Md Mascall died born Dec ye 6th 1671. My Mistress.
	25	Susan Weldon Drowned near Blackmanstone.
Oct	6	Chas 1st Begun Officate in ye Excise Office
	14	I sent Chas ye 1st letter to ye Excise Office
	16	Mr Hull hanged himself at Mr Knights he was Minister of Gt Chart
Nov	19	I was arrested in Mr. Plummer's suit for £2.8.8½., & Loftys charges 12s. 10d. Bayley's 2s. Plummer paid all
	29	Chas wrote that Mark Walk had smallpox
Dec	1	Chas came from London to Acrise ye 3rd inst.
	20	J. Atwell and I played about Romney got 18. 7½ each
	23	Stephen Wicks & I played about Lydd got each 3. 3.
	26	Chas came from Acrise to see us.
	29	I went with Chas to Acrise, home a Foot 30th

1743

Jan	10	Sent Chas box with ye first clothes by ye Carrier
	17	I. Brown turned Butler's light colour'd coat for me
Apr	9	Chas Miller Took with smallpox at Lee
	16	Chas's Pox at ye Height
May	25	Jno Breads of Rye condemned
June	8	John Breads of Rye hang'd
	26	Bought 3 shirts for Chas of Mrs Banewell 8¼ ells of Holland at 2s.6d. £1. 0. 6. & 17d, 2 Nails of Cambrick at 3s.6d. and 9 buttons £0. 3. 11¼ Total £1. 4. 7½
Aug	19	Chas put in again to officiate in ye Office to Sept. 10 next
Sep	5	Wido: Gibson put in my Mother Brown's Hospital
Aug	22	I set up my shelves in my school for my books &c
Sep	26	Wm Crittenden whip't here, stealing Mr. Moore's shirts
Nov	15	Bot. 7½ yds of cloth for sheets at 10s.7d.

	27	I rode up to Do: brought Chas down at night to go to London
	27	E.M. I pair of more sheets as on ye 15th Instant
Dec	1	Chas went from Romney to London on Mr. Wightwick's Horse.
	6	Chas Estab'd in ye Excise Office at 40 £ per year to . . . .
	20	Chas remov'd to ye Office to £50 pd a year to 25th June 1746 and then £55.

1744

Jan	16	Chas begun Board Wh Mr Gaylad at £20 a Yr. Board Washing & Lodging to July 9th 1744.
	19	First plaid to Ye Assembly at Ashford with Jos: Gipson
Feb	7	Thomas Miller 1st learnt to play on Violin
	13	Adms: Matthews & Lestocks' battle in ye Mediteranean seas
	18	Thos Miller went home with Mr H. Briquall to Guldeford Rye
	22	A Squadron of 15 Frenchmen of War anch'd off our Town & laid to ye 24th in ye night. Sir Jon Morris came in sight of them ye 24th with 32 sail!!
Mar	15	Mr. Hen. Strover and Mr. Houghton were ye witnesses to ye execution of Chas' £300 bond for ye Excise Office. Is: Brown and Wm Slodden his Bondmen. A spent 5s.
	31	Mrs Tucker of Lirr drown'd in Kite Well.
	31	War proclaimed at London, against France. Sir John Norris resign'd being Admiral
Apr	10	War proclaimed at Romney against France
	11	Fast Day. I went to Wye afoot, to Ashford ye 12th. Plaid to ye Assembly ye 3rd time. Home ye 13th.
	18	Thos. and Isa: bou't each a rabbit of Brown at 6d each
May	3	Mr. Parris (of Dimchurch) new platted my Fro hair
	7	John Birch, John Dory, John Gibson and James Hunt entered on Board ye Dover privateer
	13	Thos and Is: had each new breeches from Lidd each 4. 6.
	17	Bot. Is: a coat 3/6, Hat 1/. me a Wigg 3/6. all at Wye
	18	A Confirmation at Ashford. Bish. Asaph. Tex 13 Heb 17
	25	E.M. went to Folkestone afoot & home ye 29th with Wid: Gipson.
June	4	Tho. Tonpenny died at ye Warren Ho: of smallpox
	25	Bot. 4 ells of Canvas for a Frock, 11d an ell 3s.8d. E.M. made it.
	28	Mr. Carter boug't Rome House of J. Hayward
July	15	Uncle and Aunt Basit here stayed all night
	27	Sir Wm. Boys died. Born Sep 21st 1657, created Dr. 1690. Married 1691 and Knighted By King George 1716.
Aug	6	John Miller had ye measles
	28	My Apocrypha Book Bound by Mr. Hogben Ashford 1s. 6d.
	29	The Wreck in West Bay of Chequees &c.
Oct	1	In ye night ye Victory man of War was foundered

	13	Begun Burn a light in a Glass with bone fatt
	16	Dug a sand-hole in little Garden on Carpenter's side
		E.M. asked Mr. Vavazor to stay to Xmas for ye 3£.
	18	I shall write to Chas from hence every Thursday
Nov	22	Mr. Wybourn of Rye died & Wm Hogben had his school
	29	Mr Nicholas Rolfe begun with me on ye Violin
Dec	6	I rod to Dover to see ye Iron weighed for our men 14 ton 11 @ £4 a Ton

1745

Jan	4	Wm Hook the Joiner was hanged at Canterbury agd. 45
	21	Rec'd 25 Yds of Holland from Chas made Him 7 Shirts Holland is 2/8d a yd. yt is 3s 4d an Ell. Cambric 10/6d.
Feb	5	A Wreck point of Great Stone. I got Cotton
	16	Mr. Parton J. Lee & Co Boug't their Boat.
	18	Had a box from Chas. weig'd 27lbs with his brown and blue coat, 3 waistcoats, 4 pair of breeches, Wig, 2 shirts all for Thos.
	25	H. T. Crundwell altered my fiddle stick
Mar	14	Wm Dunk shot by Christ: Barret of Folkestone
	16	Mr. Slodden went to London did not see Chas.
	18	Earl of Oxford died. Born Aug't 4 1674
	19	Wm Dunk burried at Hythe. Tex 26 Matt: v 1.2.3. & 4.
Apr	7	Mr. Wightwick told me, 1411 ac's of land in Hope Parish
	12	I rode to Faversham and came afoot to Wye. Chas rode and laid at Wye ye night and ye 13th he rode to Romney & I walked and staid till Monday ye 29th. He rode to Ashford in order to go with Mr. Dunce ye Ashford carrier.
	27	Capt James Pelham of Lidd died
	29	I boug't me a pair of breeches of Wm Fitzpatrick 7/6d.
	30	The battle of Tourney
May	27	Sold Mr. Raven my cotton 17½ lbs @ 8d just 11s.8d. Bot Mary a gown and me a pair of Stockings (2.6.)
	30	Ric'd Castle shot by soldiers at Seabrook
June	2	Whitsunday – My sister, John Launcefield, Jas. Walk and Mr. Downe's maid came all afoot and staid all at Mr. Walk's till Tuesday 10th. E.M. and my sister had words, when she came in, & she would not stay here nor I did not speak to any one of ym but James Walk
	2	I caught our Cock Linnet in ye Chamber
	8	Mr. Rich: Rolfe bot Jno Culverhouse's Violin for a guinea
	21	Rec'd by Mr. Slodden a parcel from Chas of 2 shirts, 1 green silk waistcoat, 1 Court Kalender, 1 Seal of a Goats Head & 64 old Pens.
	29	I had my black wig curl'd by Mapleback ye soldier

July	1	My daug't Ann born just 3½ o'clock (& died March the 22nd 1747) in ye afternoon of a Monday. (Laid by Mrs. Ward. Born, she, Mrs. Ward July 6 1676)
	8	Our new pump put down at Ye Corporacons' charge
	20	Master Stephen Pilcher killed at Honeychild tun a fall from a Horse
	25	Chas Miller was at Winsor Castle 23 miles from London ye 28th at Layton Stone in Essex
Sep	3	Grand Duke of Tuscany chose Emperor & crowned ye 23rd
	4	Chas to Northend by Fulham
	11	Ye Sconches put up in our Church by Mr. Coates
	13	I. Brown made Isa: blew coat out of Chas's
	29	Mr. Wm Dan's house was broke open by Ed. Tabraham
Oct	7	Begun burn coal
	13	Edw. Tabraham put in Canterbury Jail for breaking Mr. Dan's house & was hang'd for it 3 Apr 1746
	29	I hired Rev Mr. Head a room for a bottle of wine a yr
Nov	8	William Rolfe buried at St. Mary's
	20	Thos Freebody come to Town from on board ye Lynn Man of War
	24	Mr. Wm Thomas set out for London on Mr. Tookey's business
	29	Steph Finn's goods seized by Mr. Kingsnorth for rent
Dec	3	Sir Francis Dashwood married to Lady Ellis
	5	Lewis Earl of Rockingham died
	11	Our gun carriages broken in pieces in order for new ones
	15	In ye utmost confusion because of ye French making an Invasion.

1746

Jan	29	Jno Shrubsole brought his Dulcimore here
Feb	3	Mr. Jer Smith bought ye Mill Close 40£ Pd.
Feb	4	The first field day of our Militia
Mar	1	Weaver John died in ye Dolphin stable
	11	A man found drowned at Old Romney
	17	I paid 3s. for ye Highways
	31	Had 25 Highlanders come to Town till 14 April 1746
Apr	3	Edwd Tabraham (and 4 more) hanged at Maidstone
	7	Jno Epps come to Board and school with me to be 52 weeks compleat for 11 pounds to be paid by Mr. Noakes
May day		Rome house pulled down to be rebuilt by Mr. Horn
	6	Mr. Carter and Mrs Sarah Tyghe Married by Mr. Thomas at Hope
	18	(Whitsunday) My son John Miller was put into breeches.
	24	Jno Hogman a soldier of Capt. Cockburn's Company, of Honb. Beauclerk's regiment had 400 lashes for stealing Mrs. Parton's watch and sold it at Tenterden about ye 12th inst.
	27	I had of Mr. Russell, Bayley's Dictionary for J. Gray

June 14 Mr. J. Fowles horse & a pony ran from Hythe to Romney. Pony best.
25 Chas Miller was removed from the plate duty into ye Correspondence office ie 50 to 55£ per annum
26 Sent Chas a Chest, deal box &c, Coles (Wm Jennings) Dictionary by J. Masters to Hythe to go by Mr. Mitton's Hoy
July 19 Mr. Baker, Carpenter (of Hythe) died of the smallpox, and she married again to Mr. Avards of Romney 13th Decemr 1747.
Aug 5 Nurse King died aged 82½ yrs.
18 Earl of Kilmarnock and Lord Balmerino Beheaded on Tower Hill
23 Bot of (Mr Barnwell) 4 Ells of Canvis at 10d, for a Frock
Sept 1 Box from Chas. Weighed 21 pd. 2 Coats, 1 Hat, 1 Wig (White) 1 Cap, 4 Pencils, 2 pair Stockings, 100 new and 246 Old, 28'0 (pens) 1 Green pocket book, 21 pictures & 1 Quire & 18 sheets of paper.
11 Mrs. Haffenden affrighted ye Lower way to O. Romney
29 Mr. Walk resigned ye Mill & Mr. John Stace took it and he kept it until 8th Dec 1747
Oct 9 Thanksgivng Day. Tax Mr. Thomas Psm 21st v 11. singing Ps.72 & 1,2,3,4,v. 18 Psm & 5 last verses & 5th Psm & 4 last vs. I set up Candles. Mr. Cobbs at O. Romney 33 Psm: 12 v. Mr. Kight at Lydd 122 Psm: 6v.

1747
Jany 3 A Hog (Mr. Firmenger) 11s 17lb, at 4,6 just £2.13.3.
7 A general Fast
Feb 21 Lid: Johnson took mad
Apr 4 Mr. Avade entered ye Dolphin and took his sign down again Oct 20. 1747
9 A pair of breeches for myself of N. Dutton 7s.6d.
Lord Lovat beheaded on Tower Hill
May 25 Wm Wills entered for a foot soldier
June 11 Wm Priggs up at Dimchurch Lath:
22 J. Brown E.M. quarrelled before Boys from school assembled
26 Wm Priggs broke out of Lidd Jail with Sam: Priory
July 8 Thos. Inkpen whip't here
13 Bot Isaac a frock at Fair 10/6d. Bot set of China for 4s of Mrs Minster of Folkestone
21 Sam: Priory brot back to our Jail 28 carried away
27 Isaac & Abra: Brown to school to Hythe
Aug 6 Margaret Welsh bound in her bed
22 John Miller broke his arm
Sept 16 Mrs Vavazor gave me a razor
30 Mary Miller to live with Mr Minis
Chas from Mr Shaw's to Mr Humphery's in Basinghall St.
174

Oct. 10 Dr John Potter Ld a B.C. (i.e. Lord Arch'p of Canterbury) died
29 Mr Jon Skinner and Mrs Grace Bannerman Married at Fairfield
Nov 5 E.M. Bought Bet a cloak 7/6d, and Mary do at Wye 7s.
8 Geo. Hammond Took with the smallpox
17 John Hales, Fras: Marketman and Sam: Priory out of Maidstone Jail
18 Jon Smith of Old Romney fell down Dover cliff & was killed
19 Tho Fuller Hanged at Tyburn
Dec 13 I was sworn (with 20 more) on ye Jury for Mr Johnson
Dec 19 Chas sent me a list of the Parliament &c, by Mr. Ansel
26 Jno Lancefield and sister Ann Miller married at Wye & another couple married with them

1748

Jan 21 Thos & I to Hythe to meet Mr. Pierce the Collector, about his taking Thos Miller but did not agree
22 John Walk opened an Ale House, took sign down in Feb
27 Mr. Vinal opened an Ale House and took his sign down 16 Feb
28 Jno Miller begun Write
30 Mr. Newman gave Jno Miller a coat
Feb 20 John Gray, Susan Gray, Ann Maria Bachelor, Ann Bachelor, Eliz: Bachelor, Margt Bachelor, Margt Coates, Ann Coates, Jane Edwards, Ann Wilson, Ann Lee and Thos Wilks all went to Wye to be inoculated for ye smallpox.
25 My Sparticles by Mr. Pierce from London
Mar 4 Mr Robt Hampton ye Exciseman was drowned at ye Bridge beyond Old Romney stocks at Cold Harbour
25 Mary Miller from John Minis there — — 1747
Apr 3 Mr. Smith and Bet to London for Shop goods, ye first time
24 Wm Allen died of ye smallpox at ye Warren House
27 Bet: Smith begun Keep shop
May 18 Our 6 bells took down and carried away in 3 waggons
30 Mr Veryck's Play come to Town away 13 June 1748
Mrs Goodards carried to Maidstone Jail
June 23 Mr Snip the schoolmaster of Brookland died
July 27 Young Frosty (kiss in a corner) won the £50 plate on Barham down
Aug 6 Chas Miller came to Romney & staid until ye 23rd
12 Catherine Marten was put into Rye Joal and ye 24th whip't at the Cart's Tail for thieving from Mr. Wilson's & Mr. Nortons.
John Hales cast for Transportation for 7 years at Rochester
14 Mr Thos Alderney a Cabinet maker was here from Audley Street
23 Chas Miller and Mark Walk went away. I to Can'y with them
Eliz: Miller, Isaac Miller, Goodwife Creasey, Ann Creasey, Goodw: Holmes & 2 daugts. Goodw:, Young & 2 daugts & Sarah

Eastland went to Hopping at Mr. Tresses at Sandhurst. Home 13th Sept.

	24	Catherine Marten whipt at ye Cart's Tail (3 strokes) at Rye.
Sept	1	Jno Bingley begun make shoes. Set up for him &c.
	3	I rode to Sanders to Mr. Fras. Tresses to see Eliz: Miller there a Hopping out Satterday 11 hours. There (thro' Newingden level) just 3¼ hours.
	13	E. Miller home from hopping 7 doz Bushl at 1¼ pr bushel 8s. 9d 13 doz & 10 bushells at 1d a bushell 13s. 10d. Picking only £1. 2. 7. Had given them each 1s in all £1. 4. 7. E. Miller bought Isaac a coat 6/6d and Mary 6yds of shaloon for a gown at 1/6d a yd at Tenterden.
	17	E. Miller & Thos Miller to Dover on Jon Eastlands Mare, to get Mary a place, home the 18th a Sunday.
Oct	6	Had a new bottom to our warming pan Had our bellows new leather'd by Mr. Mate
Nov	7	Had a box from Chas wth £4. 10.0 for Mr. Weldon, a Blew Coat, Waistcoat & Breeches for Thos & a wig for me.
	9	Our organ sold to Rd. Savage for 10s. this day carried away
	14	Our bells came home from 29th May last
	22	Begun burn Coals 3/4 pr Chaldron Being Tuesday was the 1st time our 8 bells was rung by the following men . . . Jon Atwell 1st, Jos Acton 2nd, Mr. Humph: Wightwick 3rd, Mr. Wm Freebody 4th, Mr. Ed. Carpenter 5th, Thos Halks 6th, Mr John Russell 7th, and Mr. Wm. Slodden 8th. I, Thos, Is: and John was up and saw ye first peel rung.
	23	Dover men here ringing.
	25	Wye men here ringing & ye 26 Rung 5040 Gd Triples in 3 hours and 23 minutes by Thos Jarman 1st, Wm Drayman 2nd, James Mace 3rd, Jno French 4th, Dan'l Fagg 5th, Robt Baker 6th, Thos Tabraham 7th and Francis Hills 8th

1749

Jan	2	Harrisham men here rung 5040 Bob majors in 3H. 19 min.
	6	Jeremy Inkpen, Old Romney died Smallpox
	16	Had Almanack and ring of string from Chas cost 7d.
Feb	3	Edmond Richards carried thro' our Town to Horsham Jail Isaac had my breeches made fit for him, by J. Ruffen
	7	Henry Crundwell shott his left hand off
	17	Thos Miller had a Canvas Frock 6/6 of Mr. Godfrey Lidd Friday Eliz. Miller, J. Walks Wife & Thos Bannewell set out Jon Walk & Thos Miller carried them beyond Elham & Thos brought

ye Horses home yt night, they to Mark Walk's at Bourn and lay there. A Satterday (ye 18th) they 3 to Canterbury (Jon Walk home today) dined at Mrs Mounts (Mary Burden's as was). At 4 o'clock got into ye Caravan by 7$\underline{o}$ to Whitstable and on board Mr. Coultrup's Hoy. Up at Bear-Key 1$\underline{o}$clock on Sunday (ye 19th) to Mark Walks 2$\underline{o}$clock laid there that night. Cha' come to them 12$\underline{o}$ clock a Monday (ye 20th) E.M. had lodgings in Red Lion Street Clerkenwell & Tuesday spent her time with Mrs Walk and Chas. A Wednesday (ye 22nd) Chas and she about London, the same to Thursday (till) 5$\underline{o}$clock in even: & then went on board a Feversham Hoy & come to Bro- Fox's just 5 o'clock on Friday (24th) and staid there till Monday (ye 27th) & then to Wye in a waggon. To Mr. Law's (for) tea by 3 o'clock but laid at Mrs. Back's. At 10 o'clock (ye 28th) she come out of Wye on foot. (Thos Law come to Billsington Cròss wth her for 1s & spent 5d) & home just 4½ o'clock being Tuesday in good health & had fine weather all ye time.

	20	Henry Crundwell come to lodge at Mr. Mate's with his arm
	24	Mr. Avarde gave me a map of London
	28	I sett an Elder Hedge round my Walnutt Tree
Apr	8	Thos Miller went to live at Appledore with Mr. Hodges
	10	T. Miller begun to teach School at Appledore
	24	Eliz: Miller begun to learn make Mantuas of Cath. Walk till May Day 1750 away June 8th 1749
		Hen. Crundwell begun teach school at Brookland.
Apr	25	Thanksgiving for the Peace
May	13	I had a pair of shoes of Mr. Thos Wood 5s. and speckled stockings 2s.
		I afoot alone to Bro. Lancefield's. Made his Father's Will home on Whit-Thursday
June	9	My Sons Thos & Isaac confirmed by Arch:B.Cant. at Ashford
	18	Moorland brot up from ye sea, drowned ye 16th and buried at Romney the 20th inst. Laid in Mr. Welsher shop.
	19	Chas sent Thos 2 Hats, 2 pair breeches, 2 pr Stock'ngs, 8d.
July	16	Dr. Clare of Hythe died
	17	My son Thos Begun board himself at Appledore
		My son Chas Miller came and stayed till 31st inst.
	28	Mr. Robt Parris made us 2 new heaters mended the iron 2s.
Aug	13	Rev. Mr. Richd Jacob took possession of our Living.
		Preached. Tax St. Jno 13c 17v.
Sept	21	Mr. J. Gray and I measured Old Romney Court Lodge House
	23	Thos Miller left Appledore school from 10th Apr 1749. Just 24 weeks
Oct	2	Thos Miller begun teach school at Sanders. Board Mr. Bennett

	7	Three Dutchmen put into the Cage for stabbing a man at Vinals
	22	Thos Miller had a box from Chas Miller containing 3 dozen of books, 3 qire paper, 200 new and 100 old pens, 1 pair of Breeches, 2 guineas and 2 letters.
Dec	1	The Scotch Greys come to Town

1750

Jan	20	Wm Vinals other eye knocked out by a Dragoon
	25	Had a new Tea Kettle lid from Hythe 9d, carriage 1d, in all 10d
Feb	8	An Earthquake in London, just 12½ of a Thursday
	12	Chas sent 7 shirts to mend and me a Calendar
	18	Sara Hyham died at ye new House on the Warren
Mar	8	Earthquake in London, as Feb 8th past, Chas felt both
	31	Appraised Wm Welsher yard & goods £102. 17. 8½ pd 50£ Down
May	12	Mr. Woodman bound my Dr Harris' History 2/6d
July	16	Mr John Rolfe elected Town Clerk in Mr Loftie's Room
	24	The Brotherhood and Guestling held at Romney. Rev Mr. Bunce preached the Sermon Tax 1.Pet.2c, 17v and It ended 26th Inst. Robt Langdon Esq, Mr Ricd Ellis, Mr Benj Cobb, Mr Augt Greenland and Mr Geo Carter for Romney and Mr Wm Temple, Bailiff. Rev Mr Thos Cobb, Mr John Lee, Mr Thos Denne, Mr John Skinner was for Lydd. 5 out of each place, in all 15 places, 75 in no. besides Sergents &c.
Sep	2	Fras Rigg & Mary Miller asked
	17	Mr Chas Rolfe's (Miller) horse won a saddle here, 3 started Mr Nichols of Elham and Mr Mumk of Appledore
	23	Francis Rigg and Mary Miller married at Romney by the Rev Mr Edward Thomas being Sunday
Oct	12	Francis and Mary Riggs begun housekeeping
Nov	7	Bett Miller lame at Lydd lodged at Mr. Battham's under Dr. Holland costing me 15s. home 23rd Inst.
Dec	24	Tommy from Sandhurst to 5th Jany
	31	Chas sent Tommy and I each a Calendar

1751

Mar	5	My Grandson Chas Riggs was born about half an hour after 10 o'clock of a Tuesday night. Baptized March 31st by Rev Mr Cobb, Adam Terry, Antony Hickmott and Mary Temple his sureties
	20	Prince Frederick died Born 20th Jany 1706
Apr	16	My Grandson Chas Riggs was here the first time he and Heny Gravenor both laid in my Cradle being the first time of each Mr. Pierce new did my clock had 5/s.
May	11	Bett cut John Miller's hair off

178

	23	Had me grey Coat and Breeches and Black Waistcoat of Geo Favis of Lydd £3. 6. 5.
Aug	17	Bet Miller learnt to make baskets of Mr. Williams
	23	Tommy and Francis Trees here for to tell the Hoppers
	29	Eliz: and 15 more went a hopping, Mr. Tress's. Home 23 Sep
Oct	20	Halks the Glover come in Nich: Ruffens room
Nov	4	Our 4th Bell broke down
	19	Isaac learnt his first tune
Dec	1	Is: Miller had a pair of breeches of Mr. Halks 6s. John Martin & Hum: Wightwick went to Northiam to be incogulated for small-pox

1752

Jan	7	Bot a desk of Mrs Sanders for a 5/-
	15	Bot a black tea-kettle of Mr. Smith for 2s.
Feb	4	I had my dream yet I should live but a little time longer
	11	Bot my iron spade of Mr. Pierce for 4/s.
May	11	Mrs Bannevell bot Mr Sanders house for 25£
	24	All my 6 own children Fras & Grandson Chas at dinner with me
June	6	E.M. & Son on Mr Smiths horse to ye Culverhouses Lympne
	24	I bot my saw of Mrs Ward at Mrs Sanders sale 1s
	30	Mrs Newman left the Rose & Crown & Mr Ellis took it
Aug	12	Jno Miller fellin a fit in Church in Prayer Time on Wednesday
	26	A tedious storm begun 3 o'clock, morn, lasted all day
Sept	26	John Miller begun summing
Nov	26	Had 2 Bantham fowles of Robt Baker of Mersham
Dec	14	Bot 6 chairs at Mrs Blechynden's sale 3/-
	23	Tommy come afoot Is: met him at Appledore

1753

Jan	3	T. Miller and I played to a Ball at Mr. Wightwicks
	12	Mr Fowle died at Bath aged 56 yrs, buried at Dimchurch 21 Jany
	20	Mr T. Bannevel to Ashford for Instructions for Excise, to Ashford, to 8 April
Feb	5	I am 50 years old, born 5th Feby 1702
	25	John Culverhouse brougt me his Violin in pawn for 7s/6d I lent
May	10	Mr. Baker, begun my windows on Mr. Mascall's acct
	14	Chas Miller sent Isaac 2 coats, 1 waistcoat, 3 pair of stockings, nothing else
June	5	Walker tore with the Mill. I see him got loose.
	15	I talked at Romney with Squire Papillon from the market to Mr T. Smith's
Sept	9	I made oath before Mr. Cobb that the Rev Mr John Wilson, Dr.

		Walter & Peter Rouse, & T. Norman as Churchwardens did sign a Petition to get Margt Wilson into St. Luke's Hospital
	11	Mr Wightwick's sign of Bacchus was hung up
	23	Jno Ansell and Elizth Miller was asked
Oct	9	John Ansell & Elizabeth Miller mar'd Romney
	15	Thos Bannevel to Lincolnshire in the Excise
	23	Mr. Smiths Play come to Town in Mr Steeds Barn
	26	Geo. Lancefield come to school here
Nov	17	My great Coat £1.4.6. E.M.'s hood £1.1.3. of Mrs. Hunt

1754

Jan	2	My Uncle Lancefield of Crundall dyed
	16	John Ansell and wife to Deal, home 27th
		Fras Riggs to France. Jon Miller with him to Sandgate Castle
Feb	7	Thos Miller & Catherine Longley married at Romney
Mar	9	Ann Worrmall (Mrs. Rolfe's maid) drowned at St Marys
		Thos Miller to Tonbridge about ye School
	16	Mr Wm Hills of Otterpool drowned at St Marys, found a Thursday the 21st by R. Hunt, T. Wilks, Geo Hammond, Thomas Warrington and Isaac Miller, had 2 guineas. Spent the odd 2 shillings, (8/- each).
Apr	4	Jane daugt of Thos and Catherine Miller was born at Mr Bennet's in Sandhurst, just 10 minutes after 8 o'cl. of a Thursday night. Bapd a Monday the 15th inst and Mr Bennett, Mrs Longley and My wife was sureties for her, the 6th E.M. went to nurse her home 28
	15	Sir Fras Dashwood and Henry Furnese Esq: chose Member for Romney without opposition
	20	Thos Miller to Tonbridge in order to begin Teach School there, this Monday the 22nd, but did not, he come to Sandhurst again a Thursday the 25th, he there again Satterday the 27th.
May	1	I & 2 The Election for the County of Kent and ye Candidates and ye Poll stood thus:— Lewis Watson 5235 — Fairfax 5137 Ld. Ed: Deering 2959
	19	Bot a Wigg of F. Riggs for 4s, Is: one 5s all 9s, his cut mine curled
	20	Thos Miller. wife, goods &c from Sandhurst to Tonbridge
	31	E. Miller bot a set of China of Mrs Gravenor for 4s.
June	2	I carried E. Miller to Crundal being Whitsunday home the 8th Inst.
	28	E.M. and Isaac on Fras Riggs horse to Folkestone Fair home ye 29th
	29	Rev Mr Jon Head (my Master) died at Sellings
July	24	Mr Geo Wickes and Mr Ed: Blechynden Tookey made Freemen
Sep	1	Sunday Mary Riggs laid of a son, Wm between 9 & 10 oclock in

morning. E.M. there ye 2nd, to nurse her ye 5th Inst, & then ye 3rd and 5th & 8th Nurse Brook there and Dr Gipps ye 9th, she died 19th inst.

Oct   3   I with John Ansell to Heny Morrises to measure 5a 1r 18p. of wood sold Wm Kennet at £5 an acre £26. 16.3½. home round by Crundal & Wye the 5th

      10   Jno Pierce took the Mill from Wm Pierce

Nov   6   Rev. Mr Edward Sedgwick took Romney free school

     27   Mr Wilson Tap'd for dropsy had 12½ quts water (drawn)

Dec   9   A vessel run a shore with rum and sugar at the Warehouse

1755

Jan 22   John Ansell & Is: Miller afoot to Deal, home 3rd Feby

Feb   3   Mr. Carter's family from Wye from ye smallpox

     17   Mr Thos Wilson tap'd ye second time, had 11½ quarts water taken

     19   Do. died. Born in July 1702

Mar 14   Hired part of ye Dolphin of Mr. Pierce for 40/s till Michas next, 10 Octo, 1755

     27   Left teaching in ye free school, come from 2d Octor 1732

Apr   9   Removed to the Old Dolphin from ye free school

     28   The King to Hanover

Aug   1   Rev Mr Lanes and Mr. J. Philpot played single cricket for 5 guineas each and won by Mr Lanes

      6   Isaac Miller won the silver cup at Dimchurch

     12   Measured Mr Wilson's pea field 8a. 22rs. 3½per.

     13   Isaac Miller won the Hat at Dimchurch

CHAPTER 12

The Charters of Romney Marsh

The imminent danger of loss of land by flood, is borne out by a lease of 1202 where provision is made for a decrease in the Rent of 6d, for every acre lost by violence of the sea. To protect such lands from the sea, sea-walls were built so that by the thirteenth century a drained and protected area had come gradually into existence. In the course of time local regulations relating to sea defence and land drainage began to be enforced and the district became known as "The Level of Romney Marsh" and by the grant of chartered privileges to the inhabitants "The Liberty of Romney Marsh" was created. The need for this special administration was the necessity of constant attention to fresh water drainage and sea defence to prevent inundation. Scarcely a grant of land was made in the Marsh without some provision for the upkeep of walls and water-ways and as early as the twelfth century there is reference to the obligations of tenants in the Marsh in this respect.

Sometime between 1100 and 1135 grants of land at Appledore were made by the Prior of Christ Church, Canterbury, with this covenant:— *Et debent wallas et waterganges custodire et defendere contra friscam et salsam; et quotiens opus fuerit, eas reparare et firmas facere secundum legem Marisci."* i.e. "That the tenants engage to maintain the walls and sewers against the fresh and salt water and as often as there shall be need to repair and strengthen them according to the Law of the Marsh."

Another Lease of Samson de Guestling undertook to repair the Walls:— *"Secundum quantitatem illus terrae inter et extra."* i.e. "According to the quantity of his inlands and outlands."

The cartulary of Horton contains nine similar agreements, although none of these is earlier than 1263, several renew earlier obligations, – *"Sicut antecessores mei."*

To maintain this efficient sea defence and land drainage throughout the Marsh an administrative organisation was necessary to enforce the obligation of the tenants. The Court Rolls of Appledore show that this Manor had its own keeper of the walls and made its own repairs of banks and waterways. As early as the twelfth century there had thus come into existence a recognised body of custom referred to as the *"Lex marisci",* the Law of the Marsh.

By the thirteenth century these officials consisted of XXIV sworn men or Jurats, elected by the Commonalty to enforce the contribution of land-holders within the Marsh towards the maintenance of sea-walls and watercourses for the common benefit and safety.

During the thirteenth century owing to the severe storms to which the coast of Kent was exposed the worst effects of such tempests as that of October 1250 were described by Holinshead, ... "The sea flowed twice without ebbing, and appeared in the dark of the night as it had been on fire, and the waves to strive and fight together after a marvellous sort."

The vital need for the drainage of these Marshlands and for their protection from the violence of the sea called for special regulations, King Henry III granted a Charter — "to the four and twenty lawful men of Romney Marsh time out of mind hereunto chosen and sworn, distress ought to be made upon all those which have lands and tenements in the said Marsh, to repair the walls and watergauges of the same Marsh against the danger of the sea." The Charter is dated the 2nd of September 1252.

CARTA HENRICI REGIS ANGLIAE DE ORDIŃATIONE
MARISCI DE ROMENE

Henricus Dei gratia, Rex Angliae, Dominus Hiberniae, Dux Normanniae, et Comes Andegaviae. Omnibus ballivis suis et fidelibus suis, ad quos praesentes literae pervenerint. Salutem. _{Carta Henri tertii Regis}

Quai per viginti quatuor legales homines de Marisco de Romene, a tempore quo non extat memoria, ad hoc electos et juratos, debent districtiones fieri, super omnes illos qui terras et tenementa habent in predicto Marisco, ad reparandum Wallias et Watergagia ejusdem Marisci contra Maris periculum, et etiam super omnes, qui ad reparationem praedictarum Walliarum et Watergagiorum obligati sunt et tenentur: Nos concessimus eisdem viginti quatuor, quod pro securitate dicti Marisci, districtiones illas fieri faciant, ita quod aeque fiant, secundum portiones majores et minores quas homines habent in eodem Marisco, et secundum quod quidam ad hoc obligantur at tenentur. Et ideo volumus et concedimus, quod nullus Vicecomes nostre Kanciae, vel aliquis Ballivorum suorum, de districtionibus illis per considerationem praedictorum viginti quatuor Juratorum factis propter praedictum periculum evitandum in aliquo se intromittant. Quicunque enim de consideratione ipsarum districtionum, ad nos querelam detulerit, nos ei in curia nostra justitiam fieri faciemus, et illam justitiam nobis vel Mandato nostro speciali, specialiter reservamus. In cujus rei Testimonium, has Literas nostras fieri fecimus Patentes. Teste meipso apud Sanctum Edmundum, Secundo die Septembris, Anno Regni nostri tricesimo sexto.

184

THE CHARTER OF HENRY III KING OF ENGLAND
CONCERNING THE ORDINANCE OF ROMNEY MARSH
(Close Roll, 36 Henry III, m.4) 2 September, 1252

Henry by the Grace of God, King of England, Lord of Ireland, Duke of Normandy, and Count of Anjou. To all his bailiffs and faithful subjects, to whom these present letters shall come, Greeting. Because, by four and twenty lawful men of Romney Marsh, time out of mind hereunto chosen and sworn, distresses ought to be made upon all those which have lands and tenements in the said Marsh, to repair the Walls and Watergages of the same Marsh against the danger of the sea, and also upon all those which are bound and charged for the reparation of the said Walls and Watergages: we have granted to the same four and twenty, that for the safety of the said Marsh, they cause those distresses to be done, so that they may be made equal according to the portions greater and lesser, which men have in the same Marsh, and according to that to which some are bound and charged. And therefore we will and grant, that no sheriff of ours in Kent, or any of his bailiffs, do in any wise intermeddle touching those distresses made by consideration of the aforesaid four and twenty Jurats to avoid the said danger. For whosoever shall bring complaint unto us, in consideration of those distresses, we will cause justice to be done unto him in our court, and that justice we reserve specially to ourself, or at our special commandment.

In witness whereof, these letters we have caused to be made patent. Witness myself at S. Edmunds the second day of September, in the six and thirtieth year of our reign.

―――――――――――

The granting of a second Charter to Romney Marsh, two hundred years later, was not connected in any way with land drainage or sea defence. It is remarkable for its unusual length. First, it grants to the . . . . "the inhabitants and residents within the bounds and limits of the Marsh . . . . that they shall be one body in deed and be one perpetual corporate community of one Bailiff and twenty-four Jurats and the Commonalty of the Marsh of Romney . . . . for ever", and . . . . "that they may have a common seal". Power was given to the officers to frame reasonable ordinances and constitutions for the public good and . . . . "wholesome government", and to raise taxes . . . . "for the necessities and conveniences" of the Marsh. Civil jurisdiction was conferred on them with a right of holding a three-weekly court, this court was known as "The King's Court of Record". Cases dealt with included debt, trespass, robbery with force and violence and pleas of land. But by far the most important privilege granted was that of exercising criminal jurisdiction throughout the Liberty.

"Yearly at the feast of St. Michael, the Bailiff, Jurats and Commonalty may choose from the aforesaid Jurats four of the most discreet and sufficient

185

Jurats as Keepers of the Peace . . . . for the year following." Power is given to . . . . "the same four, three or two of them of whom the said Bailiff for the time being shall always be one," to exercise full criminal jurisdiction, including the right of erecting gallows for the execution of felons. The justices were empowered to act as coroners within the Liberty, while the profits from both criminal and civil jurisdiction were granted to the new Corporation. All Royal Justices were excluded from interference or the exercise of any jurisdiction within the Liberty. Romney Marsh thus received the fullest judicial liberties which could be given to a Corporation and its officials were placed on a footing with those of the most privileged Boroughs. The most valuable and unusual privileges conferred was that of exemption from all national taxation, by which the men of the Marsh came to share the liberties enjoyed by the Cinque Ports since the fourteenth century.

CHARTER OF EDWARD IV TO THE BAILIFF, JURATS AND COMMONALTY OF ROMNEY MARSH,

23 February, 1461/2

(P.R.O. Charter Roll, 1 Edward IV, part 2, m. 4)

The King to the Archbishops Bishops &c. Greeting. Know ye that wheras we are bound to provide for the defence of our kingdom of England and our liege men and subjects every where and especially of those who lie nearest to the first assaults and attacks of our enemies, and considering that divers towns and places situated near the sea have been laid waste by the spoiliations and burnings of the said enemies, and on account of the withdrawing therefrom of our liege men for fear of them, the same towns and places will be left devastated, uninhabited and desolate. THEREFORE thinking it most necessary that the same be repaired or others near the same be newly built and being so built be endowed with liberties and privileges that being so strengthened they may by the resort of people be made more powerful and strong for the greater defence of the whole country; and considering that in the Marsh of Romney in the county of Kent which lies and is situate near the sea there is not now so great an abundance of people and inhabitants or labourers as there used to be, but if it should be more largely privileged a greater concourse of people and residence of inhabitants would there ensue for the greater defence of the whole county of Kent, as by the trustworthy relation of the inhabitants of the Marsh aforesaid and other adjacent parts we have been informed by persons worthy of credit. WE, considering the premises, of our special grace at the earnest request of the whole commonalty and inhabitants of the Marsh of Romney in the county of Kent, for the preservation of the said Marsh and the greater security of the towns adjoining, have given and granted and by these presents give and grant to the inhabitants and resiants within the bounds and limits of the said Marsh that they shall be To be Corporation. one body in deed and name and one perpetual corporate community of one

186

Bailiff and twenty-four Jurats and the Commonalty of the Marsh of Romney
Marsh in the county of Kent for ever. AND THAT the said Bailiff Jurats and
Commonalty shall have perpetual succession and they and their successors be
called described and named by the names of the Bailiff Jurats and
Commonalty of Romney Marsh in the county of Kent for ever, and that they
and their successors be persons fit and in law capable to purchase lands and
tenements and other possessions whatsoever to them and their successors to
hold in fee and perpetuity. AND THAT they may have a common seal to serve
for the affairs and businesses touching the same Bailiff Jurats and
Commonalty and their successors. AND THAT they and their successors by
the names of the Bailiff Jurats and Commonalty of Romney Marsh in the
county of Kent, in any of the courts whatsoever of us and our heirs and in
other courts and places whatsoever may plead and be impleaded and answer
and be answered for ever; which same Bailiff and Jurats we will to be elected
in like manner and form and exercise and occupy the same offices and be
amoved therefrom as heretofore in the Marsh aforesaid hath been used or
accustomed to be done. AND ALSO that the aforesaid Bailiff Jurats and
Commonalty and their successors may have a certain court to be holden before
the Bailiff and Jurats of the Marsh aforesaid for the time being in a certain
place, the most convenient within the Marsh aforesaid, from three weeks to
three weeks for ever. AND THAT they may have full power and authority to
hear and determine in the same court by plaints to be brought in the same
court, all and singular pleas of all manner of debts,[1] accounts,[2] covenants,
contracts, trespasses with force and arms[3] or otherwise, done in contempt of
us or our heirs, deceits, detinues of charters and muniments and chattels,[4]
unlawful distress and of other things and actions personal and real whatsoever
arising or happening within the Marsh aforesaid, although the same debts,
accounts, covenants, contracts, trespasses and other actions amount to or
exceed the sum or value of forty shillings. AND THAT the said Bailiff and
Jurats and their successors upon such pleas and plaints may have power and
authority to draw into plea the defendants against whom such plaints shall
happen to have been preferred or removed in the court aforesaid, by
summonses attachments and distresses according to the custom of our
kingdom of England, to be directed to the ministers of the same Bailiff, and
for default of the land and chattels of such defendants within the Marsh
aforesaid where or by which they might be summoned, attached or distrained
by attachment of their bodies; and all and singular the things aforesaid
severally to hear, and by like processes considerations judgments and
executions of judgments to try and determine the same as similar pleas are
tried and determined in our courts, and that execution of the processes and
judgements be made and had by the ministers of the aforesaid Bailiff for that

---

[1] Actions brought upon debts for rent, etc.
[2] e.g. actions against officers to secure account of their receipts.
[3] All actions of trespass in which the words "vi et armis" are used in the declaration of the cause.
[4] Actions where goods or records alleged to be kept for the use of another are refused on demand.

187

purpose appointed. AND MOREOVER of our more abundant grace we have granted to the aforesaid Bailiff Jurats and Commonalty and their successors that they may have full return of all writs and precepts of us and our heirs as well of assizes,[1] certificates,[2] attaints of juries,[3] as of other writs whatsoever and also summonses of the exchequer of us and our heirs, and executions of the same to be made within the Marsh aforesaid by the Bailiff aforesaid for the time being, in any courts whatsoever of us and our heirs, as well before us and our heirs as before the justices assigned to hold pleas before us and our heirs as before the justices of the bench of us and our heirs, barons of the exchequer of us and our heirs, justices assigned to take the assizes in the County of Kent and justices itinerant and other justices and commissioners of us and our heirs whomsoever returnable to be returned or issuing therefrom. AND MOREOVER We have granted to the aforesaid Bailiff Jurats and Commonalty and their successors that they yearly at the feast of St. Michael may choose from the aforesaid Jurats four of the most discreet and sufficient Jurats as keepers of the peace within the Marsh aforesaid to have and exercise the office of keepers of the peace within the Marsh aforesaid for the year then next following. AND THAT the Bailiff aforesaid for the time being, and the same four Jurats so chosen as keepers of the peace for the time being, shall be keepers of the peace and also justices of us and our heirs for keeping the peace within the Marsh aforesaid; and the same four, three or two of them, of whom the said Bailiff for the time being shall always be one, may have power and authority to enquire by the oath of good and lawful men of the Marsh aforesaid of whatsoever felonies, trespasses, riots, routs, conventicles[4] ambidextries,[5] conspiracies, contempts,[6] concealments[7] and other misprisons[8] offences and misdeeds whatsoever done or perpetrated within the Marsh aforesaid and of all manner of forceable entries made and to be made in any lands or tenements within the Marsh aforesaid. AND ALSO of all manner of entries made peaceably or by force power or strength, held and to be held, made or to be made, in such lands and tenements within the said Marsh. AND ALSO of all manner of articles of the statutes of Liveries of Cloths and Caps, Labourers Servants and Vagabonds, Carpenters Plasterers Artificers, Weights and Measures, Victuals, Tanners of Leather, Tilers, Innkeepers, Hunters and all manner of other statutes to be enquired of before justices or keepers of the peace within the kingdom of England. AND TO have full power jurisdiction and authoririty thereupon and in all other things to do and execute that which

[1] Writs to institute actions decided by inquest or recognition.
[2] Writs to institute actions decided by the testimony of facts, certified by some proper authority.
[3] Writes to institute actions to reverse the wrongful decision of a jury and to convict them.
[4] An unlawful assembly of 2-12 persons; it is a rout if such persons start to carry out their intention, and a riot if they actually effect it. (cf. Jeake, *Charters of the Cinque Ports*, p. 149).
[5] Double dealings, i.e. the action of jurors who take money from both parties for giving their verdict.
[6] Wilful refusal to abide a lawful trial or to appear when summoned.
[7] Concealments of facts by jurors.
[8] Negligences (French "mespris").

to the office of keepers or justices of the peace elsewhere within the aforesaid kingdom pertains or in anywise so ever may pertain to be done, and to hear and determine all and singular the same according to the law and custom of our kingdom of England. AND THAT the aforesaid four Jurats so to be chosen as keepers of the peace for the time being and to continue for one year or so soon as they shall be chosen as keepers of the peace, shall be coroners of us and our heirs within the Marsh aforesaid and do exercise and execute the

ners. office of coroner and all and singular which things to the office of coroner pertain within the Marsh aforesaid, for the time in which they shall be keepers of the peace there, and shall take an oath for well and faithfully doing and exercising the same office of coroner as taken and made by the same four Jurats before the aforesaid Bailiff and any others of the aforesaid Jurats in the place aforesaid, before they take upon themselves the office of coroner. SO THAT none of the justices or keepers of us or our heirs assigned or to be assigned to keep the peace within the county of Kent, nor any other of the justices or commissioners whatsoever of us or our heirs whether assigned to hold pleas before us and our heirs or itinerant justices of us and our heirs assigned in any manner in the county aforesaid inquire of any felonies trespasses misdeeds riots routs and conventicles or other articles or things whatsoever done or perpetrated or to be done or perpetrated within the Marsh aforesaid, nor in anywise howsoever intermeddled therein. AND IF any inquisition presentment or indictment, concerning any such felonies trespasses misdeeds riots routs conventicles or articles or things done or happening within the Marsh aforesaid, be taken before any such justices or commissioners of us or our heirs without the Marsh aforesaid, such inquisition, presentment and indictment should be void and of no force and considered as nothing. SO ALSO that no sheriff, escheator, coroner or officer of us or of our heirs in the said county of Kent or either of them in anywise howsoever do enter into the same Marsh to do or execute any his or their office or offices within the Marsh aforesaid nor he or they interfere in any way in anything within the Marsh. AND THAT the aforesaid Bailiff Jurats and Commonalty and their successors

eants may have one or two of the resiants within the Marsh aforesaid as serjeant or
e serjeants or ministers of the Bailiff aforesaid for the time being, to be chosen
en. by the same Bailiff Jurats and Commonalty whensoever they will. AND WE further grant that all mandates precepts and warrants of the said Bailiff, Jurats, keepers of the peace, justices and coroners being within the same Marsh be directed to the same serjeant or serjeants or ministers or either of them to execute and serve and that the same serjeant or serjeants or ministers shall serve execute and return all the same mandates precepts and warrants according to the form thereof. MOREOVER we have granted for us and our heirs as much as in us is, that the aforesaid Bailiff Jurats and Commonalty and

ect their successors may erect a gallows within the Marsh aforesaid, and the same
ws. Bailiff and Jurats may do full execution and judgment on felons and other malefactors who shall happen to be taken and apprehended there, according to

the law and custom of our kingdom of England, without the let or impediment of us or our heirs, justices coroners escheators sheriffs or other our bailiffs or ministers whomsoever. ALSO We have granted to the same Bailiff Jurats and Commonalty and their successors, that the aforesaid Bailiff and Jurats for the time being may have for ever all fines for trespasses, misprisons, offences negligences, oppressions, extortions, deceits, conspiracies, contempts, To ha concealments, regratings,[1] forestallings,[2] maintenances,[3] ambidexters, &c. forgeries, escapes of felons, clerks convicted, or persons attainted and for other misdeeds whatsoever, fines for licence of concord,[4] fines for vert,[5] and venison, fines for false claim, and all and all manner of fine redemptions,[6] murders,[7] forfeitures, issues and amerciaments as well of any of the resiants aforesaid whomsoever as of all townships tythings hundreds[8] places and lasts[9] and of their pledges and mainpernors[10] within the Marsh aforesaid in any one or more of the courts of us and our heirs aforesaid to be made adjudged forfeited and affeered; and also year and day waste and strep[11] of all and singular and aforesaid resiants whomsoever and of their pledges and mainpernors and of their hereditaments, and whatsoever to us and our heirs might pertain for the year and day waste and strep within the Marsh aforesaid or within any parcel thereof, and all manner of forfeitures for murders, escapes, rapes of women, and felonies whatsover as well of all and singular such resiants aforesaid as of the townships, tythings, hundreds and places aforesaid and of the pledges and mainpernors aforesaid as well by the King's writs of *decies tantum* and *premunire facias*[12] as by other writs, mandates and records whatsoever adjudged and to be adjudged in any of the courts whatsoever of us and our heirs or in any other court whatsoever it shall happen that the said resiants, townships, tythings, hundreds and places, pledges or

[1] Buying up market goods to sell again at a profit.

[2] Anticipating market sales by buying up goods beforehand to enhance the price.

[3] Giving financial support to a plaintiff or defendant to maintain a plea, in which he has no proper interest.

[4] A fine paid for licence to alienate or sell lands, etc., paid when the concord or final agreement is made in Court.

[5] A fine for cutting green undergrowth suitable for deer coverts.

[6] Ransoms.

[7] In Saxon times a composition was paid to the relatives of a murdered man, but the reference here is probably to the fine to which, under Norman law, villeins were liable who lived in the district in which a murder took place.

[8] The occupants of each Hundred (a sub-division of the Shire) were in Saxon times divided into groups of ten known as tithings, for purposes of surety.

[9] The Lathe or Last is an ancient land division of Kent including several Hundreds.

[10] Sureties or pledgers.

[11] The lands of a felon condemned to death descended to his heir, but the King (or those to whom he granted the right) held the profits of such lands for a year and a day, and might commit what waste or strep (or strip), e.g. by cutting timber, that he liked during that time.

[12] *Decies tantum,* a writ which lies against a juror who has taken money for giving his verdict. So called because its effect was to recover ten times as much as the offending juror took. (Stat. Ed. III, ch. XII and XIII). *Praemunire facias* (i.e. Take Warning), a writ directed to infringers of the Statutes of Praemunire (25 Edward III, Stat. 5, cap. 22; 16 Richard II, 5) against drawing persons out of the realm to answer for matters belonging to the king's court. The Statute was directed against the jurisdiction of the Papal Court and the obtaining of Papal Bulls. Infringers were punished by loss of lands, tenements and goods, were to be attached by their bodies, and were placed outside the King's protection.

mainpernors aforesaid are fined or amerced or shall forfeit issues or forfeitures as well in the presence of us and our heirs as in the absence of us or our heirs or before us or our heirs wheresoever we shall be in England, or before the treasurer and barons of the exchequer of us and our heirs, or before the justices of the bench of us or our heirs or before the steward and marshall, or coroner, or clerk of the market of the household of us or our heirs for the time being, or in any other of the courts whatsoever of us or our heirs or before the justices itinerant of us or our heirs, the justices assigned to hold common pleas, pleas of the crown and pleas of the forest, or before the justices of us and our heirs assigned to take assizes or for gaol-delivery, or other the justices officers or ministers whomsoever of us or our heirs, assigned and to be assigned, appointed and to be appointed as fully and freely as we and our heirs should have had the same although the same resiants or any of them or the pledges or mainpernors aforesaid be or shall be the sheriff, escheator, coroner, collector, taxer or justice assigned and deputed an officer or minister of us or our heirs or hold or shall hold of us and our heirs or of any other person. AND THAT the same Bailiff Jurats and Commonalty and their successors may levy receive and have all such fines, murders, forfeitures, redemptions, issues, and amerciaments and retain the same to the use of the same Bailiff Jurats and Commonalty and their successors without the let or impediment of us or our

Courts
.eet.

heirs, justices, barons of the exchequer, sheriffs, escheators, bailiffs or other ministers whomsoever of us or our heirs. AND THAT the same Bailiff Jurats and Commonalty and their successors may for ever have within the Marsh aforesaid view of frank-pledge,[1] leets,[2] and law days,[3] with all profits to such view, leets and law days in anywise whatsoever appertaining or belonging from the resiants whomsoever within the bounds and limits of the said Marsh, and sheriffs tournes[4] to be holden before the Bailiff and Jurats of the Marsh aforesaid, and whatsoever to view of frankpledge and sheriffs tournes doth or might appertain in any way whatsoever. AND ALSO all manner of sums of money called tithing pennys,[5] cert rent,[6] homestall silver,[7] common fines or fines certain,[8] sheriffs aid and hundred silver sheriffs yeld[9] and sums of money whatsoever from such resiants aforesaid so that they be not hindered for suit and ward and fair pleading[10] and for view in anywise howsoever appertaining

---

[1] The court held periodically for the production of the members of a tithing (later − for a hundred or manor).

[2] A hundred court in the hands of the Lord of a Manor.

[3] A session either of a sheriff's court, or of a court Leet.

[4] The tour or circuit made by the sheriff twice yearly, in which he presided in each hundred court to receive presentments and pleas to transfer to Justices.

[5] Payments taken by the sheriff from every tithing.

[6] Cert rent, a fixed annual rent − no allowance being made for variations from year to year.

[7] Quit rent payable to the lord for the farm in silver coin.

[8] A common fine paid by residents of several Manors to the overlords for keeping of the Leet.

[9] Dues paid to the sheriff.

[10] Beau-pleder (fair or correct pleading), a writ lying against those who levied a fine for the amendment of a plea.

to us or our heirs. ALSO WE have granted for us and our heirs to the aforesaid Bailiff Jurats and Commonalty that they and their successors may for ever have within the limits and bounds of the Marsh aforesaid, wreck of the sea, infangenethief[1], outfangenethief,[2] and all and all manner of goods and chattels of resiants whomsoever within the bounds and limits of the same Marsh, and over every parcel thereof, as well of fugitives as of felons of themselves and of other felons whomsoever in anyway condemned, convicted, attainted, proscribed, or adjudged of or on account of any felony, or put in exigent[3] of or for any felony, or of or for any felony or any other offence whatsoever or for whatsoever cause outlawed or chattels forfeited whether it be at the suit of us our heirs or the suit of any other person or party whomsoever; and all and singular the goods and chattels of all such resiants aforesaid whomsoever forfeited and confiscated, and to be forfeited and confiscated, and chattels called manuopera (mainour[4]) by any of them disavowed, or to be disavowed, as well at the suit of us as of others whomsoever[5] or otherwise before us or our heirs, or before us or our heirs wheresoever we shall be in England, or before the justices of us or our heirs assigned or to be assigned to hold pleas before us or our heirs, or before the justices of the bench of us or our heirs assigned or to be assigned, or before the chancellor of England of us or our heirs, or before the barons of the exchequer of us or our heirs, or before the justices itinerant of us or our heirs assigned and to be assigned to hold common pleas of the forest or pleas of the crown, or before any other commissioners offices or justices whomsoever of us or our heirs, so that if any such resiant within the bounds and limits of the Marsh aforesaid shall commit any offence, or fly and will not stand to judgment, for which he ought to lose life or limb or his goods and chattels, wheresoever justice ought to be done concerning him, whether in the court of us or our heirs or of others whomsoever, all the same goods and chattels shall belong to the said Bailiff Jurats and Commonalty and their successors. AND THAT it shall be lawful for the same Bailiff Jurats and Commonalty and their successors by themselves or their ministers to put themselves in seizin of all the same goods and chattels, and to take seize have and retain the same to their proper use without the impeachment of us or our heirs or the officers whomsoever of us or our heirs, although the same goods and chattels were before taken or seized by the ministers of us or our heirs. AND ALSO that the same Bailiff Jurats and Commonalty and their successors may have all and singular whatsoever escapes and evasions as well of felons as others adjudged and to be adjudged, and of others whomsoever[5] and of all manner of fines

Escapes &c.

[1] The right of trying and amercing a thief siezed within the Liberties.

[2] The right of pursuing a thief outside the limits of the jurisdiction and bringing him back for trial, and of keeping his goods on conviction. The meaning was already conjectural by the thirteenth century.

[3] i.e. served with a writ of Exigent commanding the Sherriff to summon the defendant to appear and deliver himself up on pain of outlawry.

[4] Stolen goods found in possession of a thief.

[5] In the fourteenth century, prisoners escaping were adjudged felons and their goods therefore fofeit.

forfeitures and sums of money and amerciaments for such escapes and evasions in anywise howsoever happening or arising within the Marsh aforesaid. AND THAT the same Bailiff Jurats and Commonalty may freely levy receive have and retain such escapes, and evasions and the fines, forfeitures, sums of money and amerciaments for the same, after they shall have been adjudged to the use of the same Bailiff Jurats and Commonalty, without impediment or hindrance of us and our heirs justices sheriffs escheators bailiffs or other ministers whomsoever of us and our heirs. AND MOREOVER of our more abundant grace we have granted to the aforesaid Bailiff Jurats and Commonalty and their successors that they in the court of us and our heirs, as well for holding pleas before us and our heirs and before the justices of the bench of us and our heirs, as before any other justices whomsoever of us and our heirs, may have cognizance of all pleas real personal and mixed as well of writs of assize novel disseizin[1] and mort d'ancestor,[2] juries, attaints[3] certificates as of other writs whatsoever concerning as well all lands and tenements being within the Marsh aforesaid, as all contracts covenants trespasses and other matters and causes whatsoever in anywise howsoever arising or happening within the same Marsh. AND THAT the same Bailiff Jurats and Commonalty and their successors by the Bailiff aforesaid for the time being, may challenge and demand and have cognizance of all the pleas aforesaid in the courts aforesaid and every of them, and may determine all the same pleas according to the law and custom of our kingdom of England in the aforesaid courts to be holden before the aforesaid Bailiff and Jurats for the time being within the Marsh aforesaid, and thereupon to do justice to the parties, and may receive record and engross the fines and recognizances thereupon in the courts aforesaid to be holden before the aforesaid Bailiff and Jurats concerning the lands and tenements being within the Marsh aforesaid between the parties thereupon to be levied or made, although the same Bailiff Jurats and Commonty or either of them be parties agents plaintiffs defendants or deforceants[4] in any such pleas and writs or either of them and although the same pleas and writs concern us and our heirs. AND MOREOVER we have granted to the aforesaid Bailiff Jurats and Commonalty and their successors for ever, that they be quit of all royal tallages[5] and aids[6] and of scot[7] and geld,[8] hidage,[9] carriage,[10] toll, with soc and

(margin note: ·gniz- ·ce of Pleas.)

(margin note: it of ll &c.)

---

[1] A writ brought by a person dispossessed in order to recover his seizin (instituted by Henry II).

[2] A writ brought by an heir on death of his ancestor to recover his inheritance (instituted by Henry II).

[3] A writ lying in cases of false verdict.

[4] One who keeps another unlawfully out of possession of an estate.

[5] An arbitrary tax levied by Norman and Angevin kings upon towns and demesne lands of the Crown, later used for any arbitrary tax.

[6] A money grant to the King, especially for the knighting of his eldest son, the marriage of his eldest daughter, or the ransom of his person.

[7] A tax or customary contribution.

[8] A tax or tribute.

[9] A tax paid on the hide of land. The hide was the amount of land which a family could till with one plough in the year, normally 100 acres.

[10] Either a toll, or the servile duty of carrying hay or corn for the Lord of the Manor, or the money paid in commutation of such a service.

sac,[1] thol and theam,[2] infangenethief outfangenethief, gredwyte,[3] bloodwyte,[4] flitwyte,[5] fleswyte,[6] hengwyte,[7] letchwyte[8] flemenesfrith,[9] hordel[10] and croft within time and without,[11] danegeld,[12] horngeld,[13] hosts,[14] lastage,[15] stallage,[16] shires, wards,[17] warde-penny,[18] hundred penny, tithing penny and all murages,[19] works of castles and bridges,[20] ways,[21] aids and all manner of inclosures and of all carriage, sumage,[22] and manige,[23] and building of royal houses,[24] and all manner of works, and all payments for their merchandize good and chattels at all fairs and markets, and in all passage of bridges and ways by sea and land throughout our whole realm of England. AND MOREOVER we have granted and do grant to the same Bailiff Jurats and Commonalty and their successors that whensover the commons of our realm of England in the parliament of us or our heirs or otherwise shall 'grant any fifteenth or tenth[25] or any quota tax or tallage or aid charge or subsidy[26] whatsoever or any part thereof, either of their temporal goods or movables or

[1] Soc and Sac anciently conferred jurisdiction. Soc is the right of a Lord to claim suit at Court, and sac the right of doing justice and of taking the profits of justice.

[2] Toll may be the right to take toll, or to be free of toll, but is often the right to tallage one's villeins. Team is the right of hearing and taking the profits of cases in which the procedure of vouching to warranty is used (i.e. the procedure whereby the possessor of goods alleged to be stolen, defended his title by reference to a third party). From the eleventh century grants of sac, soc, toll and team are usual in all land charters.

[3] Fine for breach of special peace.

[4] Fine for drawing blood.

[5] Fine for quarrelling.

[6] Fleswyte, probably fledwyte, i.e. freedom from amercements when a fugitive comes to the peace of the King; also fines connected with fugitives (or may be exemption from a tax on fleeces).

[7] Fine for allowing a thief to escape.

[8] Letherwite, a fine for the corruption of slaves, also spelt leirwite.

[9] Penalty for harbouring criminals.

[10] Share of treasure (treasure trove) or possibly the right to administer oaths, or adjudge ordeal trials. In any case it seems curious that an immunity is granted from what appears to be a privilege. It suggests that the compilers of the charter were copying ancient words of which the meaning was not realized.

[11] Probably the right of folding sheep within lambing time and without.

[12] A land tax, originally raised to protect England from the Danes.

[13] Cornage, a form of rent fixed by the number of horned cattle.

[14] Service with, or contribution to, the fyrd, or popular army.

[15] Toll at fairs and markets.

[16] Tax for a stall in a market.

[17] The duty of performing watch or ward.

[18] A rent paid to a superior in commutation of military service.

[19] A toll levied for building or repairing the walls of a town.

[20] The duty of military service and of repairing bridges, castles and roads was known as the *Trinoda Necessitas*. This threefold service was often excepted when liberty from other services was conferred.

[21] Duty of repairing roads.

[22] Sumpter service.

[23] Text doubtful. Probably instead of M read either IN or 'N − Navigio, i.e. naval service; if the M is an error, it was copied in later confirmations.

[24] An unusual duty, exemption from which is sometimes given in Charters, e.g. Charter to St. Peter's York, 1305 *(Cal. Close Rolls,* III, 57).

[25] A tax imposed on personal property of a tenth or fifteenth part of the value of a man's land or goods or both, amounting to a tenth in towns and a fifteenth in villages.

[26] An aid or tax granted by Parliament to the Soverign to meet special needs, levied upon the goods and lands of all subjects.

of their lands, tenements, possessions or rents, to us, our heirs or to other persons, although the same persons shall have granted the same fifteenth, tenth, quota, aid, subsidy, tax and tallage, charge or any part thereof to us or our heirs, or we or our heirs shall cause our, demesne throughout England to be tallaged, the lands, tenements, possessions, goods and chattels of the same Bailiff Jurats and Commonalty and their successors and of the resiants aforesaid or any of them shall not be taxed assessed or tallaged to the use of us or our heirs, nor the same Bailiff Jurats Commonalty and resiants nor their successors nor any of them in such their lands tenements goods or chattels by occasion thereof be distrained charged in anything or grieved, but from all such fifteenths and tenths and other quotas, subsidies, aids, charges and other tallages, and from every part thereof payable to us and our heirs, shall be quit and discharged for ever, although the same Bailiff Jurats and Commanalty and resiants and their successors or either of them, be parties agents consenting or granting such grants of fifteenths and tenths and other quotas, subsidies, tallages or taxes or any part thereof granted to us or our heirs or any other persons whomsoever as aforesaid. MOREOVER we have granted for us and our heirs to the aforesaid Bailiff Jurats and Commonalty and their

ɔ make rdinan s and ɔnstitu- ɔns &c. successors that they from time to time may frame and make reasonable ordinances and constitutions agreeable to good faith and reason for the public good of the said Marsh and the sound and wholesome government thereof and for the common utility of the inhabitants and resiants there, and may use and execute the same within the bounds and limits of the said Marsh, and may also be able to alter the same and every of them as shall seem best expedient for ever. AND THAT the said Bailiff Jurats and Commonalty and their successors for the necessities and conveniences touching the said Marsh may assess amongst themselves tallages and impositions upon the goods, lands, tenements and merchandize of the inhabitants and resiants, being within the bounds and limits of the said Marsh and otherwise as shall seem best, and may impose and levy the same without impediment of us or our heirs, justices or ministers whomsoever of us or our heirs. AND FURTHER we have granted for us and our heirs to the aforesaid Bailiff Jurats and Commonalty and their successors that no one of them their heirs or successors hereafter be put or empanelled in any assize, juries, recognizances attaints or other inquisitions whatsoever without the bounds or limits of the Marsh aforesaid, nor be compelled to go out of the said bounds or limits to be put on any juries, inquisitions, assizes, recognizances, attaints or matters whatsoever, although they concern us or our heirs, neither shall any of them be or be made an assessor taxer or collector of the tenths fifteenths or of any part thereof, or of any charges, subsidies, tallages, taxes of quotas whatsoever granted or to be granted to us or our heirs, nor collector of reasonable aids to make the eldest son of us or our heirs a knight, or to marry the eldest daughter of us or our heirs, nor any of them be ordained or appointed a constable, tithing-man,[1]

---

[1] Anciently the chief man of a tithing, later a petty constable.

borsholder,[1] bailiff or other officer or minister of us or our heirs without the bounds and limits of the said Marsh against his will. AND IN case that any one of the same Bailiff, Jurats, and resiants or their heirs or successors be hereafter chosen ordained or appointed to any charge of such offices or occupations or to undertake, perform or occupy any other office without the Marsh aforesaid against the force form and effect of our present grant, although he shall refuse to undertake, perform or occupy the same offices or charges, nevertheless he shall in nowise incur any fine, contempt, forfeiture, loss or damage in body or goods, but that the present letters shewn forth by him before any justices and ministers whomsoever of us and our heirs in any place of record whatsoever throughout our whole realm of England upon the demonstration thereof, shall remain in their strength and effect and be allowed to them without any writ or process thereupon to be further sued forth. ALTHOUGH express mention in these presents be not made of the true yearly value of the liberties, franchises, acquittances and grants aforesaid or of other the premises or either of them or of other gifts or grants heretofore made by either of our progenitors to the Bailiff and Jurats of the Marsh aforesaid or their predecessors or either of them or any statute, act, ordinance or restriction to the contrary thereof made, passed or provided in anywise notwithstanding. SO THAT our present charter turn not to the prejudice of the liberty of the Venerable Father in Christ Thomas Archbishop of Canterbury. THESE being Witnesses, the Venerable Fathers, Thomas Archbishop of Canterbury Primate of all England and Legate of the Apostolic See, L. Bishop of Durham, G. Bishop of Exeter our Chancellor of England, and our most dear Brothers George Duke of Clarence and Richard Duke of Gloucester, and also our most dear Cousins John Earl of Worcester, Henry Earl of Essex our Treasurer of England, and William Earl of Kent our Uncle, Steward of our Household, and our beloved and faithful Sir William Hastings of Hastings Knight our Chamberlain, and Sir John Wenlock of Wenlock Knight, and our beloved clerk Master Robert Styllyngton Keeper of our Privy Seal and others. GIVEN by our hand at Westminster the 23rd day of February. BY the King himself and of the date aforesaid by authority of Parliament.

---

[1] Anciently the chief of a frank-pledge, or tithing, later a petty constable.

BIBLIOGRAPHY

Perambulation of Kent	William Lambarde
History of Kent – Vol. 3	Hasted
Roman Ports and Forts in Kent	Somner
Villare Cantianum	Philpott
Rural Rides	Cobbett
History of the County of Kent – Vol. 2	Ireland
History of Romney Marsh	Holloway
Rambles in Kent	Cox
Saunters through Kent	Igglesden
History of Murders	A Gentleman of Chichester
The Kentish Coast	Harper
The Level and Liberty of Romney Marsh	M. Teichman Derville
The Cinque Ports	A. G. Bradley
The Constitutional History of the Cinque Ports	K. M. E. Murray
The White and Black Books of the Cinque Ports	Edited by Felix Hull
The Parish Chest	W. Tate
Journey Round the Coast of Kent	T. Fussell
Records of Lydd	Arthur Finn
The Martello Towers	S. Sutcliffe
The Ancient and Rightful Customs	Edward Carson
The Bulwark Shore	Caroline Hillier
Smugglers	Harper
British Lighthouses	W. J. Hardy
Archaeologia Cantiana – Various Volumes	

Church Guides:

Brenzett and Snargate	Sharman
Fairfield and Snave	Cawley
Brookland, Burmarsh, Ivychurch, Old Romney and St. Mary-in-the-Marsh	Anne Roper

REFERENCE INDEX

204

208